TECHNIQUES OF SPIRAL WORK

TECHNIQUES OF SPIRAL WORK

A Practical Guide
to the Craft of Making
Twists by Hand

STUART MORTIMER

with
Illustrations by Andrew Mortimer

LINDEN PUBLISHING
FRESNO, CA.

DEDICATION

I dedicate this book to my wife Linda for her devotion and encouragement over the years.
I include my parents in this dedication in acknowledgement of their continued support and pride shown
in all my achievements.

Library Cataloguing in Publication Data

Mortimer, Stuart.
    Techniques of spiral work: a practical guide to the craft of making twists by hand/Stuart Mortimer.
        p.   cm.
    ISBN 0-941936-34-1
    1. Turning 2/ Lathes. 3. Woodwork. I. Title.
    TT201.M67   1995
    684'.083—dc20   95-34339
                                                              CIP

Published 1995 by
Linden Publishing Inc., 3845 N. Blackstone, Fresno, California 93726, USA
Tel: 800-345-4447

Set in 10½ on 13½ pt Garamond by Ann Buchan (Typesetters) Shepperton.

Printed in Hong Kong

PREFACE

I was born into a farming family in Aberdeenshire during the war years. At a very early age I was introduced to woodcarving, or whittling, by Italian and German prisoners of war who worked on my Grandfather's farm. I would sit on the concrete horse trough by the wood watching them fashion wooden toys and whistles. My upbringing was in the highland foothills in the Vale of Alford where as a boy I had the freedom to roam with my brothers and sisters, and where we made many a stick into a fishing rod to use in the burns. I treasure my upbringing and its memories amongst the trees and heather. There is no doubt this was the roots of my love for wood. During my school years I looked forward to my technical and woodwork classes under the scrutiny of Jimmy Adam and I enjoyed woodturning in particular. When I left school I wanted to be an engineer or a joiner, instead I joined the police force.

One day in 1972, (by which time I had started to dabble in woodturning), I was off my beat a bit driving a marked police car, when I saw a little car with a large lump of wood on a creaky old roof rack. That lump of wood could be used for woodturning, I thought. An elderly gentleman was driving. I stopped the car and said to the driver, 'What are you going to do with that piece of wood?' 'What's it got to do with you?' he replied gruffly. I said, 'Because I try to turn and wondered if you were a turner.' 'Follow me,' he said. We stopped outside his house and he introduced himself as Dennis White, a woodturner. I helped him unload the big lump of oak, after which he introduced me to his shed at the bottom of the garden. The shed was new and surrounded with all sorts of timber and an old lathe. Once inside he immediately put a piece of wood between centres on a Union Graduate. He started to turn. I had met turners before and I knew enough to know immediately that this man was special, he had a touch, a gift full of experience that I had never seen in turning.

From that day Dennis and I have swapped many a piece of wood. At first I would take a piece of turning with which I was reasonably pleased, for him to inspect – he would chuck it on the floor. That needed no comment. Later on, however, I noticed he was throwing them on to the settee rather than on the floor. I was improving. As a self-taught turner I tried to develop every avenue of my work. During 1990 Dennis persuaded me to enter my first competition, by which time I had developed my general woodturning to a good standard with a reasonable eye for design. Encouraged by Dennis and others, I broadened my horizons to include demonstrating, teaching and writing articles on woodturning, and made it a 'professional' second career.

Woodturning has developed considerably over the past ten years; the increased demand for equipment and the number of woodturning centres and clubs throughout the country proves this. The hunger for knowledge has led to a demand in literature, videos and teaching on the subject, not least by many more interested people taking early retirement. Like most woodturning authors I suppose, I had not considered writing a book until I considered myself to be totally experienced in the craft.

It is very difficult to judge one's own level of expertise in any field without the opinion of experts. I personally needed someone of the calibre of Dennis White, a true professional, to push me in the right direction in terms of confidence and self-assessment, and of Alan Mitchell, past editor of Practical Woodworking magazine, who persuaded me to demonstrate for his exhibitions.

My main aim in writing this book is to encourage the return of hand-made spiral work, using traditional woodturning skills within the capability of every woodturner. This publication is on plain turning which includes twists. The early stages describe spiral work, including design, the tools required and types of material to use, and safety precautions. The book goes on to explain the stages of preparation, marking out and cutting the simplest of twists. It progresses to more complicated work and anticipates possible problems with diagnoses, to a stage where readers can apply their knowledge and skills to produce a twist of their own design.

In some cases the preparation of a piece to be twisted may appear to be beyond the capability of the turner. I refer to producing a ring or hoop, thin turning, a hollow form, etc., for twisting. Do not be disheartened, have a go; follow the stages as outlined, you will find that the ability to produce this type of work will develop and become an added feature in your turning.

I think in this Preface it is worth relating briefly two experiences. At the National Exhibition Centre, Birmingham, during the Woodturning Show, a chap approached me with a plastic bag — a normal thing for a turner — he said nothing but just indicated that I should look inside. There was only one item within, a small open-twisted goblet in rosewood. The stem featured a 'twist within a twist'. It was his first attempt at spiral work after seeing one of my demonstrations. I placed it on the stand shelf with some of my own work and someone in the audience said, 'Looks like one of yours Stuart.' I left the piece on the shelf and it was admired. He was delighted and so was I.

On another occasion a good friend, George White, asked me to show him the marking out and cutting procedure for a single twist. I did so on a rough piece of pine. Some time later he handed me a perfect example of a traditional single twist in makore. I personally could count on one hand the number of times I have produced such a perfect twist. Nothing great, you may think, but George, an excellent craftsman, has a severe uncontrollable shake in both hands.

It may only be 'a piece of wood — picked up somewhere' but the primitive pleasure to the turner in finding and fashioning it into a desirable object is unsurpassed. My intention is to encourage spiral work as another area in turning where most will be able to develop the skill. It can at times, if the project is large and demanding, require hard, frustrating work but I guarantee your effort will be rewarded.

CONTENTS

FOREWORD
by Keith Rowley

To the average woodworker, the production of the various types of twists on the hand turning wood lathe is shrouded with an aura of mystery. The general perception of the majority is that it is far too demanding, both from a technical and practical point of view, and quite beyond the capabilities of other than a few 'gifted' craftsman.

Stuart sets out to dispel this type of thinking and quotes two examples in his preface where two persons, at their first attempt after seeing him demonstrate, produced items of such quality that they were greatly admired and could have been mistaken for his work.

I can add a third example. During a woodturning show where both Stuart and I were demonstrating, I asked him to show me how to set out and execute a double twist suitable for the thin, long stems of the style of pomander I produce. This he did with such clarity, I was subsequently able, at my first attempt, to produce a matching pair with left and right hand twists good enough to win a silver medal at a prestigious woodturning competition.

I consider this book to be unique. I am an avid reader of all types of woodworking books, magazines, articles etc, but nowhere have I read the kind of in-depth information on terminology, equipment and techniques relative to twist work as is contained in this book.

A prodigious amount of research must have been done in addition to guidance over the years from his friend and mentor, Dennis White. But most of all his knowledge and expertise has undoubtedly come from his own 'hands on' experience and from his obvious enthusiasm and zest for woodturning in general and 'twisting' in particular.

These qualities shine through to the reader with encouragement to shed one's shackles and inhibitions and 'have a go, it's not as difficult as you think' is a theme running through the book. Of course, to produce the test pieces to the quality depicted, a fair degree of competence in general woodturning techniques must first be attained.

The text is complemented by many exceedingly clear drawings and photographs but for me the outstanding feature is the way Stuart has successfully translated the more technical aspects of the book into an easily understandable and readable style.

Interest is maintained in a most adroit manner by including projects in ascending degree of difficulty so that the reader can, in addition to practising the various types of twists, make several very attractive pieces. Any form of adornment such as carving and twisting, should of course complement and enhance the project as a whole and certainly not dominate it. Stuart has, in my view, succeeded in this respect in all the projects contained herein and there are several that I would unashamedly wish to copy.

It is said that when one starts to read a good book, it is very difficult to put it down. On receiving the script, I read it all the way through in one evening!

I am of the opinion that this will be THE definitive work on 'twisting' for many years to come and accordingly many will treat it as their 'bible'.

It may well also prove to be instrumental in the renaissance of this almost forgotten craft.

Keith Rowley, 1995

1

INTRODUCTION AND SAFETY ASPECTS

When I started to write this book I decided to introduce the subject with a potted history. I did a little research and found that it was not possible to say exactly when the first object was turned in wood, however it is certain that woodturning was started by ancient civilisations such as the early Egyptians, Arabians, Indians and the Chinese well before the birth of Christ. These are confirmed by archaeological and tomb findings and there are surviving Roman pieces to be found in museums, one such piece exists in the Wellcome Museum, University College of Swansea.

Early lathes were hand driven with a bow or rope drawn backwards and forwards around the workpiece, sometimes by an assistant to the turner, and would have been mainly mounted on pegs or poles driven into the ground. This type of lathe eventually led to the pole lathe with which most turners are familiar. Some of these are referred to in more detail in Holtzapffel's *Turning & Mechanical Manipulation*, Volume 4, *Hand or Simple Turning.*

There is no doubt that man has always used timber for domestic purposes. The first wooden utensils would have been carved or hewn from wood using crude tools. I sometimes try to visualise a scene where the first woodturner started in this country. A group of long haired, shabby clothed people around a contraption in an ancient Saxon village surrounded by trees. Among the onlookers are the wise men of the time and the critics, who are all shaking their heads; maybe some are also grunting in disapproval or disbelief as the 'woodturner' tells his 'little lady' to start cranking the handle or pull on the ropes. The wood starts to spin in one direction or another, there is delight in his eyes and amazement in others. The thing works. The 'woodturner' stands at the machine, his stance is questionable. ' What is this I see?' someone asks. 'A skew' he answers. He bends forward and introduces the sharp edge of the tool to the wood and his first shaving flies into the air, or drops to the floor, maybe there was a loud bang. It matters not. Imagine yourself in that man's shoes, his first shaving. I like to imagine the delight on his face as he gloats over this shaving at the expense of the onlooking critics. ' I am a woodturner' he comments. From that point onwards demands were made on him by others to produce vessels, spindles and other attractive shapes. Since then there has been a small number of men and women who are fascinated by flying wood shavings and in the art of fashioning a piece of spinning wood with a hand held tool.

Every turner today, whether they turn for pleasure or necessity, can imagine how that first woodturner felt when he produced his first shaving and form. Very little has changed since then in respect of the pure enjoyment derived from woodturning. The most important factors which separate that ancient turner from the turner of today is the advancement of the lathe and turning tools.

Whether your lathe is a pole lathe or one driven by water, steam, petrol or electricity is a matter of preference. It appears that most turners use the machine which either gives most pleasure or produces work fast enough to meet a particular demand.

When woodturners start discussing lathes, most will shy off a little or say, 'mine suits me'. What they are really saying is, the perfect lathe has not yet been built. My comment, 'maybe not, but close'. There is one thing that is certain, manufacturers will continue to produce new, improved lathes from now until eternity and woodturners will continue to buy them.

For the modern turner whether professional, amateur or hobbyist the choice of lathes today is great and for the beginner it can be a confusing decision to make. The same decision can be just as confusing for the professional.

The only advice I will give is to obtain the lathe that suits your personal requirements or space in the shed or workshop.

SAFETY

When I discuss safety to students, the first thing I mention is the lathe. The lathe is designed to spin material at high speeds. A lathe is only as safe as its operator. It therefore follows that all safety precautions to prevent an accident *must* be taken by the operator before starting up the machine.

1. Check the speed setting of the lathe before mounting a workpiece.
2. Make sure that if spectators are present they are guarded against flying waste material, by the use of perspex (or similar) shielding. Keep other people well away from the machine until you are satisfied there is no danger.
3. Prepare material properly before mounting on the lathe. Make sure it is sound, with no loose bits which are likely to fly off.
4. With spindle work, centre and countersink both ends of the timber to ensure that both drive and tailstock ends are deeply located to ensure positive drive.
5. In the case of faceplate work, regardless of the method of mounting, make sure the material is reasonably well balanced before starting up the lathe. One of the best methods of doing this is to turn the workpiece at stages freehand then let it go. The heavier side will normally turn and drop downwards towards the bed of the lathe. If the drop is dramatic, trim excess weight off until you are satisfied that the piece is reasonably balanced.
6. Once the material is mounted always turn the work piece by hand to ensure the material is not fouling the machine or rest. It is also advisable to check the material for splinters on the edges.
7. Ensure that the tailstock and tool rest are properly secured before starting the machine.
8. Make sure your stance is correct for the tool and the intended cutting action.
9. Check speed before starting. Always start at slowest speed and work up rather than vice-versa.
10. Once the workpiece has been worked on for several revolutions, stop the lathe and re-check the mounting. With spindle work in particular it tends to loosen off with working. Tighten the tailstock as necessary.
11. Beware of vibration as this is an indication that all is not well, stop the lathe.
12. Keep hand and tools clear until you are ready to start work.
13. Listen for unusual sounds in the timber such as sharp clicking or hollow sounds and do not touch or put your hand on the workpiece whilst turning unless you are certain of the material. Large revolving splinters and cracks can cause severe injuries.

Stop the machine to check the stability of the material before touching or sanding. Never turn suspect material. If in doubt seek advice.

14. Always wear protective goggles and a dust mask.

15. Do not wear loose clothing, such as neck ties, open jackets or loose cuffs. Use clothing designed for the purpose.

16. Tie up long hair near revolving belts or a workpiece, Loose long hair dangling over a working lathe could result in a very nasty accident.

17. Make sure you are in a position to switch off instantly at the first sign of trouble.

18. Always keep tools sharp and the lathe in good working condition.

19. When finishing work on the lathe, do not use large pieces of rag or wire wool. These can be whipped rapidly around the workpiece taking a finger with it.

20. Do not splash large amounts of finishing fluids on to revolving work, some are toxic and can damage the eyes and skin.

21. Do not use improvised tools made from others such as light hacksaw blades, knives or any suspect home made tool.

22. If in doubt about any aspect of woodturning do not start up, use common sense or seek advice. (Safety procedures when cutting a twist are covered in Chapter 3.)

STANCE

Additional points which incorporates safety, ability and agility, when combined enable a woodturner to cut in a smooth flowing action. This cannot be achieved without the correct 'stance' when addressing the workpiece. Always place your feet in a position which will allow you to execute the complete proposed cutting action in one pass. Any jerking, pausing or alteration of the stance along the length of the cut will result in ridges on the workpiece.

In addition to the stance, when turning larger pieces it is obvious that the body will have to be moved during cutting. When the stance has to be altered, do not attempt to continue the cut whilst moving until sufficiently experienced to do so. Fade out the cut . ('Fade out' is where the cutting edge of the tool is slowly lifted from the material by dropping the handle of the tool, allowing it to rub the 'bevel'. The bevel is the area between the sharp edge of the tool and the 'heel', and the heel is the ridge nearest the handle at the end of the sharpened section.) See illustration on Page 17. Alter your stance to suit and backtrack to where fade out started, bevel the tool before the fade out point, angle the tool to pick up the original line of cut. The experienced turner will automatically find the natural areas or breaks on the workpiece to change his stance in order to keep the cut flowing smoothly.

The reason I mention stance at this stage is because it is during the change of stance that a dig in is likely to occur. 'Dig in' is caused when the tool is introduced at the wrong angle, when control of the tool is lost and it is drawn into the material, or where the correct angle of cut is lost, the tool may turn in the hand and a dig in will result. There is normally a bang, resulting in damage to the workpiece, the tool and possibly the operator. When the stance is stretched the turning position and angle could be awkward. Altering the stance with the tool on the workpiece automatically changes the mode of the tool in relation to the workpiece. If the flowing cutting action has to be interrupted, fade out the cut to avoid the tool snatching and digging in. Do not attempt to reverse cut until experienced.

Dig in can also occur when the turning tool is hurriedly introduced or withdrawn at the wrong cutting angle to the workpiece. It will almost certainly occur when the operator is distracted or is waving the tool around like a pointing stick.

Dig ins are dangerous, we all try to avoid them.

USE OF TWISTS

Let me suggest, with tongue in cheek, that twists could be as old as carving. There is little doubt that the first twists were probably made by furniture carvers. On the other hand some enterprising turner may have started the whole thing off by offering a cabinet maker some twisted spindle work. In Britain, spiral work has been around for about four hundred years and it was a particularly popular feature on Jacobean furniture.

During the first quarter of this century most apprentice wood turners would have been able to set out and cut traditional twists. Much of this hand craft work was later superseded by automatic twist making machines similar to lathes with overhead routers or cutters which move over the rotating workpiece at a regulated, geared speed, in relation to the desired pitch.

Regardless of their appearance, the setting up of a twist, if taken stage by stage, is relatively easy. I say this first off to encourage those sceptics who doubt their ability to produce a twist.

The following general rules apply to most work:

a) In furniture, twists should de designed to suit the piece, not the other way round.

b) Where you decide to choose an odd number of twists on the exterior of a piece the twist bines should be in the same direction.

c) Traditionally, a piece of furniture such as a table, dresser or cabinet, etc., should have left and right twists on their respective sides.

d) A round or square table can have alternating left- and right-hand twists on even numbered legs.

There will be examples throughout this book where a particular twist may be used. As you progress through the book you will see that the twists get progressively more difficult and, hopefully, to a point where the reader will have the confidence to design and cut his or her own particular pattern.

An example of a Jacobean-style period chair with spiral work

2

THE TWIST

The twist is a spiral cut on a designed piece of timber. The cutting of a trough or hollow at a pre-determined angle produces a bine or bead along the length of the blank giving the appearance of a twist. A twist can be lengthened or shortened, made thin or thick, have as many hollows and bines that the material is capable of accommodating. Certain twists can also be 'opened', this expression refers to hollowing out the centre of a twist. 'Breaking through', is the term used for cutting through the bottoms of the troughs or hollows into the hollow centre which has been drilled through the middle of the piece, thus separating the bines. (It then has the appearance of a coiled spring.)

The name Barley twist was given to a twist in wood in Victorian times as it resembled twisted barley sugar, a popular children's sweet of the period. However, it appears to be a matter of conjecture whether all twists were referred to in the same way.

The main categories, or designs, are these:

a) Single twist (occasionally called Barley twist). This has a single line of twist or bine worked from one starting point to its finishing point.
b) Double twist (always referred to as a Double Barley twist or a Double Open). This has two lines of twist or bines worked from the starting point..
c) Triple twist (very rarely called a Barley twist). This has three lines of twist or bines worked from the starting point. A Ribbon twist also has three lines of twist.
d) Multi-start twist (never referred to as a Barley twist). This has more than three lines of twist or bines from the starting point. These twists are often identified by the number of bines. For example, a four bine twist may be referred to as a 4-Start twist.
e) Cable or Rope twists (never referred to as a Barley twist). These twists by tradition have at least nine lines of twist or bines, they must be pitched to resemble a cable or rope.

Before going any further, examine the Double Barley twist illustrated below. Try to keep this particular twist in mind whilst progressing through the early chapters of the book.

The points to note: 1. It is a Double Barley twist in the process of being cut and Opened. 2. The Pitch is double the width of the material or blank. 3. Note, at the left of the illustration, an indication is given to a drill hole through the centre of the material. 4. The left end of the opening is nicely rounded. 5. Take special note of the vertical and diagonal lines that can be seen at the right end of the illustration.

The main emphasis here is that at the stage of marking out and the cutting of any twist one should be able to visualise the finished product. The Open Double twist illustrated is partially cut. Note the lines running across and diagonally along the top of the bines, these are the marking out lines fading away as the twist is cut. The most important point in twisting and designing twists is the marking out. With sufficient practice marking out and identifying a twist will become second nature.

TERMINOLOGY

In most cases the visual appearance of twist work is easy enough to understand. What is slightly more difficult perhaps is the explanation of particular shapes or forms and clarifying some of the semi-technical terminology used in this respect. The following list will, I hope, be a useful guide through this potential maze.

Plain turning is the description given to all types of hand turned work (including spiral work) and whether spindle, bowls, platters or hollow forms there are standard terms for all shapes and forms. Plain turning features may include flats, pummels, 'V' cuts, beads, coves, hollows, spigots, shoulders or fillets etc. There are other terms such as jug, reel, plinth and columns, these incorporate several features to make up a recognised shape. Others, which are self-explanatory, are neck, bellied, waisted, tapered and teardrop. To a turner this is everyday language and quite easily understood. Even to a lay-person these terms conjure up a shape in the imagination. They are also used in ornamental and automatic turning.

Apart from the turning terms there are also expressions and technical jargon which vary from region to region for woodturning in general and spindle work in particular. Some of the terminology used in this respect may appear to contradict traditional engineering terms.

However, this book deals with traditional spiral work in wood, an area for which there appears to be few 'official' terms, therefore I have used considerable licence in order to make reading and explanation more easily understood. These and other terms are explained in the Glossary, Chapter 27.

PITCH

This book is mainly about spiral work or twisting. The main term which is used throughout to describe a twist is the 'Pitch'. Once the meaning of Pitch is understood it is very easy to visualise the type of twist referred to.

As in all spindle work, particularly copying, accuracy is very important. When it comes to spiral work accuracy is vital. In order to maintain accuracy when cutting a twist it is equally important to understand stage by stage what makes up a particular twist. Every twist is different, so it follows that each stage is also different. To change the shape of a twist or section of a twist, the main ingredient, apart from the thickness and material used, is the Pitch.

Pitch describes the angle of the bine and hollow along the twist. For the purpose of marking out, the Pitch is determined by the thickness of the material and distance between the ridges (apex to apex) on a thread or bine after one full circumference of the material used. The majority of pitch angles whilst working in wood vary between 10 and 60 degrees.

PITCH LINES are used to mark out the length of an individual pitch on a piece of material. The area of material between pitch lines is a pitch segment.

The distance between the Pitch Lines is calculated in proportion to the thickness of material used. In the case of all twists in wood, and for the purpose of explaining and illustrating marking out procedures in this book, the pitch is measured between apex to apex of each individual thread, bine or bead. For example, if I refer

Traditional Pitch variations

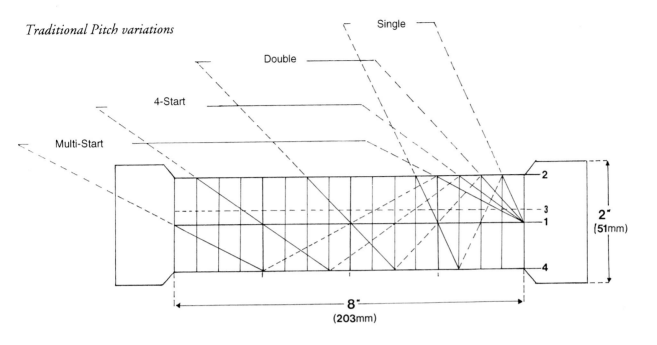

The above refers to Single, Double, 4-Start and Multi-Start twists only. The Triple and other twists
are referred to in later sections of the book. Start Lines are marked on the right-hand side
2, 3, 1 & 4 (horizontals). Pitch Dividing Lines are marked between Pitch Lines (verticals).

to a Double twist with a 4" (102 mm) pitch, there will
be one pitch measurement for each bine along the first
4" (102 mm) of the twist. The bine apex falling within
the first 4"(102 mm) after cutting is purely a pitch
reference point. There will not be two 2"(51 mm)
pitches.

PITCH DIVIDING LINES

These are the lines marked at equal distances between
the Pitch Lines, and these divide the pitch segment
equally into smaller segments to assist in controlling the
marking out, the angle of pitch and cutting. These will
be referred to in illustrations as Pitch Dividing Lines.
The area of material between each Dividing Line will be
referred to as pitch segments.

START LINES

Start Lines are the horizontal or longitudinal lines that
divide the cylindrical section or blank which will accommodate the twist. These lines must divide the blank
into equal sections otherwise there will be an imbalance
in the final result. The number of Start Lines is dependent on the number of hollows or bines. The Start Lines
cross each pitch segment to intersect with the Pitch and
Pitch Dividing Lines. These intersections or crossings
are reference points for the Pitch Control Lines which
are critical to the marking out of a twist.

Start Lines also determine the number of bines and
hollows which will form the twist. For example, a Triple
twist has three bines and three hollows, therefore it will
need six Start Lines. A Double Barley twist has two

bines and two hollows, it will need four Start Lines.

The Start Line is so named because it is at the beginning of each Start Line on its intersection with the first Pitch Line that the cutting of the hollows and bines start. For a traditional twist the cutting for each individual hollow should also finish on the same Start Line. These lines are normally numbered for cutting purposes.

'PITCH CONTROL LINES' is the combined name for 'CUT CONTROL LINES', 'BINE APEX LINES' and the 'WIDTH CONTROL LINES'.

CUT CONTROL LINES.
Cut Control Lines are the cut lines marked diagonally, from the beginning of each Start Line to each intersection with the Pitch and Pitch Dividing Lines; marking from right to left and left to right will decide whether the twist is a right- or left-hand twist. These lines also determine the pitch angle for cutting.

BINE APEX LINES
The Bine Apex Lines indicate the apex or top of each bine along the length of the twist.

COMPLETE MARKING OUT
Complete Marking Out is the term used to complete a second set of Start Lines, Pitch Lines and Control Lines in order that the hollows and bines can be cut to the required width. It is in fact a duplicate set of all the lines described above. These run parallel to the original Pitch, Pitch Control Lines and the Start Lines to produce a second set of Pitch Control Lines. This extra set of control lines is an accurate guide when cutting the hollows. Complete Marking Out should always be done in a different colour pencil across the intersections in the same manner as the Cut Control Lines and Bine Apex Lines. These lines may be varied according to the required width of bine or hollow. They may also be

regulated to produce a tapered bine. I refer to these lines, which are the result of the Complete Marking Out, as Width Control Lines.

WIDTH CONTROL LINES
When you mark out your first twist it is best to use the Complete Marking Out in order to get the Width Control Lines. For an experienced 'twister' the Width Control Lines are not always required when cutting a twist. In some cases, the blank to be twisted is sometimes too small to accommodate this procedure. However the Width Control Lines are a must for accurate cutting and very large twists. As experience is gained in cutting spirals, you will know when to drop the Complete Marking Out procedure.

At stages throughout the book I advise when Width Control Lines are not necessary and when to omit the Complete Marking Out.

TRADITIONAL PITCH OR MEASUREMENTS

SINGLE TWIST: 1 to 1¼ times the width of material.

DOUBLE TWIST: 2 times the width of material.

TRIPLE TWIST: 2½ to 3 times the width of material or vary the pitch as desired.

RIBBON TWIST: 3 times the width of material for a three bine. Stretch the pitch for each additional bine. (See Chapter 14)

MULTI-START and CABLE TWIST: A Multi-start can be a four bine twist and upwards with no limit on bines. A traditional Cable or Rope twist is a nine bine twist. The pitch should be around 4 times the width of material. This twist gives you license to have as many bines as you like provided you have the thickness of material to accommodate the bines or spirals without losing the balance of the piece.

OPEN or HOLLOW TWIST: This term is used to describe where the hollows between the bines have been cut through to a recess in the middle of the twist, exposing the bines as individual spirals along the length of the twist. All twists can be opened except for a Single. Note: In the case of an Open twist, the shorter the pitch, the thinner the bines, resulting in a weaker twist. To strengthen an Open twist you must stretch the pitch to suit the material used. This is explained in Chapter 14. on Stretching a pitch and Lengthening a twist.

A twist can be made on virtually any thickness of material down to just under $\frac{1}{8}$"(3 mm). It obviously gets more difficult to cut a twist on thinner material. A twist can be cut on practically any shape whether straight, on a knob, ball, bend or ring.

LEARN TO TWIST THE TRADITIONAL WAY

a) The method I use throughout this book is, I believe, the quickest and most accurate. I will mark Start Lines (horizontal), Pitch Lines (perpendicular), and Cut Lines (diagonal) in pencil in preparation for cutting. Colour pencils are used where necessary.

b) Once you have decided on a design and the pitch, mark the angle in pencil. Use thread or tape to pick up the pencil line around the workpiece. Measure between the tape as each circumference is completed for the desired pitch around the workpiece. To establish the number of bines, repeat the taping procedure at equal stages around the blank according to the required number of bines. Mark out or cut along one edge of the tape.

c) Cut a piece of cardboard, wrap it around the blank workpiece and tape the cardboard allowing it to revolve loosely around the blank. Cut the cardboard to the desired angle of pitch. Convert the Pitch Line in pencil from the angled cardboard by rotating the workpiece, keep the pencil line parallel to the angle on the cardboard until you have a full Pitch Control Line along the workpiece. Repeat the marking out for the required number of bines.

d) On larger pieces I recommend the above methods, but on small pieces, particularly where the material is dark, or on thin material where marking out could be difficult to execute or see, use the freehand method. This is explained within Chapter 19 Thin Twisting.

Do not be too ambitious at first. Start with a Single twist which is relatively easy; advance through the book, stage by stage, building your confidence and expertise until you are able to make the most advanced of twists. From there you can develop your own style and designs.

TOOLS REQUIRED

1. For the larger twists you will require a tenon saw.
2. A ¾" (19 mm) 'twisting gouge' (see illustration below). ground to thumb nail shape and sharpened fully round the leading edge to the heel of the tool. The bevel should be hollow ground. Hone the tool to a keen edge.

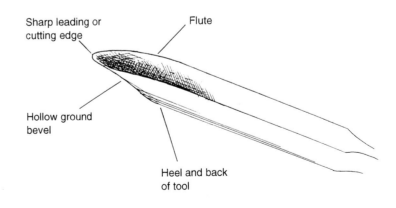

Twisting gouge

Sharp leading or cutting edge

Flute

Hollow ground bevel

Heel and back of tool

To use this tool properly it must be very sharp. Ideally, it should be 4" (102 mm) long and fitted with a standard chisel handle.

3. A palm plane (See photo below) of the type with a captive blade. A plane with an open ended blade will foul and tear up the bottom of the trough or hollow. Keep this tool as sharp as possible.

4. A range of rough and smooth rasps. Some modern rasps, Surforms and heavy duty files are very useful. See photo right.

5. Shape a piece of wood (e.g. as below) to use for sanding. Wrap sandpaper round this tool and use in a sawing motion. Dowelling may also be used.

6. For a single twist a 1½" (38 mm) carpenter's chisel is required and a ½" (13 mm) chisel for Open twists.

7. For the small twists a range of small wood files or rasps are needed to suit the individual hollows or troughs. There are several brands on the market and they can be purchased at most large hardware and tool stores.

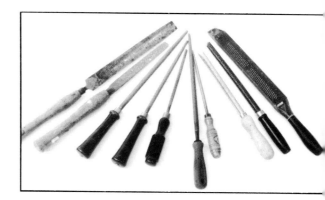

A range of large rasps

Chisels and dividers

Base of the palm plane

INCORRECT
With this plane the edges of the blade has a tendency to tear the bottom of the hollow

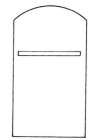

CORRECT
The ends of the blade on this plane is protected in a captive housing

Tenon saw, twisting gouge, palm plane, rasp and shaped piece of wood for sanding

3

PREPARATORY CONSIDERATIONS

PRODUCING A TWIST BY HAND

As shown in the last chapter, the tools required for cutting twists are relatively simple and with a little practice should present no problem in their use. Whether an amateur or professional woodworker the ability to cut a twist should make little difference, provided the proper procedures and marking out are followed. The use of sharp tools whilst cutting a twist can be dangerous, therefore the whole procedure is a discipline and must be strictly followed both for safety and to obtain the result you desire.

When you attempt your first twist it is likely that frustration may set in. It may be that tools are not sharp or the material is too hard, so commence with soft wood and keep sharpening your tools. Should you be unable to sharpen the tools properly seek help or get someone to teach you sharpening techniques.

Your second twist will take half the time, the marking up procedure will improve and quicken with practice as will the cutting. By the time you have cut four or five twists you will be confident enough to tackle a more difficult twist, even an Open twist. At this stage you will be capable of producing a 9"(229 mm) Double Barley twist in soft wood within 30 minutes. So prove me right.

The Double Barley twist is the easier twist to cut, so it may be that readers may wish to tackle it first. There is also an added advantage with a Double. It is more versatile and is only three simple processes from an Open twist. It is also more flexible when it comes to designing an Open twist.

As with any subject or craft, the process of learning is progressive. The same applies to woodturning and twisting. Go through each section stage by stage; the system of marking out and cutting a twist will become second nature. Do not be tempted into the next stage until you understand what is required at each stage.

For the complete novice to turning and twisting I refer you to the Glossary of Terms section at the back of the book. There is not too much to learn and it is better to be equipped before reading the book in detail. Spiral work is a discipline and one should follow the instructions implicitly to achieve the best result.

To many experienced turners today, the traditional methods of marking out and cutting spiral work carry a little mystique. This is mainly due to the reduction in demand for this particular form, in fine furniture, etc., and thus the lack of knowledge. In the case of the younger turner it is like a forgotten art. I suggest that the experienced turner, with some knowledge of twisting, selects the type of twist he wishes to copy from the book, then transfers the marking out to his selected workpiece and follows the cutting procedures from the appropriate chapter.

I have taught and demonstrated to amateur and

professional turners with varying degrees of expertise using the methods described in this book. Many have since produced some very nice pieces, some also expressed surprise as to the speed success was achieved.

For the flamboyant turner, several of whom I know but will not mention by name, I would say take the bull by the horns, dive in, select a twist wherever you like and try it.

SAFETY PROCEDURES

1. When selecting timber for a twist ensure there are no shakes or large knots as they can prove difficult when central to a bine. A shake can cut across a bine or central stem and render the piece dangerous and useless.

2. Never use large pieces of rag or emery cloth on a rotating spiral, whether solid or open. Note: As a beginner take care when sanding. Open-twist sanding should be carried out with the lathe stopped.

3. Should you decide to hand sand with the lathe in motion, reduce the speed to around 400 r.p.m. (revolutions per minute) and use *sandpaper* only, underhand rather than overhand. *Never* hand sand an Open-twist with the lathe in motion.

4. As a precaution, particularly on your first twist, it may be advisable to un-plug the lathe, remove or loosen the belt to avoid inadvertently starting the machine.

5. Always wear goggles, particularly when turning a twist which is already cut. An Open-twist is particularly dangerous if it breaks at high speed.

6. Do not attempt to cut a twist with the lathe in motion, or attempt to re-tool a completed twist whilst revolving.

7. Do not turn a partially cut twist, it may be that one side of the material is lighter due to the removal of waste material, the piece will vibrate and is likely to break up whilst spinning. Turning unbalanced materials can be dangerous. This applies to both large and small pieces.

LATHE CAPACITY

As in all woodturning, the size of the lathe 'between centres' and 'the swing over the bed' will determine the maximum size of the finished product, unless you are prepared to join finished pieces together.

'Between centres' means the maximum distance between the centre point of the headstock and tailstock centres for that particular lathe. 'The swing over the bed' or 'through' refers to the maximum width of material capable of being turned by a lathe.

Regardless of the lathe size one should be able to cut a twist. However, twisting is mainly confined to spindle work such as legs, stretchers, columns, rails, newels, banisters, balusters etc. These pieces are normally 24" (610 mm) long and upwards, therefore should you wish to turn and twist such items your lathe will have to be at least 30" (762 mm) between centres. For smaller items, such as candlesticks, goblets, Open-twist lamps, thin twists, pineapple twists, twisted knobs and boxes etc., a small lathe of 12" (305 mm) between centres will cope. The capacity of the lathe will not restrict your ability to cut a twist. In any case, even if you are not a woodturner, a twist can be cut by hand carving or supporting the piece centrally between two fixed points with sufficient clearance to rotate the work and use the tools.

There are lathes with obvious and considerable advantages over others in all areas of turning. A relatively recent innovation and introduction to lathes is variable speed with a reversing facility. For speed comparisons in cutting twists all lathes are similar, however when it comes to sanding and finishing a twisted piece the variable and reversing facility is invaluable. No changing gears or ' turning over' the workpiece. (This will be explained in the appropriate chapter.) This does not detract from any individual producing a turned and

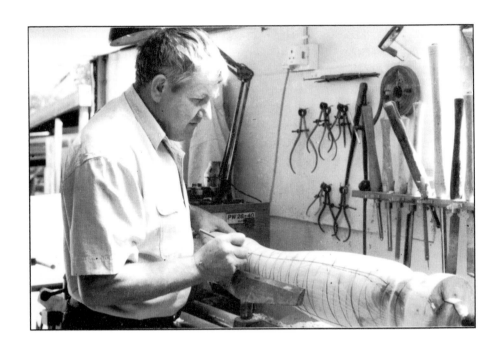

Lathe capacity: Poolwood and Little Gem lathes with twists between centres for comparison in size of machines and workpieces

twisted piece on the simplest of lathes, whether pole, metal or any other device designed to hold material between centres.

MATERIALS USED FOR TWISTING

Virtually any woodworking book, regardless of the subject, should make special reference to one of the most valuable and beautiful resources on our planet Earth. The tree and its beauty throughout the world has given man, from the earliest times, protection from violent elements, food and a means to develop domestically and creatively in many and various ways.

Today, timber is much in demand for its beauty and, sadly, much unnecessary destruction of the world's forests is taking place for other reasons.

Where there is a demand for timber and its products, the timber importers, merchants, manufacturers and woodworkers in general will try to meet that demand and have done so for centuries.

At one time it must have appeared to man that the supply of trees was inexhaustible. Who could have thought that within a short period of a hundred years, the situation regarding the world's vegetation could change so dramatically. I firmly believe that the vast majority of woodworkers love wood and the trees and detest the wilful and needless destruction of our natural forests for land. According to the 'experts' there is ample timber for everyone through re-planting, proper farming, cultivation and using timber felled through natural means.

In the case of woodturning, any type of wood may be turned provided it can be safely mounted, even timber that has been dead for years and has begun to rot. Spalted timber or timber which has all sorts of grub holes and knurled bits is a valuable find to a turner. It follows therefore, that the same applies to twisting. However, when selecting material for twisting, try to select sound, knot free, straight grained timber that is dry, and always twist across the grain where possible. Should you decide to glue shakes, knots or glue pieces together for turning and twisting, make absolutely sure the glue has cured and worked properly before use. Traditional turnings with twists are mainly from oak, beech, ash, elm, yew, walnut, mahogany, pine and some species of fruit trees. My favourites are yew, mahogany, holly, elm and walnut in that order. All these timbers are home grown except for mahogany. All my mahogany is second-hand discarded doors or furniture and any other pieces I can beg, borrow, and obtain from friends. I draw the line at stealing! I am also very fond of some exotic timbers such as ebony, sonekeling, padauk and cocobolo and these can be used for more decorative pieces. Twisting these species takes a little more time than the softer varieties and, in the main, the twists are smaller in any case.

4

ASPECTS OF DESIGN

Woodturning in itself is a very rewarding occupation, whether amateur or professional. The enjoyment in making a piece of work from wood is an experience that pushes the turner on to producing better and more complicated pieces. They do not always work, but there is pleasure in the pursuit anyway.

As a child I used to think that wood turnings were the shavings and pieces of wood on the floor. Even to this day I question the woodturner's aim. Is it to make beautiful shavings or to make something out of wood? How many times do we get carried away by the sheer pleasure of seeing those nice green wood shavings and end up with a smaller piece than originally intended? I still consider that some of the best turned pieces are on the floor of the workshop.

I may be about to upset some of my peers. No design or shape can be claimed to be totally new or original. Over thousands of years shapes have been made from all types of materials. How can we be sure a particular shape has not been made before? We cannot.

I look at a particular piece of material, (not spindle work), try to picture the shape in my mind to decide a design. After turning it I try to view it in a critical sense. I obviously like it or I don't. I have decided to take off a very fine shaving here and a little there. After a few minor adjustments I may be satisfied with the result. It is also a fact of life that, after very many minor adjustments, all

you end up with are designer shavings and firewood.

We have all experienced this feeling of loss. Looking at the floor we think, where did that piece of wood go?

There is one thing that is certain. All the shapes that I made during the destruction of that particular piece of wood have been made before. Make sure when practising a particular shape to use a cheap piece of stock.

Somewhere in that piece of cheap material is the shape you are looking for. It may leap out at you immediately or you may have made numerous alterations or shapes before attaining the one you like.

The most important aspect in woodturning design is that the profile must flow from one feature to the next in a clearly defined line which is pleasing to the eye. Any irregularity or break in a curved profile will be spotted immediately.

Should difficulty be experienced in getting into a particular design or style, start with traditional shapes. These may be varied to get very pleasing results. I find there are shapes everywhere: furniture, buildings, bridges, etc. Look for them to give inspiration. One particular piece I did was a hostess trolley. It features on the tray, a gallery with pillars similar in design to the stone work gallery on Henley-on-Thames bridge. Personally, I am not so concerned where the shapes originate, whether from the mind, stone or steel. If it looks good, have a go, convert it to wood.

There are however, some very pleasing shapes and styles which have been refined and reproduced over and over by some turners. Some of these styles can be identified as a particular turner's work or 'trade mark'.

Whenever a particular shape has been achieved, regardless of its origins, if you really like it, develop it to your *own* style.

There are considerations regarding copying more recent turners' designs or work. If the design is painted, carved, burned or otherwise worked to an individual, perhaps artistic style, acknowledge it, admire it or not, see its potential — but don't blatantly copy it.

The more recent developments in woodturning, such as burning, colouring, carving, fine segmenting etc., as well as twisting may be added to your repertoire. Woodturners throughout the world are continually striving to achieve the ultimate design. Whatever their speciality, the list is endless.

As general woodturning gives the turner great pleasure, the pleasure from finished turnings passes on to the purchaser or owner. I find that the owners enthuse over such pieces as they would a new car, whether they are items of furniture, bowls, boxes or other wooden trinkets.

To the trained or untrained woodturner's eye no piece escapes judgement, whether it is a masterpiece or piece of wooden art gone wrong. Turners are critical individuals who, in the main, love every piece of wood, even the shavings. When a critic views a piece that he is not sure of, or dislikes, the usual comment is, it's a lovely piece of wood. What they are saying, in truth, is, shame about the design. Sometimes it may be the other way round. 'What a lovely design; could have used a decent piece of wood'. An important point to remember is the type of timber selected. In some cases stability is important, particularly if shape is to be retained.

I consider that design, quality of turning and selection of material are the three most important aspects in woodturning. If I were to be complemented on my work I would hope the comments would also be in that order.

I, personally, have several critics. In the main they are members of my family.

My eldest son James is traditional in taste and likes most things I make.

My son Andrew is an artist. He tends to like the more modern look. The best critic of all is my wife Linda who, without fail will pick out any imbalance in a piece. Sometimes I will have a re-think and sometimes not. I don't always do what I am told! Joking apart, a good critic is normally someone close or someone will not mince their words.

I consider that the main purpose of the majority of woodturners is to achieve the most desirable shape from a particular piece of wood, and to bring out the natural beauty of the material to enhance the design. Design and turning technique also determine the level of craftsmanship. Design is particularly important where the wood is painted or masked in some other way. In this instance design is critical.

Most woodturners can be a little vain. They will say 'I don't mind constructive criticism', when all the time they may be thinking, what does he know about it. I have to admit, I have done it. We have all made and seen them — those pieces made from a beautiful piece of timber. With a little more thought to the shape, we would have loved them ourselves. It gives me a great deal of personal pleasure when people admire my work.

I know that the turning and the finish are all important, but the first thing that will attract attention is the design.

My main reason for going into design aspects in detail, is that it is one of the most important factors in twisting. The design of the spindle, whether a leg, stretcher, column, etc, has to balance before it is twisted. Treat the twisted area as another feature, just like any other.

It is my personal opinion that a twist is the most attractive form in spindle work. It also takes a lot of beating on a hollow form or bowl.

We all have memories of some of our favourite and treasured pieces that hopefully grace a home, place of work or meeting place. I have such favourites.

Bill Rice, a dear friend for many years, all the time I knew him, never saw my work or me. He had been blind for 30 years before he died.

He would ask to see all my work and I would respond by showing him every piece I could and describe the wood. I consider myself privileged to have had such a friend, who would, with tactile sense, see everything in my work that others more fortunate may take for granted. I also take heart in the pleasure it gave him during his latter years, confirmed by words and facial expression.

When Bill passed away, his wife and her sister, asked me to consider making something in his memory for our village church. Our vicar and I got together and decided that a fitting memorial would be a pair of candlesticks in oak for the altar, Bill's favourite timber.

It gave me great pleasure to make the pieces and have them accepted in his memory to be used in our place of worship.

5

THE SINGLE TWIST

Before starting any of the following twists, make sure you have a small stock of fresh, good quality joinery pine, not too tightly grained and free from knots and shakes. Four 16" (406 mm) × 1½" (38 mm) × 1½" (38 mm) will do to start with.

PREPARING THE WORKPIECE

Before starting this twist, decide whether you want to use it for a lamp, candlestick or just keep it as your first attempt. Consider it as a practice run.

Prepare a piece of soft pine 16" (406 mm) × 1½" (38 mm) × 1½" (38 mm), mark and centre punch both ends deeply with the lathe centre 4 or 2 prong drive in order to obtain positive drive at either end of the piece. The twist you are about to prepare for, will be 9" (228 mm) long, single bine with a 1½" (38 mm) pitch. (See page 15 for pitch details). The pitch in this case is exactly the same as the width of material.

Centre your blank between centres, pencil mark 3" (76 mm) from either end, turn the central 10" (254 mm) section down to a smooth and parallel 1½" (38 mm) blank cylinder, the central 9" (228 mm) section of this blank will be your twist. Leave the two 3" (76 mm) square ends.

Small lathes

Reduce the length of the blank to suit your lathe. You may also consider reducing all the marking out measurements by ¼" (6 mm) if your lathe is less than 12" (305 mm) between centres. For those who wish to try traditional twisting in miniature, there is no reason why an eighth of the size should not be done on the first attempt. (See Chapter 19 for thin and wire twisting).

Preparing a blank for twisting

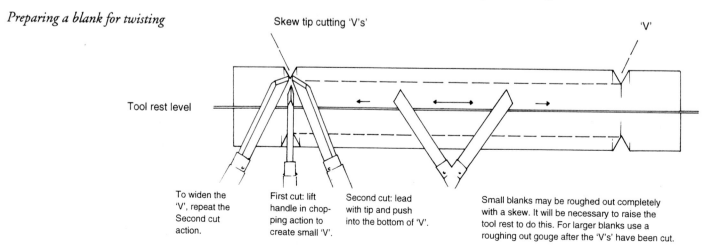

Skew tip cutting 'V's'

'V'

Tool rest level

To widen the 'V', repeat the Second cut action.

First cut: lift handle in chopping action to create small 'V'.

Second cut: lead with tip and push into the bottom of 'V'.

Small blanks may be roughed out completely with a skew. It will be necessary to raise the tool rest to do this. For larger blanks use a roughing out gouge after the 'V's' have been cut.

MARKING OUT

Stage 1: Start Lines

Mark in pencil, four horizontal or longitudinal lines across the 10" (254 mm) blank at four equal points around the circumference. If you have an index facility all the better, if not, line up the tool rest against the square corners of the blank and draw a pencil line, using the straight edge of the rest as a guide along the 10" (254 mm) prepared section. Do this at all four corners. You now have what I term, the 'Start Lines'. Number these lines 1 to 4.

Stage 2: Pitch Lines

Mark the 9" (228 mm) section into 3 equal 3" (76 mm) sections and split the 3" (76 mm) sections again to 1½" (38 mm), making sure these marks are clear enough to be seen with the lathe in motion. Start the lathe and mark at all seven points. You should have seven circles around the blank, each circle crossing the Start Lines at four intersections. These vertical circles are what I call the 'Pitch lines'. I will refer to them from now on as Pitch Lines rather than Vertical Lines.

Union Graduate in action preparing a workpiece

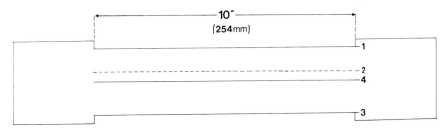

Four horizontal Start Lines for a Single twist with a 1½" (38 mm) pitch

Stage 1: Start Lines

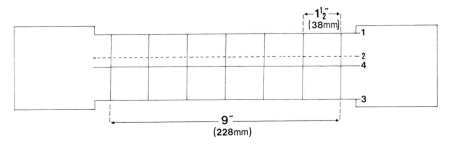

Setting the Pitch Lines for a Single twist

Stage 2: Pitch Lines

Stage 3: Pitch Dividing Lines

You now have six segments or pitches along the length of the blank each measuring 1½" (38 mm). Divide these segments twice, to ¾" (19 mm) then ³/₈" (9 mm). You now have twenty-four segments. These are the Pitch Dividing Lines, their intersections with the Start Lines will determine where the 'Pitch Control Lines' will be.

Stage 4: Pitch Control Lines or Cut Line

This stage is where the diagonal lines are marked out. This line is crucial and is the end product of all the marking out labours. Begin at Start Line 1, mark this line heavily in pencil across the segment from right to left clockwise, diagonally around the blank towards line 2 to 3 and 4 along the full length of the twist. That line is the course for the cut. I call it the 'Cut Line'. Go to Start Line 3, mark with a green pencil in the same manner. This green line is the top of the bine, and therefore the 'Bine Apex Line'. Repeat the process at lines 2 and 4 in red pencil. These red pencil lines indicate the width of the bine and hollow. They are the 'Width Control Lines'. You have now completed the marking up for a 'Single'. I call all these diagonal lines the 'Pitch Control Lines'. You will note that the Pitch Control Lines, start and end on the same Start Line. This is the measure of a true traditional spiral twist.

Stage 3: Pitch Dividing Lines

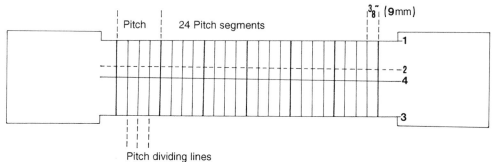

Pitch   24 Pitch segments

³/₈" (9mm)

Pitch dividing lines

Divide the Pitch segments twice to get the Dividing Lines
After which there should be 24 Pitch segments

Stage 4: Complete Marking Out

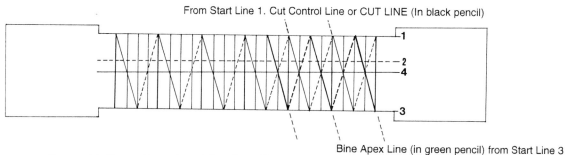

From Start Line 1. Cut Control Line or CUT LINE (In black pencil)

Bine Apex Line (in green pencil) from Start Line 3

To complete the marking out, mark in red pencil
Control Lines from 2. and 4.

Obviously, should you so desire, you may use any colours you wish, but keep to the marking out procedure. The use of colours in this case is purely for identification purposes.

The Marking Out Procedure for a Single twist is the basis for all marking out regardless of the design of twist.

Stage 5: Cutting the Single

The piece is ready to cut. The square corners are left in order to give you grip with your free hand whilst cutting the twist. It may be necessary, should you find the corners are too sharp, to start the lathe and remove only the sharp edges to prevent damage to the hands. You will soon discover that the square ends are vital in obtaining a smooth cut.

The depth of the hollow (or trough) in the case of a Single twist is about one third the width of the material. ½" (13 mm) in this case. Before you start cutting with the tenon saw remove the tool rest from the lathe. Take the tenon saw and with your free hand hold the left square end.(Left-handers see below). Start to cut along the heavily pencilled Cut Control Line. Cut across the first segment only, to a depth of approximately ¼" (6 mm). Keep the heel of the saw in this cut, rotate the piece anti-clockwise with your left hand, continue the forward cutting action as you rotate the piece into the direction of the cut. Make sure to keep the saw at the correct angle at all times. You will find co-ordination is vital. Following each stroke of the saw return the blank to the starting position with the left hand. Repeat the action until the required depth is reached. Once depth is reached on each segment, instead of returning the blank to its original position, rotate the piece and saw into the next segment.

The intention is to count the strokes of the saw whilst your free hand is simultaneously turning the wood to the forward cutting action. Continue this action along the full length of the Cut Control Line without crossing the end Pitch Line.

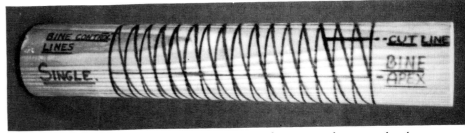

The Single twist marking completed

Note for Left-handers

If you are left-handed you will find cutting a right-hand twist a little awkward just as a right-handed person would find cutting a left-hand twist. A left-handed person should take hold of the opposite square end with their right hand and cut with the same rhythm. You may also find it easier to stand on the other side of the lathe to make this cut.

You can use a saw with a depth control bar, although I personally dismiss this type of tool as a little bit of fun. Count roughly three cuts on each segment and there is no need for a depth control bar. However, the cut should be accurate in depth as well as accurate in line.

The cut is there to assist the cutting action of the next tool, the gouge, not to determine the depth of the hollow. Do not cut too deeply, or, try to reach what you consider is final required depth. You will only mess it up. This cut is also critical in allowing the waste material from the first pass of the gouge to break out without tearing up the other side of the cut and ruining the piece.

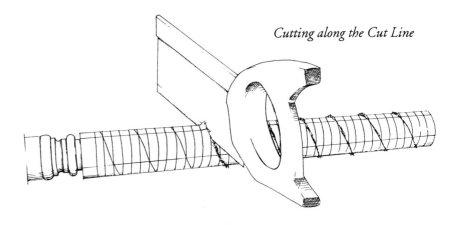

Cutting along the Cut Line

Stage 6: Cutting the trough or hollow

Take your twisting gouge, make sure it is sharp. Set the tool rest just under level with the centres, turn the gouge on its left side with the flute facing the headstock, place the gouge on the rest. Introduce the sharp tip of the tool on to Start Line 1 against the first Pitch Line, push and turn the tool at the same time until it is on its right side. This should make a nice fingernail type cut in the corner of the two lines. Incline the gouge on to its right side and start to cut from the left edge of the fingernail mark. You should see the saw cut approximately ¼" (6 mm) to the right of the gouge and the proposed angle of cut. To control the direction of cut all you need do is alter the angle of the gouge by moving your body either left or right. Your feet must be properly placed and the body must be 'locked on' to the gouge. The angle should be about 45 degrees to the workpiece. You must also ensure that the gouge is on its side at all times in order that the sharp edge leads through the material. Start the cut, when you and the gouge are set, by turning the workpiece with the left hand firmly anti-clockwise into the sharp leading edge of the tool. Do not attempt to push the gouge or move it along the rest. All you have to do is keep it at the correct angle of cut and depth. The gouge will automatically follow its cutting edge and angle of least resistance as the waste material breaks off at the saw cut.

Keep a parallel and even cut to the saw cut line. Do not try to remove too much material in one pass. The ¼"(6 mm) shaving should roll off the tip of the gouge into the saw cut. Make sure you do not cross over the red line otherwise you will damage the bine. Keep the gouge firmly in position at the same time continue to turn the workpiece until ½" (13 mm) short of the last Pitch Line. Then slowly turn the gouge tip to point at 90 degrees to the horizontal Start Line, at the same time pulling firmly but slowly into the cut with the left hand. On reaching the last Pitch Line you should have a nicely rounded corner. Pull steadily down with the left hand making sure to cut along the Pitch Line and into the saw cut. That should leave a nice clean shoulder at the end of the bine.

Turn the workpiece end to end between centres on the lathe and repeat the procedure on the other side of the saw cut. This will prove to be a little more difficult and firm control of the gouge is called for. (*The alternative method to this is not to turn the workpiece; use the gouge on its left side with the flute facing you and cut to the right of the saw cut. The shaving will roll towards you into the hollow. This method of cutting will improve with practice.*)

Complete another two passes with the gouge as above. You will find that the saw mark will be removed, possibly leaving uneven and fluffy waste material at the bottom of the hollow. Remove this waste, by turning the gouge completely on its back into the bottom of the hollow. Using the bevel of the gouge to control the depth of cut, rotate the workpiece as before with the left hand, and cut the waste as it comes over the horizon of the hollow. You now know the basics of using the 'twisting gouge'. To gain depth and width, repeat the passes as required.

During the hollowing process make sure the red lines are not removed. Go tightly up to these lines with the gouge but never over. Otherwise you may change the design of your twist.

Left-handed person

When preparing the workpiece use a 20" (508 mm) length instead of 16" (406 mm). Leave 5" (127 mm) long square sections at either end. This will give you room to cut with the saw and the gouge. With the gouge in your left hand, turn the workpiece at the tailstock end with your right. Follow the same procedure and cutting action as above.

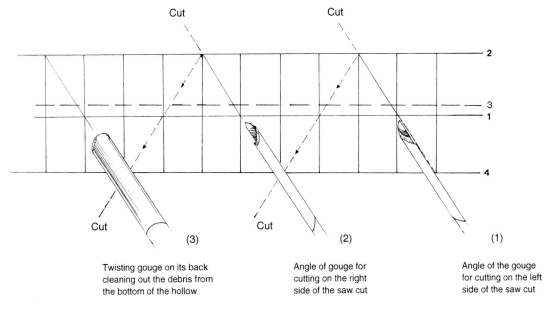

Cut

Cut

2

3
1

4

Cut

(3)

Cut

(2)

(1)

Twisting gouge on its back
cleaning out the debris from
the bottom of the hollow

Angle of gouge for
cutting on the right
side of the saw cut

Angle of the gouge
for cutting on the left
side of the saw cut

The order of cutting is from right to left.

The twisting gouge in its cutting modes in the correct order

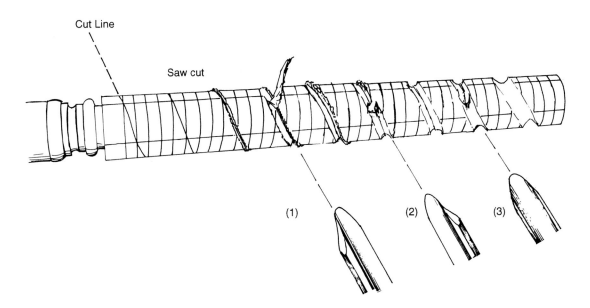

Cut Line

Saw cut

(1)

(2)

(3)

The body is 'locked' on to the gouge

Once you gain experience in using the gouge, it is by far the fastest and cleanest method of removing waste. particularly on softer material. Other methods can be more labour intensive, however, on really hard materials for example, where it is very difficult to use the gouge. Tools such as rasps, round files, drills etc., are very useful for such occasions. In some cases where the material is cross grained, the waste material may be removed with the saw and chisel by cutting V's between the two red Pitch Control Lines in the areas of difficulty. (See illustrstion on the facing page) When using this method do not go too wide or deep. Tidy up with the gouge, plane, rasp and sandpaper as normal. See Chapter 10 Alternative Methods Of Cutting a Twist.

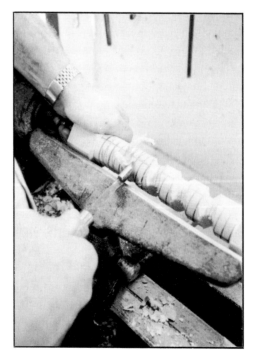

*Turning the workpiece into the leading edge
of the angled gouge*

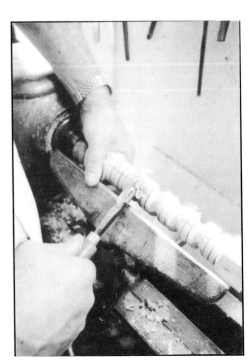

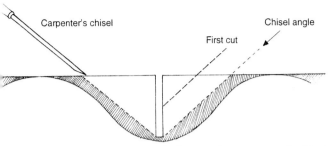

Cutting or roughing out a hollow with a carpenter's chisel

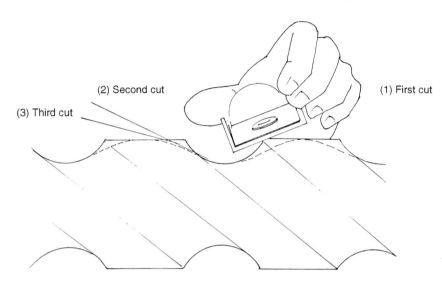

The palm plane in its cutting mode. Note the cutting angles

Stage 7: Using rasps and files

The next stage is to ensure the hollows or troughs are clean and regular and that the bine is reasonably even throughout its full length.

Perhaps the best method to do this, is with one of the modern round files or rasps as near in size to and just under the width of the hollow. Use the rasp with long even strokes whilst turning the workpiece with the free hand as before, taking care not to create flat spots (Flats). Using this tool slightly angled left across the hollow you will be able to tidy the sides or shoulders of the bine and also even up the widths.

Stage 8: Rounding the bine

The next stage is to round off the bine with a palm plane. Place the plane in the palm with the blade body in the crease between thumb and forefinger. Place the plane over the top of the bine, incline the plane to the left and into the hollow. Use the same rotating action as before with the left hand to pull the material into the blade, simultaneously pushing the plane forward and round the bine. Keep the left edge of the plane in the hollow during this cut. The next cut with the plane should be on the brow of the bine and the third just over the brow. (Note: during these three strokes, the red line has been removed. Do *not* remove the green line at any cost. To do so will

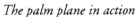

The palm plane in action

change the shape of the twist.) With the left hand rotating the workpiece as you did during sawing keep up this planing action along the length of the bine, continually checking the shape of the bine behind the blade. In order to plane the other side of the bine, turn the workpiece over in the lathe and repeat the process on the other side. Any irregularities should be trimmed off with smaller and even passes with the plane. Check your work to ensure the bine is perfectly rounded. Do not go on to the next stage unless you are satisfied.

Should you not possess a palm plane, the same result can be achieved with a heavy duty flat rasp or Bastard file. The finish may not be as smooth so more work will be required at the sanding stage.

Stage 9: Shaping the bottom of the hollow

The bottom of the hollow must be cut to give that true tight spiral effect seen on most traditional Single twists. To do this use the 1½"(38 mm) carpenter's chisel with a keen edge. Hold the workpiece as normal with the left hand, the chisel in your right like a dagger, with the heel of the chisel away from you. Push the chisel tightly against the left shoulder of the bine with the sharp edge into the extreme right edge of the hollow. Push firmly straight down into the hollow and rotate the spiral anti-clockwise onto the chisel.

This action will have a ploughing affect on the material with a shaving rolling into the middle of the hollow. On reaching the end, stay there, turn the chisel round in your hand and repeat the same process backhand and rotating the workpiece clockwise until reaching the starting point. Repeat this process until satisfied with the regularity of the 'V' finish.

The piece should now be ready for sanding.

Shaping the hollow with the carpenter's chisel

Stage 10: Sanding the Single

The procedure for sanding must be co-ordinated just as is saw cutting and planing. Take the wooden sanding tool and wrap a length of 60 grit paper around its full length about of 18" (457 mm). Wrapped in paper the tool must fit snugly into the bottom of the hollow 'V'. In a long stroke sawing action and using the left hand as before to rotate the work sand the entire length of the twist. Clean up the ends and any areas where the grain may have been torn. Use the same sanding tool in a rolling action round either side of the bine. Do not sand in one spot. Keep the workpiece moving otherwise flat spots will occur. Use this tool for rough sanding only.

Take a 4" (102 mm) square piece of emery or sand-paper, bend it round the index and middle finger. Holding the paper with the thumb against the index finger, on the lowest speed start the lathe and with the sandpaper hand stroke the top of the bine lightly from right to left until you catch the bine lead. Time this action for sanding by pushing into the hollow, lower or increase the speed of the lathe to suit the timing. You will probably find the lathe speed may be increased to around 300 to 400 r.p.m. and still be able to control this sanding procedure. This process will regularise the bine.

To clean the top of the bine, take a small piece of sandpaper measuring 4" (102 mm) × 1½" (38 mm). Place it under the index and middle fingers with the apex of the bine pressed on to the sandpaper between the fingers to form an arch over the bine. Use the free hand to turn the workpiece as before. This time you can also rock the workpiece backwards and forwards to assist sanding evenly throughout the length of the twist. Sand until the green line is removed and the apex is clean and even. Go through the grit range for the desired finish. (For other methods of sanding refer to Chapters 6 and 7).

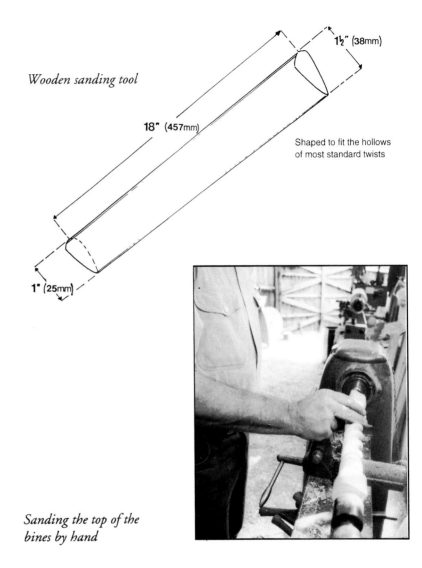

Wooden sanding tool

1½" (38mm)

18" (457mm)

Shaped to fit the hollows of most standard twists

1" (25mm)

Sanding the top of the bines by hand

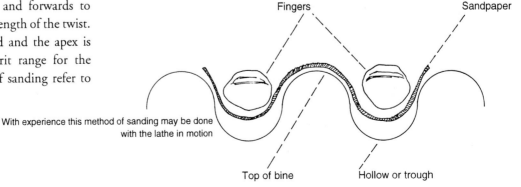

Fingers

Sandpaper

With experience this method of sanding may be done with the lathe in motion

Top of bine

Hollow or trough

Stage 11: Finishing the ends of the twist

To complete the twist and finish it off in a traditional manner turn a cove or hollow at either end of the spiral to about a quarter of the depth of the material, or as desired. Some traditionalists may say that these coves should be turned before cutting the twist. Start the coves on the end Pitch Lines. It may be necessary to pinch about an 1/8" (3 mm) of the bine to get the proper effect. Remember this when marking up and cutting for its partner (mirror image) when making a pair. Should the cove require sanding take care not to damage the clean sharp end of the bine.

A Single twist can be used on many designs of furniture, and as it is one of the stronger twists it can, in my opinion, be one of the most attractive. Like any other twist there should be a left and right (mirror image) in matched pairs.

(Cutting a left-hand twist is explained in Chapter 9).

The finished piece

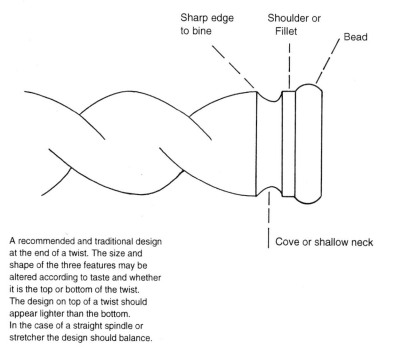

Sharp edge to bine — Shoulder or Fillet — Bead

Cove or shallow neck

A recommended and traditional design at the end of a twist. The size and shape of the three features may be altered according to taste and whether it is the top or bottom of the twist. The design on top of a twist should appear lighter than the bottom. In the case of a straight spindle or stretcher the design should balance.

Matching pairs (mirror image) of c. 1930's oak table legs with single twist

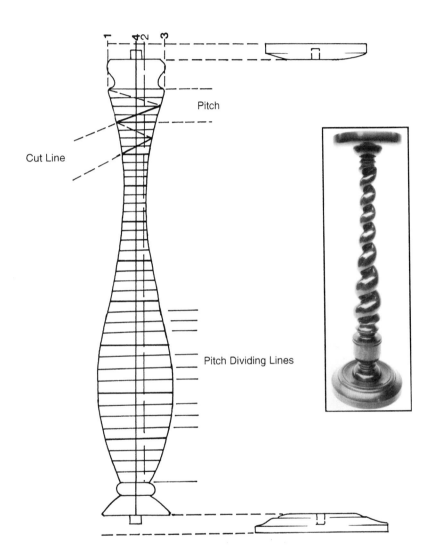

Project drawing for a torchere which has been marked out for a Graduated Single twist. (See Chapters 16 & 17). Overall height 36" (914 mm).
Inset: a similar torchere with a Tapered and Graduated Single twist

6

DOUBLE BARLEY TWIST

The Double Barley twist is a real old favourite and is found on a variety of furniture going back over the past three to four hundred years. It may be cut in any wood although it appears that the Double in oak was particularly favoured with the oldest examples surviving on oak tables, chairs and hall stands. The pitch may be varied according to taste and type of material. It may be tapered, shaped as a teardrop, waisted, arched or even cut on a hoop or ring. A most fascinating aspect of the Double barley is the fact that it can be opened to produce the 'Open' or 'Hollow twist' which is definitely my favourite — and most other people's as well. In this chapter I will take you through the stages to make this most attractive form and in the next chapter I will show you the procedure to open the same twist. I refer to these twists as the 'Double' and 'Double Open'.

Whilst marking out and cutting the Double in this chapter, to avoid repetition I refer back to some procedures in the previous chapter which cover the same ground.

Stage 1: The blank
Select a piece of straight grained softwood, free from shakes, knots etc. 16" (406 mm) × 1½"(38 mm) × 1½" (38 mm). Prepare the blank as described in Stage 1. Ch. 5. Remember to keep the two 3" (76 mm) long square sections at either end and, if necessary, take off the sharp edges. Centre punch both ends with the lathe drive centre.

Stage 2: Start Lines
Mark the four horizontal or Start Lines from the square corners as previously described, p27, and number them 1 to 4 clockwise at the extreme right end of the blank.

Stage 3: Pitch Lines
The pitch for a Double is normally double the width of the material or blank. In this case the pitch will be 3" (76 mm). Mark centrally on the blank a 9"(228 mm) section, this will be your twist. Divide the 9"(228 mm) section into three 3"(76 mm) sections and mark heavily in pencil. These are the Pitch Lines indicating the length of the pitch.

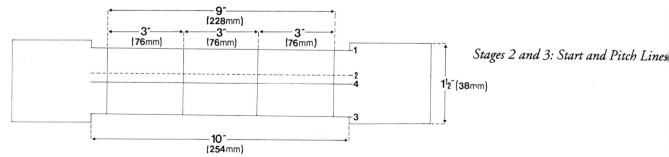

Stages 2 and 3: Start and Pitch Lines

Stage 4: Pitch Dividing Lines

In the case of this double, split the pitch segments twice to get your three control lines and therefore your four equal segments ¾"(19 mm) wide, making a total of twelve segments.

Dividing Lines divide the pitch segment into equal smaller segments between the Pitch Lines, in the case of a Single, Double, or 4, 8, 12, or 16-Start, the divisions are always equal in number. They intersect with the Start Lines to determine the angle of the Cut and Pitch Control Line.

In the case of a Triple, or 6, 9, 11 and 13-Start, the process is different. This will be explained later.

Stage 4

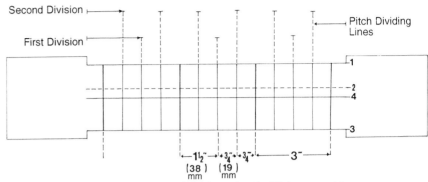

This illustration shows the equal divisions after the Pitch segment has been divided twice

Stage 5: Pitch Control Lines

As mentioned in the previous chapter the Start and Pitch Lines determine the angle of the control lines. In the case of a Double there are two Cut Lines and two Bine Apex Lines.

Mark in red at 1 on the first Start Line diagonally across the first segment to the second, third and fourth Start Lines. Continue to the end of the blank. (Note: at this point the first cut line is marked out). Repeat the process in the same colour at Start Line 3. (Note: at this stage you have two red cut lines or Pitch Control Lines along the length of the blank). Repeat this process at Start Lines 2 and 4 in green pencil. The two red lines are the Cut Lines and the green ones are the Bine Apex Lines. Make sure all the control lines cross the intersections of Pitch and Start Lines accurately. The marking out for the Double is complete and ready to cut.

Some readers will say, 'Hey, what about the other Pitch Control Lines, the Complete Marking Out?'. Okay, you asked for it. (Other readers may carry on to the next stage).

Stage 5

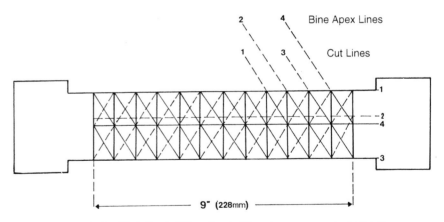

Double Barley Pitch Control Lines (control lines is a common name for all the diagonal lines.)

For the Complete Marking Out take an orange or any other brightly coloured pen and mark a fresh set of four Start Lines evenly between the originals.

Divide the segments equally between the original Pitch Dividing Lines. There are now twenty-four segments. Using the same new colour, from right to left, mark very carefully across the red intersections, to create a new set of Pitch Control Lines. These lines indicate the width of the hollows and bines and they provide accurate control when cutting the hollows and forming the bines. The piece may look cluttered. However, this is what I term as the Complete Marking Out. This procedure will ensure a very accurate twist although it is not always necessary to use.

Readers may have noticed that the Complete Marking Out procedure was automatically built into the earlier marking out of the Single twist by using four Start Lines.

Stage 6: Cutting the troughs or hollows

With the tenon saw cut the red lines at 1 and 3 using the same technique as at Stage 5, Ch. 5, only this time take care not to go too deep. Three light strokes of the saw, about ¼" (6 mm) deep, will suffice. Do not be tempted to regulate the depth of the hollow by using the saw cut as a guide. The saw cut is there only to allow the waste from the first two passes with the gouge to break out. One could attempt to use the gouge without a saw cut, but this it is not advisable. All that would be achieved is a ragged cut with a strong possibility of unrecoverable damage to the piece. The depth of the hollows on a Double should be approximately a quarter of the width of the twist. Take care not to cut over the two end Pitch Lines otherwise you will end up lengthening the twist.

Complete Marking Out

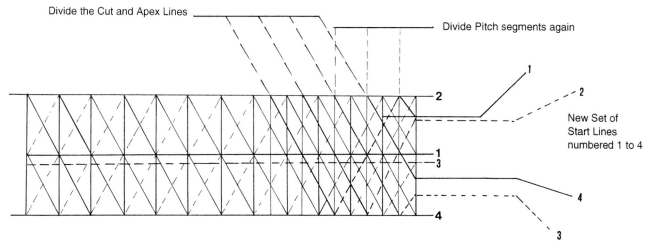

The Complete Marking Out is required only if a very accurate twist is required. Complete this marking out in bright colour

Stage 7: Gouge cutting

There is little difference in cutting a Double from a Single. The combined effort of cutting two hollows is probably more work. However it is easier due to the fact that the hollows are shallower. Use the gouge in the same manner as explained in the previous chapter. On the first pass with the gouge cut up to the orange Pitch Control Line. Be careful not to attempt too large a cut, otherwise the waste material may not break out at the cut and may tear across to damage the opposite bine. Do not cross the orange line otherwise you will spoil the shape of the twist.

With a sharp gouge, five or six passes per hollow should be sufficient to reach the required depth . When using the gouge keep a firm grip and try to keep a long continuous spiral of waste along the cut. Tidy up any debris with the gouge before going on to the next stage. See page 32 for illustration on the proposed cutting methods.

Stage 8: Cleaning or trimming with rasps and files

Take a round file or rasp that fits the hollows snugly, and use it to clean up and balance the hollows and bines as at Stage 7 in the previous chapter. When using a rasp or file which is smaller than the hollow, angle the tool horizontally in the hollow to effect cutting along the sides of the bines.

Stage 9: Rounding the bines

Use the plane or flat rasp as described at Stage 8 in the previous chapter taking care not to remove too much material or to remove the green lines. Whenever possible use a palm plane, it will give a more satisfactory finish. The plane can, if not sharp, and the rasp definitely will, tend to drag the grain and leave a rough surface, particularly on softer material. Compensate for this by leaving sufficient material to sand out defects. It is a common mistake not to allow sufficient material for cleaning up the workpiece. This can ruin the balance and profile of a spiral, in fact it can ruin any piece. With experience you will be able to avoid this type of potential error.

As experience is gained in using the palm plane, try to introduce a slicing or shearing action to the cutting edge of the plane. This may be done by pushing the nose of the plane slightly into the bottom of the hollow and turning the back end of the plane slightly outwards towards the apex of the bine; the cut will be smoother.

In cases where a rasp is used, the old fashioned type of rat tail file is a very useful tool for cleaning up the hollows before sanding.

Refer to the previous Chapter for photographs and Illustrations of the plane rounding the bines.

Cleaning and trimming with the rasp

Stage 10: Sanding the Double

See Stage 9, Ch. 5 covering sanding with the designed tool. When hand sanding the Double, the pitch has doubled in length, therefore one cannot hand sand with the lathe going at the same speed as for the Single. If you try to you will find that you will be unable to catch the timing; your sandpaper hand will whip very quickly over the workpiece without locating in the hollows. Should you be able to hold on to the sandpaper, all that would be achieved would be flat or pointed topped bines. Slow down the machine to its slowest speed and find the timing as before by stroking the sandpaper over the workpiece from right to left to catch the bine lead; increase the speed until you obtain a comfortable sanding speed. Do not remove the green lines.

You will find this action slightly different and more difficult to time than when sanding the Single. The difference in pitch will mean that the speed of the lathe will have to be reduced considerably. Another point to consider is that to sand both hollows, you may have to change the timing or synchronisation between strokes.

The most successful method I have recently discovered and employ during demonstrations, is the use of modern high quality emery, carbide or aluminium oxide cloth. For this twist, tear off a length of 100 to 120 grit abrasive cloth about 18"(457 mm) long and ½"(13 mm) wide. Finish the sanding with a similar length of abrasive cloth at 320 grit. This finish will satisfy most.

There are several methods of using this material:

1. Wrap the prepared strip of abrasive cloth once around the twist so that the abrasive side fits into the hollow. Take care that the sanding strip remains in the same hollow and does not cross the bine into the second hollow. This will damage the top of the bine.
   Take hold of the cloth at both ends. Pull it by the shortest end allowing the opposite end to be pulled towards the twist. The cloth will pass between the bines along the hollow, sanding it. Alternate the sanding between both hands in a lateral see-saw manner. As you do this, pull a little harder with the right hand and you will find the twist will rotate anti-clockwise, with the left in a clockwise direction. To sand the piece more effectively, put tension on to the cloth by pulling at both ends and continue the above process. Alternate this method between the two hollows to keep them even and well balanced. Go through the grits and a perfect finish should result.

When sanding any piece of woodturning on a lathe always use the coarsest grit necessary at first to remove any blemishes, working through to the finer grits. Do not make the mistake of using too fine a grit at first and having to return to a course grit. Sanding heats the wood and hardens the surface of

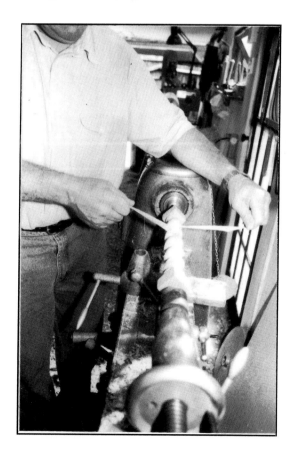

Sanding with cloth strip

most timbers. Returning to a coarse grit results in very difficult to remove sanding rings or lines. Learn to select the correct grit to do the job. Do not press too hard and so allow the timber to heat up too much, this may create heat shakes. Keep turning the sandpaper on to a fresh section and keep it moving. As a very rough guide, on soft timbers and spalted timbers after stabilising, it is sometimes necessary to start sanding with 60 to 80 grit. On soft species of timber, dependent on tooling, 150 grit is normal for starting. On some harder species start around 240 grit. Some exotics such as rosewood, padauk, cocobolo and ebony require very little sanding, starting around 320 grit and going through the grades to 800 to 1,000 grit.

2. You can also use a 4"(102 mm) square piece of sanding cloth to hand sand with the lathe in motion as above, also to clean the top of both bines as before. The finer grades of modern sanding cloth are very effective, particularly on the final fine sanding.

3. Take a piece of sanding cloth approximately 6"(153 mm) × 3"(76 mm). Fold it to 6"(153 mm) × 1½"(38 mm).

At this point make certain the lathe is in the slowest speed, the tool rest is removed, and the drive belt is loosened off and is in the slip mode. Also ensure there is no loose clothing near the workpiece.

Do not attempt this method of sanding unless you are absolutely certain and confident to do so, *or* if your lowest lathe speed is more than 500 r.p.m. *or* if your lathe is not capable of belt slip or fitted with an instant stopping device.

Start the lathe. Take the piece of sanding material in its doubled form for strength — we don't want it breaking. Grasp both ends of the material making sure the ends are safely tucked away in the palms of your hands, pull tightly with both hands leaving a taught section of material between both hands.

Place it centrally over the right end of the revolving spiral, push down on the spiral so that the centre of the material is pressed into the hollow, at the same time move it swiftly to the left to catch the timing. This is what I term as 'over the top sanding'. There is no danger provided you follow and understand these instructions. Repeat this process until you are satisfied with the result. You may also allow 'drag' on the sanding material, which will give a jumping effect along the twist in order to tidy up the top of the bines.

It is very important to keep the section of material between both hands shorter than one circumference of the material to be sanded. Any longer and the cloth may wrap itself around the material or whip itself around your fingers with possible disastrous consequences.

Using over the top sanding method

Stage 11: Finishing the ends of the twist
Re-mark the two end pitch lines, if removed during sanding, and make sure they can be seen with the lathe in motion. Cut the coves at either end of the twist as Stage 10 in the previous chapter, or to any other design considered suitable. Remember, in most cases the end of the twist should be finished off with a cove or hollow to achieve the correct style. Sand to desired finish.

The finished piece

Ebony Double Barley candlesticks

*Small rosewood goblets with
Double Barley twist stem*

Double Barley torchere

HOSTESS TROLLEY PROJECT

The hostess trolley is a combination of spindle and faceplate work.

There are four main pieces that make up the hostess.

1. The main frame.
2. Top tray.
3. Top tray dome.
4. Lazy Susan

The main frame has four legs, with two pummels each. One pummel is located at the top and the second 10"(254 mm) from the bottom. These pummels are the fixing points for the supporting stretchers. Eight outer stretchers are also turned with pummels centrally located for mounting the inner supporting stretchers and bosses.

These bosses house the inverted finials attached to which are the threaded securing spigots. The spigots are held in position within the boss by a washer fitted in a neck between the finial and the threaded location pin. The finials are glued to the threaded pins by means of a ³/₁₆"(5 mm) spigot, once located in the boss.

When the tray and lazy susan are placed on the main frame, the threaded pins protrude sufficiently to locate automatically with the centrally threaded recess at the base of each piece.

The main frame is elegant yet very rigid and strong.

The balls at the top of the uprights are capped in ebony. The caps are fitted by means of ¼"(6 mm) spigots.

The ½"(13 mm) brass casters are fitted on a tapered cup, above which there is a ½"(13 mm) ebony spat. The brass casters and the spats were turned to match the design at the base of the legs.

The main feature on the legs or uprights is the Double Barley twist with a 3"(76 mm) pitch.

Main frame

1. Four 1¼"(32 mm) × 28½"(724 mm) legs or uprights. (Not including brass casters)

2. Eight 12½"(318 mm) × 1"(25 mm) outer stretchers with ½"(13 mm) spigots at either end, for fitting to the pummels on the uprights.

3. Eight 5½"(140 mm) × ¾"(19 mm) inner cross stretchers.

4. Two 1½"(38 mm) × ¾"(19 mm) bosses for mounting the inner stretchers at the centre. These two bosses are turned with a recess to house the ½"(13 mm) threads on the tray locating pins. They are also centre drilled to ³/₈"(9 mm) to accept the spigot that, in turn, secures the finials.

5. Two 1⅛"(28 mm) × ³/₁₆"(5 mm) retaining washers centre drilled to ³/₁₆"(5 mm) to fit the finial on the threaded pin. These washers are also set into the centre bosses and should remain loose on the pin after fitting. These washers are, in fact, trapped within the centre boss between the threads at the top and the inverted finial at the bottom.

Note: The inverted finials located in the centre bosses. The threaded location spigots or pins can be seen protruding through the top of these bosses. The retaining washers can also be seen.

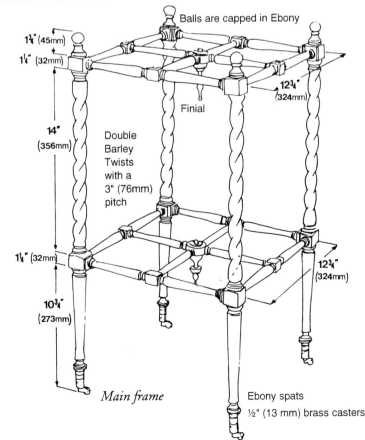

Balls are capped in Ebony

1¾" (45mm)

1¼" (32mm)

12¾" (324mm)

Finial

14" (356mm)

Double Barley Twists with a 3" (76mm) pitch

1¼" (32mm)

12¾" (324mm)

10¾" (273mm)

Main frame

Ebony spats
½" (13 mm) brass casters

Top tray

1. One 17"(432 mm) × ¾"(19 mm) mahogany base, turned as desired, and threaded centrally on the underside, with a ½"(13 mm) threading tap to a depth of ½"(13 mm). There are twenty ⅛"(3 mm) holes drilled around the circumference, on the top surface of the tray, exactly ½"(13 mm) from the outer edge. These holes must be equidistant otherwise problems will occur when fitting the gallery rail.

2. Twenty 1⅛"(28 mm) × ½"(13 mm) gallery supports in Ebony, with ⅛"(3 mm) spigots at either end.

3. Two 3½"(89 mm) × ½"(13 mm) ebony stretchers with ³/₁₆"(5 mm) spigots at either end. These are for the handle grips.

4. Four 2"(51 mm) × ½"(13 mm) ebony handle supports with a 1"(25 mm) ³/₁₆"(5 mm) spigot at one end, and a ½"(13 mm) ball at the other. These balls are drilled to ³/₁₆"(5 mm) to accept the spigots on the handle grips. The ³/₁₆"(5 mm) spigots are set into the side of the tray to form the handles. Note: The handles must be assembled and glued before they are set into the tray.

5. Gallery rail. This item is advanced turning. The rail is mahogany based with a ³/₁₆"(5 mm) ebony cap. Both the mahogany and the ebony are carefully

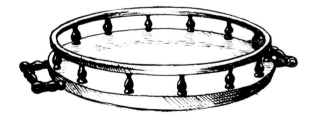

Lazy Susan tray. (The top tray is similar in construction.)

segment laminated, all in side grain approximately 4"(102 mm) long. These segments were roughly cut into shape before turning.

Brief turning technique. Glue sufficient segmented mahogany on to a wooden faceplate, taking care there are no gaps in the material. Turn roughly to oversize with a very flat surface to mount the ebony. With the ebony segments flat sanded fit and glue them to the surface of the mahogany with a non-flexing glue or resin. Make sure the joints are not opposite the mahogany ones. Ensure the glue is properly set before turning the rail to size ³/₈" (9 mm) deep and ¼" (6 mm) wide. Complete the top of the rail, cut a 'V' on both the inside and outside edges of the rail at the point of parting off. Leave an uncut centre section of ⅛"(3 mm). Sand and finish the rail to match the piece. Part off partially to the point where one can hear the thin turning tone, just before the rail is about to drop off. *Do not* part off the ring with the lathe in motion. With a Stanley or similar knife on the tool rest, revolve the workpiece by hand into the blade at the parting off point. This will ensure no damage is caused to the piece. To finish off the base. Turn a recess on the remaining mahogany or the wooden faceplate, to fit the top of the rail. Fit double sided tape into the recess and mount the rail. Sand and finish the base. Before removing the rail from the faceplate, drill the 20 holes around the circumference to match the base of the tray. Note: Also make sure that none of the 20 drill holes around the base of the rail end up opposite a joint on the ebony. <u>This is extremely important.</u> These 20 drill holes must be drilled to the depth of the mahogany only. The strength of the rail lies in the ebony at these fixing points.

6. Four 1"(25 mm) × ½"(13 mm) bun feet with ¼"(6 mm) spigots for fitting to the base of the tray when complete.

Dome

1. One 15½"(394 mm) diameter dome measuring 4"(102 mm) high. It is constructed by gluing the bottom 3"(76 mm) segmented section to a faceplate. The top of the dome is turned separately and is constructed from 16 wedge shaped segments in alternating dark and light mahogany. Each wedge shape is separated by ⅛"(3 mm) ebony strips. Once turned the top is set and glued into the base section by means of an 'L' shaped joint. The top is also locked into the base section by a ³/₁₆"(5 mm) square ebony inlay. Turn the outside of the dome leaving a 4"(102 mm) flat section at the top. Fix and centre a faceplate to this area. Mount and turn out the inside as one would a bowl. To finish the outside, mount the dome on the same faceplate used for the gallery rail above. Turn a recess to fit the base. The dome can be finished between centres, or by using a threaded length of dowelling through the dome and headstock or into the faceplate. The dome itself can be retained in position by means of a threaded wooden nut on the outside. When finished, the top of the dome is centre drilled to 1"(25 mm). This will retain the inner threaded flange.

   Note: The dome should be glued with a non-flexing glue or resin.

2. One 3"(76 mm) finial, with a ½"(13 mm) threaded spigot.

3. One 2" (51 mm) domed washer centre drilled to ½"(13 mm).

4. One 2" (51 mm) domed cap with a 1"(25 mm) × ⅛"(3 mm) shoulder, to fit the recess at the top of the dome. This cap is ½"(13 mm) centre threaded to a depth of ³/₈" (9 mm) to accept the threaded finial spigot.

   Fit the finial through the washer. Insert the threaded spigot into the recess at the top of the dome to locate with the inner cap. Tighten the finial and the dome is complete.

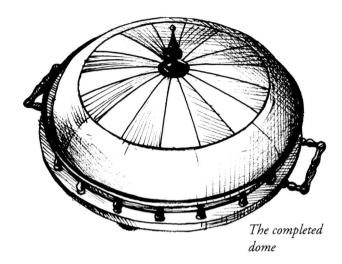

The completed dome

Lazy susan

The tray of the lazy susan is constructed of the same materials and to the same design as the top tray. Only the dimensions are changed.

The component dimensions are as follows:

1. One 11¾"(298 mm) × ¾"(19 mm) tray base. Turned with a recess to fit a 4"(102 mm) lazy susan.

2. Fourteen 1"(25 mm) × ½"(13 mm) ebony gallery supports.

3. One ³/₈"(9 mm) × ¼"(6 mm) gallery rail. This rail is constructed in the same manner as the top tray rail.

4. Two 3"(76 mm) × ½"(13 mm) ebony stretchers with ³/₁₆"(5 mm) spigots at either end, for handle grips.

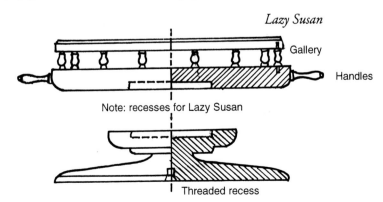

Lazy Susan

Gallery

Handles

Note: recesses for Lazy Susan

Threaded recess

5. Four 2"(51 mm) × ½"(13 mm) ebony handle supports to match the top tray.

6. One 11"(280 mm) base turned as illustrated below with a recess to fit the lazy susan. The base is centre drilled and threaded in the same manner as the top tray, to accept the ½"(13 mm) threaded locking pin. Assemble this piece in the same manner as the top tray.

All the spindle work for the main frame involves three sets of copy turning. Make sure the sizes and design are exact.

Before assembling the components, ensure all the pieces are a colour match.

See illustration p. 47 for the completed lazy susan.

With all four pieces completed, assemble the hostess, wax the locking threads for the top tray and lazy susan. I recommend that four ³/₈"(9 mm) black leather discs are glued to the top of the four central pummels on the outer stretchers, to pad the bottom of the top tray.

The completed hostess trolley
with Double Barley twist legs

7

OPENING THE DOUBLE BARLEY TWIST

The more confident turner may now wish to 'open' the Double Barley to produce the Open or Hollow Barley twist. Should one be tempted to do so, a word or two of caution. The pitch is a little short for this to be made in soft wood and it may entail stretching the pitch. However, it is possible. Should it remain intact in the process, you will find that the finished spiral will be unstable and will have the characteristics of a spring. If you decide to cut the above Double in a harder wood, such as oak, beech, yew or mahogany, there is no problem.

Start the opening procedure at Stage 2 below.

Stage 1: Preparing the blank

Select a 16"(406 mm) piece of timber of good quality as for the twists in the previous chapter. Prepare the blank as before with a 10"(254 mm) x1½" (38 mm) central cylinder with the two 3"(76 mm) square end hand drive sections.

Stage 2: Drilling for the hollow centre

For a 1½"(38 mm) Open twist a $3/8$"(9 mm) central hole is recommended, but a little smaller will suffice. Do not be tempted to go any larger, otherwise insufficient material may be left on the outer ring to form the bine. For this particular spiral, at least ½"(6 mm) thickness of material is required to achieve a cylindrical bine.

Note: For small lathes, cut the blank down to a length to suit your lathe provided you can retain the 9"(228 mm) marked out section. Should your lathe be smaller than 10"(254 mm) between centres reduce the length to suit, and all other measurements by one quarter, and make the central hole ¼"(6 mm) instead of $3/8$" (9 mm).

METHODS OF DRILLING

There are several methods of drilling. I will run through some of these and the dos and don'ts before preparing your blank.

1. Standard drilling procedures with the use of the Jacob's chuck in the tailstock. The workpiece may be between centres or chuck held.
2. Through the tailstock, using the long boring apparatus, for between centres drilling.
3. For lathes without a hollow tailstock, use a long boring apparatus which can be fitted to the banjo or tool rest, this apparatus also supports the end of the workpiece in the same manner as the tailstock. The hole is then drilled through the hollow supporting barrel of the apparatus. The material can be between centres or chuck held. A work steady may also be

used to support the tailstock end of the work to facilitate drilling.

4. Freehand, see photograph below. **Caution:** When drilling freehand, do not be tempted to use just any type of drill or auger, the result could be disastrous. For example, an auger with a worm or threaded lead screw could pull forward very quickly and could be very dangerous if used at the wrong speed. I personally will not use this type, unless the lead thread is ground off. **Do not** use the type of drilling tool with a cross handle to hold it. This may jam and cause damage to the work and worker.

   Do not drill a pilot hole, then attempt to enlarge it by hand using a larger drill.

   Do not be tempted to drill a very large hole freehand unless you have special equipment.

5. Another method that may be used to drill between centres on lathes without a hollow tailstock, but which have a hollow headstock is as follows: twist the drive belt between pulleys (reversing the drive on the machine) or use the reversing facility, to drill through the headstock. This may be done on older type lathes where design permits.

CORRECT METHOD OF APPROACH

When drilling freehand without a guide or rest, always make sure the drills used are sharp and the lathe is at the correct speed. Do not push hard or use too much exertion, as this can cause the workpiece to go off centre. With the lathe in motion this could result in injury.

SAFE DRILLING EQUIPMENT

The drills I use, and which I favour, are engineers' drills, saw tooth bits and sometimes flat bits which are held in either a Jacob's or similar chuck. For medium to long boring I use extended engineers' drills of varying sizes welded on to thinner shanks or handles with rounded knobs for handles. The reason for the thinner shanks is to allow waste material to escape along the hole to prevent binding. For long boring I use standard equipment as well as adapted engineers' drills.

DRILLING SHORT PIECES MECHANICALLY

Drilling short pieces with the aid of a Jacobs chuck held in the tailstock with the appropriate drill size, is probably the safest and most commonly used. Any type of drill can be used with this method.

Left:
Free-hand drilling
Right:
A selection of drilling bits and equipment

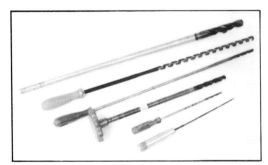

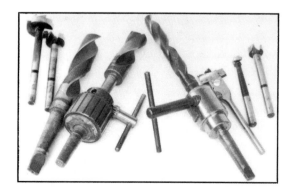

For really large hole boring, 1½"(38 mm) and over, always hold the workpiece in the headstock with a jam chuck or heavy duty jaw chuck. Fit the chuck into the tailstock and use the tailstock to push the drill forward into the workpiece to the required depth.

The safest method of drilling is to use the required size of engineers' drill on a morse taper directly into the tailstock.

DRILLING SHORT TO MEDIUM PIECES BY HAND

Hold and centre the workpiece in a 3 or 4 jaw chuck, jam or cup chuck. Start the lathe on the slowest speed, countersink the workpiece with a drill or fixed centre in the tailstock, sufficient to start the drilling. Hold the drill by hand central to the countersunk end, ensuring that the drill is parallel and horizontal to the lathe bed. Offer the drill into the lead hole and gently push. Once the drill has a straight lead in it will continue on a straight course to the required depth. To check if the lead in is straight, hold the drill very loosely in your hand and it will start turning. Should there be any wobble at the tailstock end of the drill, correct the angle to stop the wobble and continue drilling.

With care, workpieces up to 3 feet (904 mm) can be drilled using this method.

USING THE LATHE AS A PILLAR DRILL.

One of the oldest methods of drilling on a lathe is to use the lathe as a pillar drill. Put the required size morse taper drill, or chuck held drill into the headstock. Centre countersink both ends of the piece. Mount the workpiece very lightly between centres, (between the drill and tailstock), and set the lathe on its lowest speed. Hold the workpiece very firmly to prevent it revolving throughout the process. Start the lathe, and you will find that the drill has cut a recess. Push the workpiece on to the drill with the tailstock. Withdraw the workpiece at regular stages to ensure waste material is removed, otherwise binding and overheating may occur. Small pieces may be hand held.

Using this method the workpiece may also be held, assisted at the tailstock end, with a 2 or 4 prong drive.

DRILLING LONG MATERIAL

Hold and centre the workpiece between centres. Use the long auger through the tailstock. Drill to the full required length. In some cases it may be necessary to turn the workpiece round end to end in order to drill the whole way through. To make sure the hole meets properly in the middle, it may also be necessary to use a steady for long-boring thin material.

There is also a tool rest mounted jig for long boring. The jig is set to the level for boring against the end of the workpiece and acts as a hollow tailstock. Drill as above.

All the above methods are safe provided that the correct procedures are followed. Should the drill start to bind or overheat, remove it, and rub the drill with wax.

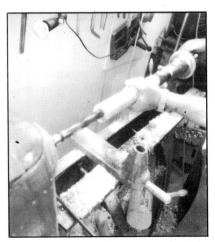

Left:
Using the tailstock
Right:
Using the lathe as
a pillar drill

DRILLING THE PREPARED BLANK

Take the prepared blank, holding it by whichever method you are equipped, centre and countersink as above. With the lathe turning at its slowest speed, drill the workpiece to a depth of 12"(305 mm). This will leave 4"(102 mm) not bored and will not affect the original drive end or final parting off, should you be using a jam or cup chuck.

Should you so desire, continue to use the chuck or remove it and cut the twist between centres as normal.

PITCH OF AN OPEN OR HOLLOW TWIST

I mentioned previously that it may be necessary to stretch the pitch of an open twist if the spiral is to be made in a soft wood. The reason for this is that the bines will be weak across the grain on a short pitch. The only method of strengthening the spiral is to: a) stretch the pitch, and/or b) thicken the bine.

In this case I intend to stretch the pitch to 4"(102 mm). It will mean this spiral will be 8"(203 mm) long with two 4"(102 mm) pitches. For stretching a pitch and lengthening a twist see Chapter 14.

Stage 3: Start Lines

On the 10"(254 mm) prepared section of the blank, mark in pencil four horizontal or Start Lines at equal distances around the blank. Number them 1 to 4 as previously described.

Stage 4: Pitch Lines

Mark 8"(203 mm) centrally on the 10"(254 mm) centre prepared section that is the length of the twist. Divide once, there are now two 4"(102 mm) pitch segments. These are your Pitch Lines.

Stage 5: Dividing Lines

Divide the two pitch segments equally twice. This will give you eight segments measuring approximately 1"(25 mm) along the 8"(203 mm) blank. These are the Pitch Dividing Lines.

Stage 6: Pitch Control Lines

Mark out the control lines, as at Stage 5 for the Double: in red at 1 and 3, these are the Cut Lines, and green at 2 and 4 for the Bine Apex Lines. These are your primary Pitch Control Lines. From this stage, the more experienced turner may cut the twist as previously described for the Double. Complete the Double, including sanding, before breaking through.

For the less experienced, and those who want accuracy, take an orange pencil, mark a new set of Start Lines between the original set and number them 1 to 4. Divide all the pitch segments. There are now sixteen segments along the blank.

Mark in orange from all four points diagonally across the segments as previously described. These are your secondary control lines and the Complete Marking Out for the Open Double. They control the width of the bines and hollows.

Follow the same cutting procedure as for the solid Double, then go on to the opening up. The result should be similar to the illustration on p. 53.

The reason I have illustrated the Open Double in this manner is to give a clear visual reference; an indication of marking out and the drilled centre hole. This will also act as a guide whilst cutting and opening the twist.

Stage 7: Cutting this particular Double

Be fully aware that this piece is to be an Open twist. Do not be tempted to go deep with the tenon saw as this will weaken the structure. If you cut through to the hole it will break. The standard Double must be cut and completely finished *before* breaking through.

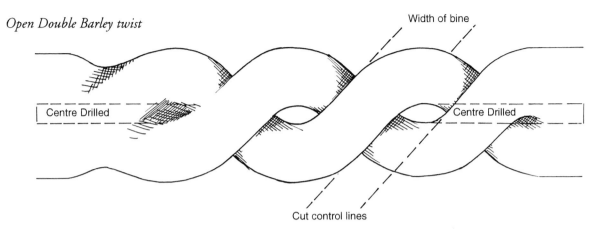

Open Double Barley twist

Width of bine

Centre Drilled

Centre Drilled

Cut control lines

Before going on to open a Double Barley twist, have in mind a clear picture of the intended twist. It may be the intention to make the bines the same width as the hollow or opening. It is sometimes advisable to make the bines a little stronger by reducing the width of the opening, as illustrated above.

To cut this twist, use the same process employed to cut the Double, stage by stage as before.

1. Saw cut at Start Lines 1 and 3.
2. Keep the twisting gouge virtually on its side, pointed in the direction of the intended cut.
3. Keep the palm plane sharp. Do not attempt too large a cut.
4. Do not press too hard when sanding. The workpiece may be weak and breakthrough may be near.

When using the twisting gouge, take care. As the pitch is longer, this tool may tend to have a mind of its own and try to follow the grain of the wood. Firm control is called for. *Do not* attempt to cut up to the orange lines on the first pass. Take a smaller cut to ensure the waste material breaks into the saw cut. *Do not* force the tool — sharpen it.

Stage 8: Shaping and cleaning the bine
Shape and regularise the bines using rasps and palm plane, adopting the same procedures as for the Double, as previously described.

FINISHING THE WORKPIECE
Turn the coves at either end of the twist before breaking through. In the case of a usable piece complete all remaining turned work, including spigots etc. Finish the piece to the desired standard.

Do not, under any circumstances, attempt to turn or re-turn any profile after breaking through, particularly at the tailstock end. The twist will not have the strength to sustain a drive at the opposite end. You will get chatter and the twist will break.

Stage 9: Breaking through to open the twist
Switch off the lathe.

Where the experienced turner has prepared a workpiece with some functional purpose in mind, it may be that the square ends have been removed. In this case great care will have to be taken against the tools from slipping as there would no longer be the protection afforded by the square ends. Turning the workpiece with the free hand whilst opening the twist, may prove more difficult.

Hold the workpiece as before with the left hand, take the tenon saw in your right and very lightly start cutting at the bottom of a hollow against the left shoulder of the bine.(*Do not* cut through into the hole at this stage.) Cut the full length of the bine, trying not to damage the bines or the end shoulders. Repeat this cutting action at the right side of the hollow against the other bine. There should now be two parallel cut lines in the hollow. Repeat this process in the other hollow.

These four light cuts are your guide lines. Sand out any damage to the bines. With the tenon saw, cut more deeply into the initial cut and through into the central hole. You may discover whilst breaking through, the waste material may have a tendency to jam the saw blade. With the free hand keep the workpiece supported whilst turning it, and you will find the back stroke of the saw will remove the waste.

With all four cuts through to the hole, drill a ³/₈" (9 mm) hole at the bottom of each hollow, ¾"(19 mm) from the end of the twist. Do this in both hollows, at both ends. The drill holes should go completely through the twist, indicating the end of the open spiral.
Note: There are other hand rasps and files on the market that are very efficient for the purpose of drilling these holes, and for ripping between the bines to remove the waste.(See photograph of tools. Page 18).

With a ½"(13 mm) carpenter's chisel, remove any loose debris from the hollow. With your free hand supporting the spiral, place the heel of the chisel against the left inside of the bine and into the drill hole. With the free hand, gently turn the spiral into the sharp edge of the chisel. Trim the inside and underside of the bine with the chisel on its back in the same manner. On reaching the opposite end, repeat this process backhand along the bine and back to the starting point. You will

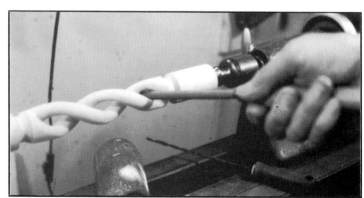

be pleasantly surprised how easy this process is. Continue to trim the bines in an even manner until you are satisfied they are reasonably round. Then use a smooth rasp or round file to clean up the drill holes at either end.

tinually on the move, otherwise grooves will form. The timing must be exact when sanding as any hesitation or jerking could cause the bine to break.

To sand around the bines, in order to keep them regular, wrap the strip of fine sanding cloth once around the bine, and with very little pressure see-saw backwards and forwards to maintain a light sanding along the bine. This method may be used to finish and polish the twist. See illustrations below.

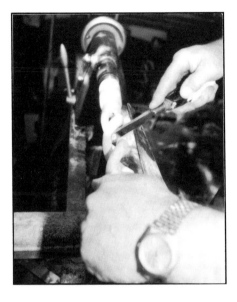

Stage 10: Sanding the Open twist

Pull the plug on the electricity supply to the lathe. Under no circumstances must the lathe be started during this sanding process.

There should be very little sanding required to the top of the bines.

Tear a ½"(13 mm) strip of 120 grit sandpaper or sanding cloth. Wrap it around the inside of the bine with the abrasive side rubbing the bine, then open the cloth to expose the area of bine facing the operator. The bine is now cradled by the sanding cloth. Hold the sanding material in the same manner as described in Stage 10/1. of the previous chapter. Take care not to pull too hard. See-saw lightly backwards and forwards along the length of the bine keeping the material con-

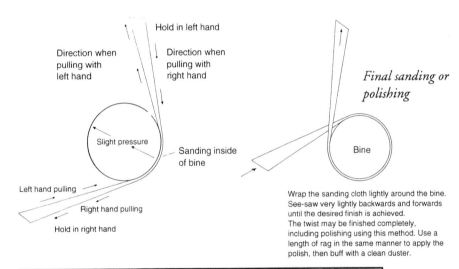

Final sanding or polishing

Wrap the sanding cloth lightly around the bine. See-saw very lightly backwards and forwards until the desired finish is achieved.
The twist may be finished completely, including polishing using this method. Use a length of rag in the same manner to apply the polish, then buff with a clean duster.

To tidy the ends where the holes are drilled, twist the sandpaper or sanding cloth into a long cylindrical cord and draw it backwards and forwards through the hole and around the bines to get the desired finish. Ensure that any uneven areas are removed before proceeding through the grits.

For the final finishing use a 4"(102 mm) square piece of 320 grit and sand by hand along the length of the bines. Try to get your fingers round the bines whilst doing so. Go to a finer grade of sandpaper for a smooth finish.

The finished Open Double Barley twist on the right with an example of a stretched Open twist on the left for comparison

A pair of Open twist candlesticks in yew

8

DOUBLE OR OPEN BARLEY TWIST CANDLESTICKS PROJECT

Once a certain amount of experience is gained, one may be tempted to attempt something a little, or even a lot, more ambitious. This normally involves a more dramatic piece of timber. It may even involve a project made up of several turned components.

Timber can be the most unpredictable of materials and every wood turner is aware of this. Some of us will use a flaw, nasty knot, rotten area etc. and fashion the piece around that feature. We call it artistic. Some turners hunt for these burrs and rotten bits of wood and when they find a piece, you could actually believe a piece of gold had been found. I know, most turners have done it, I have. However, when you discover this thing in the middle of a not so artistic piece or a twist, out comes the Super Glue.

If you are unfortunate, and if the flaw is not too serious, stabilise the area with Super Glue or other reliable glue. Should there be any doubt, discard the piece.

Due to its nature of growth a piece of cut timber may be more tightly grained or more dense on one side than the other and may be harder on one side. Take this into consideration when cutting spirals. Should this arise, and you find that there is a hard ridge down one side, it will be necessary when cutting the bines and hollows to make extra passes with the tools along the higher areas to compensate. Ensure that the hollows and bines are even.

Should very hard irregular areas be encountered, use rasps to overcome the problem.

PREPARING A BLANK FOR A CANDLESTICK

Readers may now be in a position to undertake this candlestick project with a spiral.

Remain with softwood. Select and cut a piece of straight grained softwood with an attractive grain measuring 13"(330 mm) × 2"(51 mm) × 2"(51 mm), for a 12"(304 mm) candlestick. Decide whether the twist is to be solid or open. Centre the piece in preparation for turning between centres. If it is to be an open twist, drill a $3/8$"(9 mm) hole as previously described to a depth of 10"(254 mm) from the intended base end.

To prepare the candleholder end, mount the workpiece in a suitable cup or jaw chuck, drill a $5/8$"(16 mm) hole to a depth of ¾"(19 mm) centrally at the top end, taper and sand the hole to the desired candle size.

Remove the piece from the lathe, re-mount between centres with a firm cork centred in the candleholder at the tailstock end. Turn the candlestick to the desired style. The 2"(51 mm) thistle style as illustrated below will do nicely. Turn the wax drip tray to the full width of the material. The remainder of the candlestick should be turned to 1½"(38 mm). Prepare an 8"(203 mm) section below the wax tray for a 6"(152 mm) Double twist with a 3"(76 mm) pitch. Turn 2½"(63 mm) of the remaining 3"(76 mm) into a ¾"(19 mm) spigot. For the marking out and design of a candlestick see the illustration below.

MARKING OUT FOR THE DOUBLE OR OPEN DOUBLE CANDLESTICK

As described previously on page 27, mark the four Start Lines and number them 1 to 4. When there are no square corners use the indexer, 4 prong drive or chuck jaws as a guide, otherwise measure the circumference using a tape measure to find the four equidistant and parallel horizontal Start Lines.

Mark the 6"(152 mm) twist section central to the 8"(203 mm) twist area, which will include a cove, fillet and bead at either end. Mark a central Pitch Line. There are now two pitch segments (three Pitch Lines).

Divide the segments twice to make eight segments (six Pitch Dividing Lines). At Start Lines 1 and 3 mark the Pitch Control Lines in red and 2 and 4 in green, as in Stage 5 for the previous Double. The marking out is then complete.

On this occasion omit the Complete Marking Out procedure. This would have involved dividing the eight segments into sixteen, and repeating the Start Lines between the originals, then marking the Width Control Lines accordingly. Have confidence in your ability to control the gouge without the aid of these extra lines.

The Complete Marking Out or extra control lines, need only be used for exhibition, competition or more complicated pieces, and during the introductory period to twisting. Once experienced in marking out and once confidence is gained in cutting simple pieces, you should be able to judge the equal width of the hollows and bines. In any case give it a try.

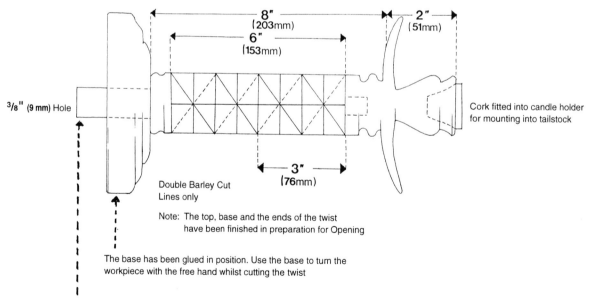

3/8" (9 mm) Hole

Cork fitted into candle holder for mounting into tailstock

Double Barley Cut Lines only

Note: The top, base and the ends of the twist have been finished in preparation for Opening

The base has been glued in position. Use the base to turn the workpiece with the free hand whilst cutting the twist

Note: The extended spigot at the base. the spigot may be held in check, or the piece may be cut between centres. If the twist is to be opened it is best to hold the spigot in a chuck

CUTTING THE HOLLOWS

With the tenon saw cut at Start Lines 1 and 3. as before, counting the three saw cuts on each segment. Keep the saw cut on the green line. Do not go too deep or over the end pitch lines.

Take the twisting gouge, make sure it is sharp.(For the full procedure see Stage 6, Ch. 5).Position the tool rest to level with centres, adjust to suit your height. Push the tip of the gouge into the corner of line 1 and the first Pitch Line, twist the gouge round forming a fingernail type cut and continue to roll the gouge on to its right side on the rest, maintaining the cut approximately ¼"(6 mm) from and parallel to the saw cut. Set your feet firmly apart in the most comfortable stance to gain an even flow when cutting along the workpiece. Try to lock the gouge hand in the correct position against your body, turn the piece into the cut with the free hand. Maintain an even and long spiral of waste material the full length of the Cut Control Line. Go back to the beginning of line 1. Turn the gouge over on its left side, with the same grip on the tool, start the second cut approximately ¼"(6 mm) to the right of the saw cut. This cut is more difficult to control and the waste will be more fragmented when breaking out. Because of this take care that the gouge does not slip. The reason the cut is being made on the right side is to save turning the workpiece round between centres. As experience is gained in using the gouge it will become second nature to turn the gouge round to cut the other way rather than turning the workpiece.

Note: After the first cut on the right hand side, the second pass will have a natural hollow and line to follow. The right side becomes the easier to cut. Repeat the process at line 3. Repeat these two passes at either side of both hollows. You will see the shoulders of both bines forming with debris in the hollow. With the gouge on its back, bevel resting at the bottom of the

hollow, incline the gouge towards the horizon and turn the workpiece onto the sharp edge to remove the waste. With practice, five to seven passes with the gouge on this material will complete the hollowing out. On harder material, take lighter cuts.

Cutting a hollow with the twisting gouge

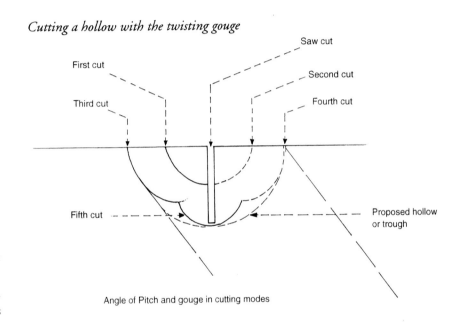

Angle of Pitch and gouge in cutting modes

BALANCING THE BINES AND HOLLOWS

Use a round rasp or file to tidy the hollows and shoulders of the bines as before. When using the palm plane to round the bines, try to co-ordinate the cutting with the action of the free hand to maintain a long and even shaving. This tool is a joy to use once proficient. (See Stages 7 and 8. Ch. 5.) Sand and finish in the same manner as for the previous Double, described in Stages 9 and 10, Ch. 6.

FINISHING THE CANDLESTICK STEM

To finish the stem, turn a cove or hollow, then a bead with a fillet at either end of the spiral. Take care that the design at the top end of the candlestick is lighter than the bottom, as illustrated on page 58.

Do not attempt to break through before fitting and completing the base. If breakthrough is attempted before the base is turned, vibration from the 'Open' twist will make it virtually impossible to tool. As soon as a tool is introduced to turn the base it will be drawn into the cut and a serious 'catch' will occur. The same procedure applies to thin turnings and thin spirals.

THE BASE

Prepare a 5" (127 mm) × 1" (25 mm) blank in similar timber, drill centrally a ¾" (19 mm) hole. Take the finished stem, glue and fit the spigot tightly into the base. Clean off any excess glue and allow to dry.the top and base in position, in preparation ready for turning the base once glued in position. Also marked out for the Double or Open twist above. No. 30.

To finish, re-mount the piece as before between centres, reduce the speed of the lathe in preparation for the larger circumference of the base, turn the base as desired. The traditional base illustrated below has been turned with a shallow hollow around the stem which will act as a well for the molten candle wax, and with an outer bead followed by a half cove to the outer flat.

Sand and finish with sealer; wax and polish the top and base only.

OPENING THIS DOUBLE

Opening this twist will be a good exercise in tool control; if there are any pitfalls to be found in opening a twist it will be experienced with this one. To achieve a good result will be success indeed.

To complete the Open twist on this particular candelstick care will have to be exercised as the material is soft and therefore weak. This is the one I can have problems with when demonstrating, particularly if my timber selection has been a little unfortunate. The candlestick is already centre drilled in order that it may be opened. First, drill the two ³/₈" (9 mm) holes in the bottom of the two hollows, through to the hollow centre approximately ½" (13 mm) from either end of the twist.

Support the piece with the free hand whilst breaking through.

This twist can be opened as normal using the tenon saw to cut two parallel cuts into the centrally bored hole, as outlined in the previous chapter.

Another method of opening this type of twist is to use a ¼"(6 mm) drill bit to drill a series of holes along the bottom of the hollows. Care must be taken when drilling the last few holes, not to allow the drill bit to grab as it breaks through into the centre hole, as this may result in the bit forcing the bines apart and cracking them. If this procedure is used often it will only be a matter of time before one experiences this catastrophe. In most cases, provided the damage is confined to a crack, the skilful use of Super Glue can rectify the situation.

Whatever method of breaking through is used, use the ½"(13 mm) carpenter's gouge to trim the inside of the bines as previously described.

Sand, using a length of sanding cloth around the bines, and clean up the drill holes at either end. Go through the grades of sanding cloth for the required finish.

Apply sanding sealer with a strip of cloth saturated in sealer and wrapped around the bines. Use the same see-saw action as used when sanding. This is the best method of gaining access for finishing and polishing the inside of the bines.

Finally, turn off and part the protruding spigot from the headstock end. Make sure the lathe speed is reduced to around 500 r.p.m. and the pressure is released from the cork at the tailstock end before parting off, otherwise the flexibility of the cork will cause the workpiece to push towards the headstock and trap the parting tool.

9

LEFT-HAND TWIST

MARKING OUT A LEFT-HAND TWIST WITH A 3" (76 mm) PITCH

START LINES

Prepare a 20" (508 mm) × 1½"(38 mm) × 1½"(38 mm) piece of softwood. Turn the 10"(254 mm) central blank. Leave two 5"(127 mm) long × 1½"(38 mm) square ends. As for the Single and Double, mark out the four Start Lines using the corners of the square ends as a guide. Number these lines 1 to 4. Not at the right-hand end of the blank as before. This time at the opposite end.

PITCH LINES

Mark a 9"(228 mm) section central to the 10"(254 mm) blank. Divide the 9"(228 mm) section into three 3"(76 mm) segments. These are your Pitch Lines.

PITCH DIVIDING LINES

Divide the three segments twice. There are now twelve segments.

BINE AND CUT CONTROL LINES

From the extreme left Pitch Line, mark in red, at 1 and 3 from left to right, upwards and across the segments.

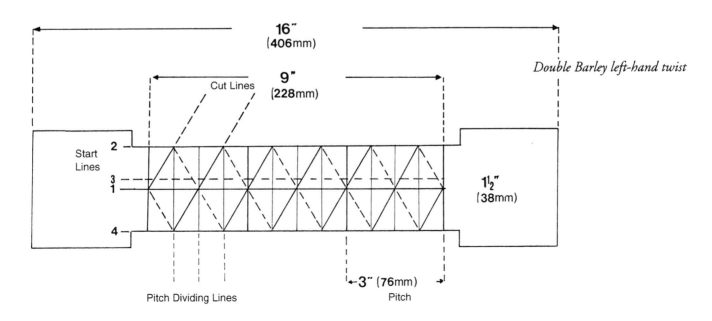

Double Barley left-hand twist

Note: Compare this marking out to the previous examples. Notice, on this piece, the two cut lines are marked in the opposite direction. Once cut, this twist will have a left-hand spiral.

MAKING MIRROR IMAGE TWISTS

In this section I outline the principle of copy turning before going on to explain how to copy a twist in its mirror image.

As in all pairs, or copy turning, the main intention is to repeat the original design, sometimes only once, at other times when demand dictates, for numerous copies. It is very important that every turned feature making up the profile of the original piece before twisting is copied perfectly, the same applies to a twist and its mirror image.

In copying work a twist tends to complicate the procedure and should be considered advanced work. Therefore I have devoted a later separate chapter spe-

cifically to this aspect (Chapter 20), and confined the work here to making a mirror image (that is a left-hand twist), to match an existing (right-hand) twist.

To turn a perfect copy of any piece there are no hard and fast rules, however there are traditional methods of copying spindle work. A template may be made from the original using several methods. The main profile features, such as beads, width of coves, hollows, flats, shoulders or fillets etc, may be marked in pencil on a plain template made from plywood the exact length of the original. These points can then be transferred to each copy in turn as if from the original. Another method is to indicate the above features with sharp pins set into one edge of the template. On the other edge of the template set in round headed nails indicating the depth of the features. All that remains is to turn a cylinder or drum the length of the turned section, introduce the sharp edge to fix the features, then gauge the depth using the round headed nail side of the template. See template illustration. The template may be kept for future use.

Marking-out template

Main profile features marked on workpiece

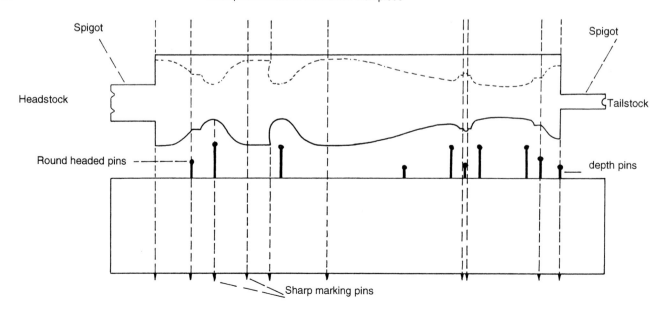

Another method for copying a small number of pieces is to lay the original along the top of the piece to be copied which is between centres. Mark the features freehand in pencil from the original to the blank. Provided that the stock or blank is the same size as the original there should be no problem in copying the piece. With practice and a keen eye a perfectly matched copy should be achieved.

When copy turning batches of work, the batch may be marked out together from the original. Lay the stock or blanks alongside the original and use a straight edge to mark out the features.

With the workpiece prepared it is now a matter of marking out for the twist and converting the copy to its mirror image.

CUTTING A LEFT-HAND TWIST, (MIRROR IMAGE)

LEFT-HANDED SAW CUTTING:
(For the left-handed person, cutting this twist will be more natural).

With the tenon saw in your left hand, hold the tailstock end with your free hand. From the headstock, cut along the red line across the first segment. Keep the heel of the saw in the cut, turn the workpiece into the saw cut and at the same time cut on to the next segment. Count three cuts per segment to ensure a regular cut the full length of the twist.

LEFT-HANDED GOUGE CUTTING:
The procedure is the same for the left-handed turner as for the right, except that you start cutting from the headstock end of the twist. Keep the gouge sharp. (Refer to Stages 5 and 6 Ch. 5).

RIGHT-HANDED PERSON:
The same difficulties arise for the right-handed person

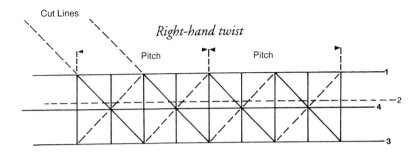

Right-hand twist

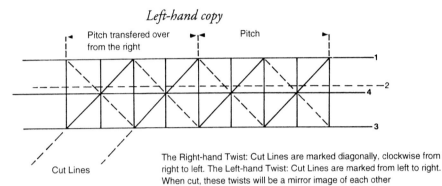

Left-hand copy

The Right-hand Twist: Cut Lines are marked diagonally, clockwise from right to left. The Left-hand Twist: Cut Lines are marked from left to right. When cut, these twists will be a mirror image of each other

cutting a left-handed twist as that for a left-handed person cutting a right-handed twist. On the first attempt at a left-hand twist, make sure there is sufficient material to retain a good grip. This is the reason for a 20" (508 mm) long blank.

RIGHT-HANDED SAW CUTTING:
To cut with the tenon saw reach over the lathe with the saw in your right hand. With your left hand turn the workpiece clockwise into the saw cut from the tailstock end. Cut from right to left and co-ordinate the cutting action. For the full cutting procedure see Chapter 5.

RIGHT-HANDED GOUGE CUTTING:
Using a gouge on a left-hand twist is awkward for a right-handed person. However, I suggest two methods:

1. When preparing the blank, two 5"(127 mm) long

square ends are left. These will give you more room to hold and control the blank. At the headstock end, hold the workpiece with the left hand. Hold the gouge in the same manner as before. Note: this time you will be cutting in the opposite direction along the workpiece. Make a fingernail type cut with the tip of the gouge, as before, at the left side of Start Line 1. Start the cut approximately ¼"(6 mm) from the red saw cut line. Turn the workpiece into the gouge cut. Try to obtain an even cut along the length of the blank. On this twist the cutting action is away from your left hand and therefore it should be safer.

2. Go to the opposite side of the lathe. Complete the above process from the tailstock end. With most lathes you will find there is more room and, therefore, is less awkward.

Use the palm plane or rasps to round the bines as before. Both right- and left-handed turners should have no problems, provided that the stage by stage procedures are followed.

The technique for sanding the left-hand twist is the same as for the right. The main difference you will find, when using the sanding cloth in a strip, is that when you pull with the right hand, the workpiece will turn clockwise, and with the left, anti-clockwise. For obvious reasons, this is the opposite to sanding a right-hand twist. It can be a little awkward at first.

When it comes to hand sanding with the lathe in motion, it is natural for the left-handed person; a right-handed person must use his or her left hand or go to the other side of the lathe. **Do not** lean over the workpiece when sanding.

Turners who are lucky enough to have a reversing facility on their lathe can use it in these circumstances to their advantage.

To finish the ends of the twist, turn the hollows at either end as before, remembering to keep the leading edges of the bines clean and sharp.

Note: On a spiral intended for use on a piece of furniture, the sharp edges described above should be very lightly sanded off with 320 grit paper. The reason for this is that these sharp edges are normally cross grain, and the slightest knock or even a firm buffing may damage the fragile edge.

There are several examples of left-hand twists throughout this book and, hopefully, they are in their correct position, i.e. to the left of its right-hand partner.

A left-hand twist is opened in the same manner as a right.

10

ALTERNATIVE METHODS OF CUTTING A TWIST

Before attempting any alternative method of cutting a twist, make sure the method is safe, regardless of how effective it appears. Safety is the main criterion.

The method of cutting a twist as so far described, is probably the fastest, safest and most labour saving of all the methods known to the author, not taking into account automatic twisting machines. There are, of course, other methods of removing waste material. Some of these aids are described below.

Tools such as drills, carving cutters, high speed cutters of various types, may be used in a hand held power drill to drill between bines or to shape a twist. In certain circumstances the use of these tools is necessary, although great care must be exercised in their application. In the main, it is a case of 'more haste, less speed'. They can rarely, if ever, be used to carry out delicate work.

Never use the tools described above in a hand held router. This is very dangerous.

Some may be tempted to use a woodcarver's cutter of the wheel type that is used as an attachment to a hand held grinder. **Do not** attempt to use such tools when cutting a twist. They are very dangerous indeed, particularly when cutting at chest level and within 12"(305 mm) of the operator's face.

There are several other methods of removing waste material which have been attempted and suggested by others, but none which the author could safely recommend.

RECOMMENDED ALTERNATIVES

The recommended alternatives described here are to assist in removing waste material. In certain circumstances, they can be incorporated with normal cutting, particularly when normal cutting gets difficult, or where the craftsman encounters large knots, very hard materials or undertakes large scale pieces. The alternatives *do not* affect the marking out. However, Complete Marking Out is necessary in such cases.

First Alternative

The first alternative method is used when cutting large workpieces, including knots. The size of piece to consider for this cutting method, may be 4" (102 mm) in diameter and upwards, or a hollow vessel.

With the marking out completed as previously described, take a tenon saw, or larger saw if necessary, and cut on the Pitch Control Line or cut line as previously described, to the required depth. Note: Take care not to cut too deep for the particular twist you are working on.

The intention is to cut a 'V', starting at the Pitch or Width Control Lines, which determine the width of the hollows and bines. Start the cut at the tailstock end for a right-hand twist. Set the saw to the proposed angle of cut, in line with the bottom of the V. Cut segment by segment, along the length of the twist forming half the V. Turn the workpiece round and cut the other side of the V. There will be a series of flats along the length of the bine. These can be trimmed in several ways:

1. Use a wide carpenter's chisel to trim the flats from the top to the bottom of the V.
2. The hollows can be completed as normal with the twisting gouge.
3. The hollows may also be formed and completed with rasps and files.

To shape the bines, use the palm plane. To complete the sanding, use the same methods as before.

The saw in use cutting a hollow

Second Alternative

With the blank marked out as above, make the saw cut as before. Support the underside of the workpiece on a saddle attached to the tool rest. Cut the V with a carpenter's chisel. Ensure that the piece is properly supported before cutting, otherwise damage may result. In the case of a very large piece, I recommend cutting with a saw. However, a chisel can be used with the aid of a mallet. Remove the workpiece from the lathe, place it in a bench vice. Cut the V with a sharp carpenter's chisel. It may be necessary to support the workpiece from beneath whilst in the vice. When this method is used, it is not necessary to turn the workpiece round in order to cut each segment in turn. Leave the piece in the vice and cut the V at each pitch along the length of the twist before turning it. Repeat this process until the chiselling is complete.

To finish the piece, use the twisting gouge and the palm plane to round the bines and sand as before. Use the wide carpenter's chisel as illustrated on page 34.

Third Alternative

The third alternative is the most labour intensive. On very hard material, where the twist hollow is narrow and too deep to use traditional tools and the use of a gouge almost impossible, use the saw, gouge and palm plane for cutting as far as possible before using rasps and files to gain the necessary depth. This method can be hard work, but the results can be most rewarding. Finish the twist in the usual manner.

The marking out procedures, taken stage by stage, are relatively simple. However, in some cases a degree of strength is called for to actually <u>cut</u> a twist. The alternatives given here may be found to be useful, particularly for younger readers or the less strong, when approaching more difficult pieces, and a combination of cutting methods in certain circumstances may be used to make the job at hand easier.

11

TRIPLE AND RIBBON TWISTS

Readers should now be familiar with the basic principles of marking out and cutting a twist. Even so,before starting the Triple, there are several terms that may require revision, so here is a quick recap to prompt the memory and to save readers continually referring back.

START LINES, are horizontal lines at equal spacing around the blank, indicating the starting points of the hollows or troughs and the bines.

PITCH LINES, are the vertical lines that run round the blank forming circles, after the length of the pitch has been decided.

PITCH DIVIDING LINES, are to divide the space between the Pitch Lines, at equal distances and form intersections with the Start Lines.

PITCH CONTROL LINES, are the diagonal lines. (From right to left in the case of a right-hand twist and left to right for the left-hand twist.)

Marked from the Start Lines across the intersections with the Pitch and Pitch Dividing Lines. These indicate the Cut Lines, the first process to form the hollows and the bines, and the Bine Apex Lines.

COMPLETE MARKING OUT means a repeat marking out of the Start Lines between the first set and another set of Pitch Control Lines dividing the existing ones. The Complete Marking Out is there to achieve

the second set of control lines which indicate and control the width of the hollows and the bines.

MAKING THE TRIPLE TWIST

Stage 1:
Prepare a 16"(406 mm) ×1½"(38 mm) × 1½"(38 mm) blank with a 10" (254 mm) central cylinder as described previously. This blank should be the same size as for the Single and Double. However, for those who wish to open this particular twist, read the section OPENING A TRIPLE TWIST below.

Remember to leave the ends square; it will be difficult to cut a twist without them. They allow for a more positive and powerful cutting action.

Stage 2: Start Lines
The Triple has three cut lines and three bines, therefore six Start Lines. Mark the blank with dividers set at 1⁵/₁₆"(33 mm). Complete three Start Lines from these marks and number them 1 to 3. A second set of Start Lines is then marked out between the originals. Number this set 1 to 3. There are now six Start Lines in two sets of 1 to 3. The first set are the Cut Lines and the second set are the Bine Apex Lines.

Note: 1⁵/₁₆"(33 mm) is not a third of the circumference. Dividers do not take into account the arc of the circumference. They work on triangulation.

Using dividers to find the Triple Start Lines

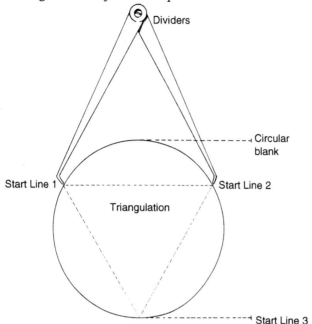

Triple twist and Ribbon Start Lines

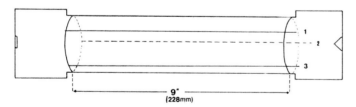

Triple twist Pitch and Pitch Dividing Lines

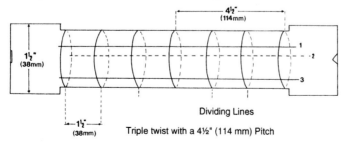

Triple twist with a 4½" (114 mm) Pitch

ALTERNATIVE METHODS OF FINDING
START LINES

The quickest method after a little practice, is to use dividers judging the divisions by eye. It is surprising how accurate one becomes in a short time.

This is the method I use when an indexer is not available. To find three Start Lines, look at the cylinder from a fixed point, judge by eye two thirds of the width of the material, set the dividers at that distance. That should roughly be one third of the circumference. Hopefully, when you mark out the three divisions you will get it right. If the dividers are too wide, reduce their width by one third of the over run, and vice versa if the dividers are too narrow. The simple rule for this method is two thirds of half a circumference is one third of the whole. The same rule applies to any other number of divisions, e.g. find ½ of the visual width, this will be ¼ of the circumference.

Another method of finding the three equal divisions for the Start Lines, is to wrap a piece of tape around the blank. Cut the tape to the exact length with a sharp blade. Remove the tape, measure, and mark it into three equal sections. Replace the tape on the blank and mark the three Start Lines using the marks on the tape as a guide. Number the lines 1 to 3. Divide the Start Lines again, as above.

The quickest and most efficient method, obviously, is the use of an indexer fitted to the lathe or chuck.

Stage 3: Pitch and Pitch Dividing Lines
To decide the pitch on a Triple, it is normally 2½ to 3 times the width of the material. In this case the pitch will be three times the width, therefore 4½"(114 mm).

Mark centrally 9"(229 mm) on the 10"(254 mm) prepared section of the blank. That is the length of the twist. Divide the 9"(229 mm) centrally into two. These are the Pitch Lines. Divide these two pitch segments into three equal sections measuring 1½"(38 mm) long. These are the Pitch Dividing Lines.

Stage 4: Pitch Control lines

Mark in red from one set of three Start Lines, the diagonal Control Lines. For a right-hand twist mark these from right to left, and left to right for a left-hand twist. These will be the Cut Lines for the hollows. Mark the second set of Start Lines in green, these will be the top of the bines. See the illustration below

The Triple can be cut from this stage. However, should you require accuracy, follow the Complete Marking Out procedure.

COMPLETE MARKING OUT

Mark in orange another set of six Start Lines between the original, this will give you twelve Start Lines in total.

Divide the Pitch and Pitch Dividing Lines in the same colour. There are now twenty-four segments. Mark all six new Control Lines in orange. It can be clearly seen that these lines will indicate, accurately, widths of the hollows and bines.

I have not illustrated the Complete Marking Out for the Triple as there are similar illustrations elsewhere in the book. (page 76 refers to the 4-Start in particular).

Stage 5: The saw cut

The depth of the hollows or troughs on a Triple are approximately $1/6$th the width of the material.

When using the tenon saw, cut the full length of all three red Cut Lines. Do not cut deeper than $1/8"$ (3 mm). An important point to remember when using the saw, it is very easy to create flat bottomed cuts leaving pointed areas between each cut. This could result in sections of the cut being too deep. Should this occur the hollows could end up deeper than originally intended.

Stage 6: Using the twisting gouge

When using the twisting gouge on a Triple or a Ribbon twist, the angle of cut will be more acute to the grain and there will be a tendency for the sharp leading edge of gouge to follow the grain. Firmer control of the tool is called for. The first cut at either side of the Cut Line should be narrow and shallow. On the second pass at either side, turn the gouge almost on to its back with half of the sharp edge protruding from the material. The waste material should break out into the saw cut. The hollow at this stage should be quite shallow.

Triple twist Cut and Bine Apex Lines

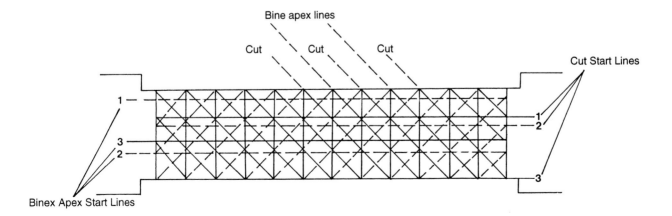

On the next pass with the gouge, cut up to the orange line to the required depth. Turn the workpiece round on the lathe and complete the other side.

To remove any waste material from the bottom of the hollow, place the gouge on its back into the hollow, with the sharp edge pointing towards the horizon, turn the workpiece steadily with the free hand onto the sharp edge of the tool. To prevent damage or going too deep, 'rub the bevel' of the gouge on the bottom of the hollow using the bevel to control the depth. See the illustration below.

Triple Twist saw and gouge cutting

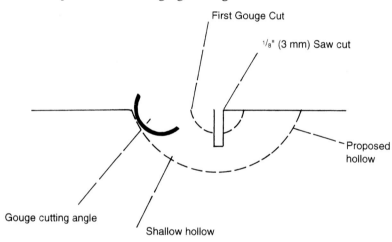

First Gouge Cut

⅛" (3 mm) Saw cut

Proposed hollow

Gouge cutting angle

Shallow hollow

1. Care must be taken not to cut too deeply with the saw
2. The cutting angle of the gouge must be shallow

Stage 7: Rounding the bines and finishing the Triple

Set the blade of the palm plane for light cutting. When rounding off the bine take long smooth strokes. Try to grip with the free hand as far around behind the workpiece as possible in order to achieve these long strokes. Pull long and steadily into the cutting edge of the plane. With practice, one should be able to adopt this action to cut all twists. As in all woodworking, techniques of using tools can be developed to a stage where less exertion is required to achieve the desired result. The same applies to spiral work. I cannot stress strongly enough the importance of keeping tools sharp.

Sand the Triple using the same method as for the Single and Double.

The cove or hollow at either end of this Triple should be no more than ¼" deep.

The finished Triple

Examples of Triple twist work

Mahogany torchere with Triple conversion

*Pair of yew candlesticks
(Compare these to the Double
twist design on p. 56)*

Goblets in ebony

OPENING A TRIPLE TWIST

If you decide, at this late stage, to open the Triple twist, the central hole may still be drilled. There should be no problems provided the correct drilling tools and procedure are adopted. The hole must be drilled perfectly central through the length of the intended twist. Any deviation and the twist could be ruined. It is better to drill the hole before cutting the twist.

For this size of twist, regardless of the number of bines, the drill size should be at least ³/₈"(9 mm). If the intention is to make thin bines, a ½"(13 mm) or even a ⁵/₈"(16 mm) hole can be drilled, as long as sufficient material is left to accommodate the bines. Before drilling the hole, consideration should be given to the following points:

1. Is the pitch long enough? and
2. Is there sufficient material of this type to accommodate three open bines?

The answer to both questions is yes, with a big IF. If you have the confidence and experience to have a go. Drill the hole as previously described in Chapter 7.

To open this twist, the Triple must be completely finished, including sanding, before breaking through.

Note: As the number of bines are increased on an open twist, it follows that the bines will be thinner, therefore weaker. When cutting the hollows and trimming the bines, great care must be taken not to exert too much pressure after the twist has been opened. If you are using soft material it will be necessary to support the twist with your free hand whilst cutting. Great care must also be exercised when sanding.

When supporting a piece by hand, make sure at all times you keep a bine between the sharp edge of the gouge and the free hand, otherwise injury could occur.

The Triple can be opened quite successfully. How-ever, for those who wish to put this Open Triple to use in a strong supporting role there are three options:

1. Increase the size of the blank to 2"(51 mm) square and prepare it in the same manner. This will mean the twist strength will automatically increase by a quarter.
2. Use a stronger species and keep the blank at 1½"(38 mm) square. For example use, Yew, Oak, Beech, Mahogany or almost any exotic species.
3. Increase the length of the pitch beyond the traditional recommendations to 5" (127 mm). This will give a straighter bine with longer grain, therefore more strength.

RIBBON TWIST

It may appear at first that the marking out for the Ribbon twist is the same as the Triple. In fact there is a greater difference in these two twists than the Single and Double.

Stage 1:
Prepare a 16"(406 mm) × 1½"(38 mm) × 1½"(38 mm) blank in soft wood as for the Triple, and make a 10"(254 mm) cylindrical centre section and the two square ends turned in preparation for marking as before. Mark the three Start Lines, (horizontal), and number the lines 1 to 3 in pencil. *Do not* add the second set of Start Lines at this stage.

Stage 2:
The pitch for the Ribbon will be 4½"(114 mm) the same as for the Triple. The twist will be 9"(228 mm) long, therefore there will be two pitches.

Mark centrally the 9"(228 mm) section and draw a central Pitch Line. Divide the two segments into three equal segments of 1½"(38 mm).

Stage 3:
Mark the three diagonal Pitch Control Lines in red.

These are the Cut Lines for the hollow.

Stage 4:

Mark the second set of Start Lines, this time in green and number these also 1 to 3. Divide the pitch segments again. There are now six Start Lines and twelve segments measuring ¾"(19 mm). From the second set of green Start Lines mark another set of Control Lines in green. These are the bine apexes.

Stage 5: Complete Marking Out for the Ribbon twist

The Complete Marking Out for the Ribbon is different to that of the Single, Double and the Triple.

At all intersections with the Pitch Lines and Pitch Dividing Lines (including the end Pitch Lines) measure ⅛"(3 mm) at either side of the green Bine Apex Lines. At these ⅛"(3 mm) points, mark in green two parallel Pitch Control Lines alongside the existing one. There are now three green Bine Control Lines on either bine, a total of nine green Width Control Lines.

Note: The distance between the Bine Control Lines

is ¼"(6 mm) and in this case the distance between the Cut Control Lines is ¾"(19 mm). These measurements are based on a traditional style Ribbon. The hollow is approximately three times the width of the bine apex. In the case of a standard twist these widths are equal. See the illustration below.

CUTTING THE RIBBON

Stage 6:

With the tenon saw, cut very lightly to a depth of ⅛". Although the hollows are wider they are also shallower and taper upwards very quickly towards the bine apex. Cut as accurately as possible to prevent damage to the sides of the bines.

Stage 7:

When using the twisting gouge take shallow cuts, otherwise the waste material may not break out properly at the Cut Lines. Do not be tempted to remove any ragged

Ribbon twist Bine Apex and Width Control Lines

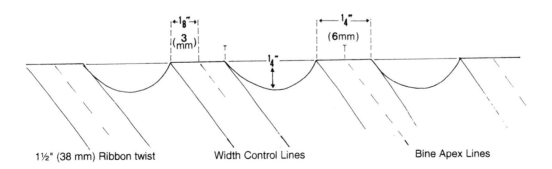

1½" (38 mm) Ribbon twist   Width Control Lines   Bine Apex Lines

waste at this stage. Turn the workpiece end to end and repeat the cutting action on the other side of the Cut Lines, this cut should remove most of the waste material, any remaining waste should be left at the bottom of the hollows. The third and fourth passes should also be light. Make sure the gouge is kept sharp in order to obtain a clean cut. When cutting with the gouge, taper the hollow gently upwards leaving the ¼"(6 mm) flat at the top of the bines. The hollow should be no deeper than ¼"(6 mm). A good result with the gouge saves a lot of unnecessary sanding. Do not attempt to remove the waste at the bottom of the hollow with the gouge, unless you are perfectly confident there will be no dig-ins. A dig-in will mean the hollow will have to be deepened and obviously that would change the shape of the twist.

Waste material may be trimmed when balancing the bines and hollows with a rasp or round file. Take care to keep the workpiece turning with the free hand into the rasp cuts to ensure an even cut. Make use of the whole length of the rasp with long even strokes.

Stage 8: Palm Plane

When using the palm plane make sure it is sharp and reduce the depth of cut. Here, there is very little planing to be done, so with the plane set correctly, two or three very light cuts should be sufficient to round the top of the bine. Do not remove the central green line and remember the bine top is only ¼"(6 mm) wide. The bine may also be shaped according to the required taste.

Stage 9:

Sand the twist in the same manner as for the Double. There should be very little sanding required to the top of the bines, as the plane should have left a very clean surface. Any sanding should be light as the bines can be very easily marked. To sand off the green line, set the lathe speed at approximately 400 r.p.m. Start the lathe and use the hand sanding method. With a 4"(104 mm) square piece of 180

grit cloth or sandpaper held between the thumb and index finger, stroke the workpiece from right to left to find the timing of the spiral. Once the correct timing is achieved exert a little pressure in between the bines to get the desired finish. Follow up the same stroking action on top of the bines. The twist should be finished when the green line is removed. The proper use of hand tools should produce quite a good result. Try not to use a course grit sandpaper on this type of twist.

A Ribbon twist is aptly named because it should look like a twisted ribbon. One could be forgiven for thinking, or daring to mention, ' But a Ribbon has only two sides not three.' There is nothing to prevent anyone from cutting a Double Ribbon. However, it would only look like a flat Double with pointed bines and would serve no useful purpose.

When cutting a Ribbon twist, which is intended to have pointed or slightly rounded apexes, cut it without the Complete Marking Out. Use only the green central apex lines as a guide for the gouge cutting and sanding. In these circumstances there is no need to use the palm plane or rasps on the top of the bines, to do so may damage or destroy them and possibly the whole twist. On this type of twist sand the hollows as normal, taking care not to cross over the tops of the bines as this may tear out grooves and spoil the shape. Lightly sand out the green line and slightly round the tip of the bine to produce the desired shape. Turn the coves at either end to a depth of approximately ¼"(6 mm).

Notes: 1. A Ribbon twist cannot normally be opened successfully. It would be very weak and the bines would be triangular shaped. Try one, you never know, it could be a very pleasing piece in the correct material.

2. Start Lines: All twists with the number of Start Lines divisible by 3, must initially start with three Start Lines, e.g. a Triple, 6-Start, 9-Start, 12-Start and other Multi-Starts. A Single, Double, 4-Start, etc. require four initial Start Lines.

12

4-START TWIST

A 4-Start may be cut with the distance between the bines at a quarter the width of the material. This would result in the angle of the bine being at the same pitch as for a traditional Single. However, the pitch would in fact be 2" (51 mm). Such a twist would be quite strong and look most attractive.

Have you worked out the thickness of the material for this twist? Yes, 2"(51 mm), the same as the pitch. This particular twist may be cut with a V at the bottom of the hollow in the same manner as the Single twist. The result would give the appearance of a Rope twist.

The pitch on a 4-Start can vary according to the design of the piece. The pitch is dependent on the thickness of the bines, and the thickness of the material intended to be twisted. In essence, here I am suggesting that the permutations are endless.

To add to the complexity of this lovely twist, it can be safely opened at virtually any pitch above 1½ times the width of the material. This is obviously dependent on the type of material used.

MARKING OUT FOR THE 4-START

Stage 1:

Prepare a 16"(406 mm) × 2½"(63 mm) × 2½"(63 mm) blank in the same manner as for the Single and Double Barley twists. Only this time leave the two square ends 2"(51 mm) long and not 3"(76 mm) as before. Remove the sharp tips of the square ends, just in case knuckles come in contact with the material. The centre blank will be 11"(279 mm) long.

The pitch in this case will be the same as for the Double, twice the width of the material, therefore the pitch will be 5"(127 mm).

Mark in pencil the four horizontal Start Lines, numbering them 1 to 4.

Stage 2:

Mark centrally a 10"(254 mm) section and divide it once into two 5"(127 mm) segments. Start the lathe and mark the Pitch Lines.

Confident or experienced turners may keep the lathe running. With a pencil divide each pitch segment twice. There should now be four segments on each pitch measuring 1¼"(32 mm) long. A total of eight segments.

Stage 3:

Mark all four Pitch Control Lines in pencil, from right to left across the segments as before. For this exercise, only the basic marking out is required. For the Bine Control Lines repeat the above marking out, to produce eight Start Lines and sixteen segments.

I have deliberately left out the Complete Marking

Out. The twist can be cut quite successfully without it.

However, for those who wish to complicate life, take another colour of your choice, repeat the Start Lines, no need to number them. Divide the 16 segments into 32. Mark the Control Lines at all eight Start Lines as before. That completes the marking out to include the hollow and bine Width Control Lines. Illustrated below is the Complete Marking Out of *one pitch only* for a 4-Start.

CUTTING THE 4-START

Stage 4:

The hollows should be no deeper than one sixth to a fifth the width of the blank. Use a tenon saw and cut at all four points to a depth of approximately ¼"(6 mm). Three or four light cuts per segment should be sufficient.

Complete marking out for a 4-Start twist

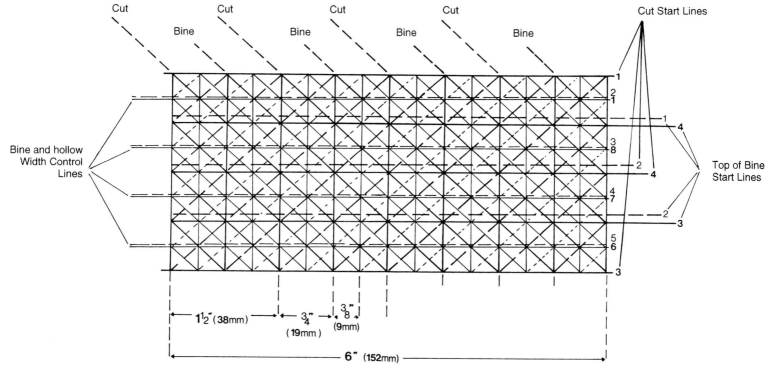

As one can see the Complete Marking Out can become very cluttered and possibly confusing.
Avoid it where possible. For accuracy and large pieces it is essential

Stage 5:

When using the twisting gouge on this occasion, it is intended to cut the hollow in stages. Widen the hollows until they balance with the bines. Great care must be taken not to over cut and damage the bines.(For those who marked out completely make sure not to cross the Width Control Lines). This is a good exercise in tool control and training for balancing the bines by eye. It also speeds up the process for cutting spirals.

On this occasion, the bines are smaller and therefore the hollows shallower. Make sure the gouge is very sharp; speed up the cutting action a little and you should find that the cutting will become more fluent and efficient. Should you find it difficult to attain fluency take lighter cuts. At first it may be difficult to control so slow up until you are satisfied with the cut. Most turners will find the cutting will become easier and, with practice, will automatically speed up.

The first gouge cut should be no more than ¼"(6 mm) from the Cut Line, the second cut should be on the opposite side of the saw cut. From this point check the width of the hollow and the bine. The next two passes should balance up the bines with the hollows. On the fifth pass the gouge should be turned on its back to tidy up the waste at the bottom of the hollow.

Cutting this twist with a sharp tool at the correct speed should give readers some idea what is required in order to speed up and cut a twist more quickly. Do not be put off even though the twist is a little messed up. I am certain, at some point during the cutting process, the perfect cut will be achieved by everyone who follows this method. Find that perfect cut and work on it, just like a golfer with his or her swing. I remember the first time I tried to cut a twist, I was digging holes, tearing up the wood along the grain and slipping off the material.

These things occur due to impatience for a quick result. It is at this stage that injuries can occur. Slow down, sharpen the gouge.

Stage 6:

The next stage is to round the bines, making sure to balance the bines with the hollows the full length of the spiral. One cut too many, on a bine or hollow, can spoil the appearance of a twist. Rounding the bines with a palm plane is by far the best method for the tighter spirals. A rasp or file tends to roughen up the bines too much. Where the material is soft and the bines are small a rasp can completely destroy the twist. Remember, when cutting a twist, the majority of cutting is across the grain. Make sure the plane is very sharp and not cutting too deep. Take light cuts, check the bines regularly after each stroke of the plane to ensure uniformity of the bines. Once satisfied, proceed to sanding.

Stage 7:

Sand the 4-Start in the same manner as the Double and Triple twists, taking care not to cross over the bines. This is a common and easy mistake with a length of sandpaper or cloth when sanding a Multi-Start. This will result in 'waves' on top of the bines.

When hand sanding with the lathe in motion, it can be difficult to catch the timing of all four bines. It may not be possible to hand sand in this manner if the hollows are too narrow to accommodate your fingers. In this event, use the sanding tool or a small length of ¼"(6 mm) dowelling with sandpaper wrapped around.

With the twist finished, turn the coves at either end as before, only this time turn these coves a little deeper than the spiral troughs or hollows. The result should be very pleasing.

Examples of 4-Start twist work

Base and column of music stand

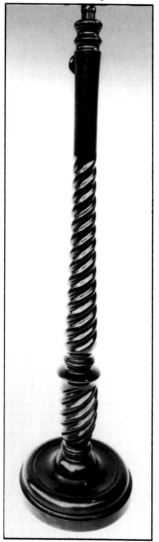

Music stand sheet rest

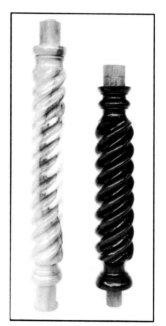

4-Start twists in yew and mahogany

13

4-START OPEN TWIST

Before starting on a 4-Start Open some of the potential pit-falls need to be explained and how to avoid possible disaster.

The 4-Start Open twist is the first departure from traditional spiral work. It is not a form commonly seen in old and antique furniture, whether fine or otherwise. Although spiral work is purely decorative and serves no purpose other than to enhance the appearance of spindle work in the main, strength is nearly always sacrificed. Therefore, in order to compensate and regain strength, particularly in the case of Open twists, the materials used must be stronger, the bines should be made thicker or the pitch stretched. Changing the thickness of the bines and the length of the pitch will obviously change the design of the twist. To retain the design, stronger material will have to be used.

Stronger material

In the case of timber this means that the species should be harder or more dense. There are virtually no restrictions on design when using this type of material. With soft materials there are restrictions on virtually every feature. For example, the bines on a Double Open twist with a 3"(76 mm) pitch in 2"(51 mm) soft pine should be cut to a combined thickness of no less than approximately half the overall thickness of the material. Any thinner and it would be too weak to be of use as a single

piece. (Such a piece could possibly be used with several like pieces to support a small table, platter or cake stand, etc). Cut a 4-Start in the same material with the same pitch and it would serve no useful purpose. However, make the same twist in yew, holly, ebony, rosewood, cocobolo or any other hard species and you will have a very strong and attractive piece.

Thicker Bines

This is where we depart from traditional marking out and design. When it comes to the weaker species of timber the bines, and in some cases the material, must be thicker to accommodate an Open 4-Start. Should one desire, keep the same length of pitch on thicker material and this will result in thicker bines giving added strength. There may still be a degree of spring in the twist. To alleviate this, I would always advise that the bines should also be stretched.

Stretching the bines

This is where the bine or pitch is stretched in order to gain more strength along the grain of the wood. This stretching effect appears to have been used in Jacobean furniture when twisting in oak, I presume for the same reason, and can be seen mainly on table and chair legs. I qualify this by saying, it is possible that spirals with stretched bines were around before then. Good quality tools are required to deal with the difficult cutting angles of a stretched pitch.

In the case of solid spindle twists, there is a limit as to how much a pitch may be stretched before it loses its effect and charm as a true spiral. In the case of the Open, there is a difference. The Open may be stretched for as long as one wishes, in fact to a point where it is still just capable of being seen as a spiral. There is a limit to the number of bines on an Open twist. I mean that, there is a stage where the material or pitch is unable to accommodate both bines and the opening, therefore access for cutting is impossible. This will become obvious when marking out.

An extra bine can be added and the pitch may be shortened as desired. However, care must always be taken that the end result is not a wooden spring.

With this information, and a little thought, one should be able to select a material that is most likely to accommodate the desired twist. Remember, however, we are dealing with a 4-Start Open. Do not get carried away and decide to cut a Six- or other Multi-Start. The formula changes with the twist. We are getting very close to designing a twist.

Refer to Chapter 14 for more information on stretching bines and lengthening a twist.

Here is an example that the more experienced turner may wish to try:

Prepare a blank in yew or similar material 12"(304 mm) long and 3"(76 mm) thick. Drill a ½"(13 mm) hole through the centre of the blank. Set the pitch at twice the thickness of the material, so 6"(152 mm). Mark out as for the double, only as far as the cut control and bine lines. Do not follow the Complete Marking Out procedure.

Cut the twist in the same manner as explained in the previous chapter. Turn the coves or hollows and any other design at either end of the twist *before* going to the next stage. Start the 'opening procedure' and follow the

directions implicitly. Sand the piece in the same manner as the Open Double. The piece should make a very nice lamp or candlestick.

PREPARING THE BLANK FOR A 4-START OPEN TWIST

There is a lot of work in cutting a 4-Start, particularly an Open one. In this case treat the piece as a usable column or stem for a candlestick, cake stand or lamp. I also recommend that a harder, more attractive species of timber is used, such as yew, cherry, plum, walnut, oak, elm or a good quality mahogany.

Plan the piece and make the top and base to suit the twist. For a candlestick, lamp or cake stand, I recommend a 4½"(114 mm) to 5"(127 mm) base with a ¾"(19 mm) thick spigot recess.

A cake stand top should be a platter approximately 12"(305 mm) diameter. In the case of a candlestick design the top to suit or copy one from this book.

For the purpose of this exercise I will explain how to mark up a 4-Start Open twist with a stretched pitch on a 2"(51 mm) blank.

The twist in this case will be 9"(228 mm) with a 6"(152 mm) pitch. This will result in one and a half pitches.

For those making a cake stand, this twist is too long. Reduce the length of the twist to 6"(152 mm), one pitch only. Follow each of the stages accordingly.

Stage 1:
When selecting the timber make sure it is straight grained. Prepare a 14"(356 mm) × 2"(51 mm) × 2"(51 mm) blank with a 10"(254 mm) central section turned into a cylinder for marking up. (The central section will be 7"(178 mm) in respect of the cake stand). Leave two square ends as before. Centre punch both ends deeply with the four prong drive.

Warning: Using the twisting gouge to cut this twist in

harder material could prove difficult to some. To overcome this, shallow cuts will have to be made, this will increase the risk of the tool slipping and care must be taken to avoid injury.

DRILLING AND MARKING OUT FOR AN OPEN 4-START

Stage 2:

Mount the piece in a 3 or 4 jaw chuck for stability. Drill a ⅝"(16 mm) hole through the middle of the blank from the end selected for the bottom of the twist to a depth of 12"(305 mm). This will leave a solid 2"(51 mm) section at the top end of the spiral for design and securing the intended workpiece top.

Drill to a depth of 10"(254 mm) if making the cake stand.

As the material selected in this case is semi-soft, I have decided to lengthen the pitch to three times the width of the material. This will mean a 6"(153 mm) pitch. There is no hard and fast rule regarding the pitch for an Open twist. The main criteria are the design, species of wood and whether there is sufficient room between the bines to cut the twist.

Stage 3:

Mark four Start Lines from the square corners on the blank across the central cylinder as before.

Stage 4:

Mark centrally to the 10"(254 mm) a 9"(228 mm) section. This is the length of the twist. Measure 6"(152 mm) from the tailstock end and a further 3"(76 mm) from the 6"(152 mm) mark. These are the Pitch Lines.

Stage 5:

Divide the 6"(152 mm) section twice, and the 3"(76 mm) section once. These are the Pitch Dividing Lines. There are now six 1½"(38 mm) segments. In the case of the cake stand stem mark out the single 6"(152 mm) pitch length only.

Stage 6:

Mark the four diagonal Cut Lines from all four Start Lines, right to left for a right-hand twist and left to right for the left twist, (mirror image).

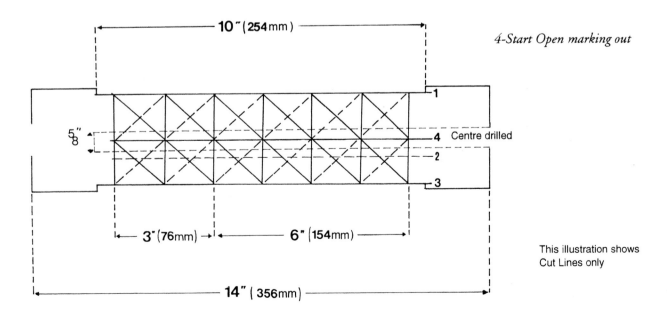

4-Start Open marking out

This illustration shows Cut Lines only

BINE APEX CONTROL LINES

For the Bine Apex Lines mark out another set of four Start Lines between the original four. Divide the pitch segments once to make twelve segments. Complete the diagonal Bine Apex Lines as before. These indicate the top of the four bines. With confidence, it will not be necessary to mark out these lines. This type of twist is quite easily cut and balanced by eye to suit the individual.

COMPLETE MARKING OUT

The Complete Marking Out for this width of material is not necessary. However if you wish to complete this procedure, use a red pencil and mark another set of eight Start Lines between the existing ones and, once again, divide the pitch segments. Complete another set of diagonal lines. There are now sixteen Start Lines, seventeen Pitch Lines and sixteen Diagonal Lines per 6"(152 mm) pitch. The Complete Marking Out for the 9"(228 mm) twist consists of 25 Pitch Lines and 24 Pitch Segments.

The Complete Marking Out for the 6"(152 mm) cake stand stem, which is one pitch only, is outlined above.

Stage 7:

When using the tenon saw do not cut completely through to the centrally drilled hole at any stage before break through is intended. This may complicate the gouge cutting.

Stage 8:

Cut this twist in the same manner as the 4-Start. When using the gouge be careful that it does not slip, as the angle of cut is more acute to horizontal than the ordinary 4-Start. For safety, keep your driving or free hand as close as possible to the end of the workpiece. Do not attempt to remove too much material in one pass. All that will be achieved is an uneven cut which will make the next pass more difficult. The harder the material, the shallower the cuts. This will ensure an even cut. Use the palm plane very lightly to round the bines as before. Complete the piece as far as possible including the coves and design at either end. Sand the piece before breaking through.

Stage 9:

To decide the end of the Open twist bines, drill a 3/8"(9 mm) hole approximately 1/2"(13 mm) from either end of the twist at the bottom of each hollow. On dense or larger material the whole twist may be opened with the aid of a drill.

Stage 10:

For breaking through use the same method as for the Open Double. (See Chapter 7).

To balance and determine the width of the bines, use the palm plane around the top and the 1/2"(13 mm) carpenter's chisel, as before, on the inside of the bines. The thickness of the bine can be decided using this method.

Do not trim the bines too thinly, the result may be a very weak springy spiral. Do not exert too much pressure, or force the bines apart with the chisel, otherwise they will break.

Stage 11:

For sanding and finishing the bines refer to the same procedure for finishing the Open Double. (Chapter 7 refers). When sanding with the strip of cloth sanding material be careful not to pull too hard. Remember to clean and sand the drill holes at the end of the twist.

PAIR OF OPEN TWISTED LAMPS PROJECT

The intention with this project is to consolidate all previous information to make a pair of matching 4-Start Open twists in yew. The marking out is not traditional, in fact all the features of these twists are unusual. It may be necessary to refer back to complete the marking out and cutting.

Reference was made earlier to a pair of 4-Start Open twists and, as with any pair, this would require a mirror image of either a left or right-hand twist. The illustration below is the perfect method of producing such a copy.

Note: The right-hand twist is at the headstock end of the lathe, also note that the workpiece may be turned end to end between centres.

1. To begin with select a 3½"(89 mm) × 16"(406 mm) blank. Turn the complete blank into a cylinder then turn a dovetail or spigot at both ends for mounting in a chuck. The piece may now be turned end to end for convenience.

2. Mount the blank in a chuck and drill a 1"(25 mm) hole through the centre. It may be necessary to turn the workpiece end to end to drill completely through.

3. Measure and mark a central dividing line. This will be the central dividing line between the left and right-hand twists.

4. Mark out four Start Lines, number them 1 to 4. In this case each twist is 5"(127 mm) long. The pitch is set at 12"(305 mm). This will mean that the bine spiral will only go halfway round the circumference of the material. In fact each twist will only be half of a true twist. Mark out 6"(152 mm) for each twist, one left and one right at either side of the centre line.

5. Mark another line 1" (25 mm) at either side of the original central line. This 2"(51 mm) central section may be retained for the design at the top of the finished twists and parting off. Note: The two 5"(127 mm) twist sections are indicated.

6. Divide the 5"(127 mm) sections once. There are now four Pitch Dividing Lines including the two central area lines. There are two Pitch Segments for each twist.

7. To complete the cut control lines for the right-hand twist start at the first Start Line at the tailstock end of the workpiece and mark diagonally towards the centre of the blank from right to left across two segments only. This will produce the half pitch required. Stop after reaching the central section Pitch Dividing Line. Mark the three remaining Cut Lines at Start Lines 2, 3 and 4 in the same way.

8. To produce the left-hand or the 'mirror image', carry out the same marking out procedure, this time start from the headstock end and mark the cut control lines diagonally from left to right towards the centre section. The cut control lines are complete for both twists.

9. For the Bine Control Lines, repeat all the marking out as above. There is no requirement for the Complete Marking Out.

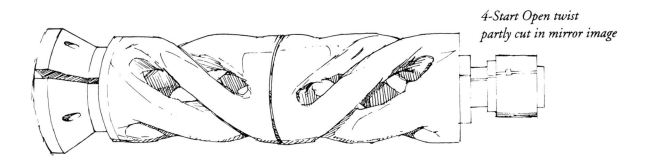

4-Start Open twist partly cut in mirror image

CUTTING A LEFT AND A RIGHT OPEN TWIST ON THE SAME BLANK

This particular twist is quite difficult to cut with the tenon saw, gouge and plane. With the central hole already drilled, with a ¾"(19 mm) bit, drill on all the Cut Lines at both ends, just inside the end Pitch Lines through to the centre hole. There should be eight holes per twist, a total of sixteen.

To open each bine use a ½"(13 mm) bit to drill a series of holes from either end along the Cut Lines to the hole at the opposite end. Try to drill the holes as close together as possible, this will make cleaning out quite easy. Use a rat tail rasp to break through the drill holes to complete the breakthrough.

To open the bines to the desired width, round the top of the bines first with a palm plane, then use the ½"(13 mm) chisel to reduce the width of the bines. Once this has been done access will be gained to the inside of the bines. These twists may require a fair amount of trimming. Once the bulk of waste has been cleared, remove the workpiece from the lathe. Trim the inside ends of the bines through the central hole with the ½"(13 mm)

chisel.

The design at the ends of this type of twist may be made to any style. It is not necessary to turn a cove at the end of the bines. However, take care not to turn too deeply and into the hollow centre. Sand and finish in the same manner as any other Open twist.

SEPARATING THE TWISTS

If it is felt necessary for safety and to prevent damage, the bines may be strengthened by wrapping them with masking tape. Mount the workpiece between centres. Carefully turn off the chuck mounting points and centrally part the twists to a point where vibration starts, this is an indication that you are deep enough with the parting tool, remember the hollow centre, do not go too deep. The final parting may be done with a saw. The result is a matched mirror image pair. Turn and fit a base to both lamps.

These twists are a good test for anyone. They may be cut using a combination of the methods previously described.

The completed lamps

PROJECT 2. CANDELABRA

On first appearance the candelabra illustrated is a complicated piece. This is not the case. The turning is relatively easy, it is during assembly that problems may be encountered. A little thought and patience is called for.

All the components are quite fragile. The piece has to be constructed in such a manner as to make maximum use of their strength. I recommend rosewood for this reason and ebony for the fittings.

COMPONENTS REQUIRED

Main stem

The main stem is turned from a 12"(305 mm) × 3"(76 mm) blank, with a ¾"(19 mm) spigot at the base.

The section at the top of the stem houses the smaller rings. This section should be turned to allow for the rings to rest on the shoulder at the top of the stem. Note: The small rings are set into a central boss at the top of the stem.

The stem is centre bored before cutting the twist. It features a 4-Start Open twist on an inverted taper.

Base

The base is made from 5½"(140 mm) × 1½"(38 mm) rosewood blank. It is recessed to accept the ¾"(19 mm) stem spigot.

Rings

Four inner rings measuring 2½"(64 mm) in diameter and 5/16"(8 mm) thick.

Two 4"(102 mm) × 5/16"(8 mm) rings. Cut exactly in half with the grain. This should leave the side grain at the bottom of the half ring intact, for strength.

Candle holders

Five candle holders with wax trays are required. These are turned from 3"(76 mm) × 2"(51 mm) blanks.

Rosewood and ebony candelabra

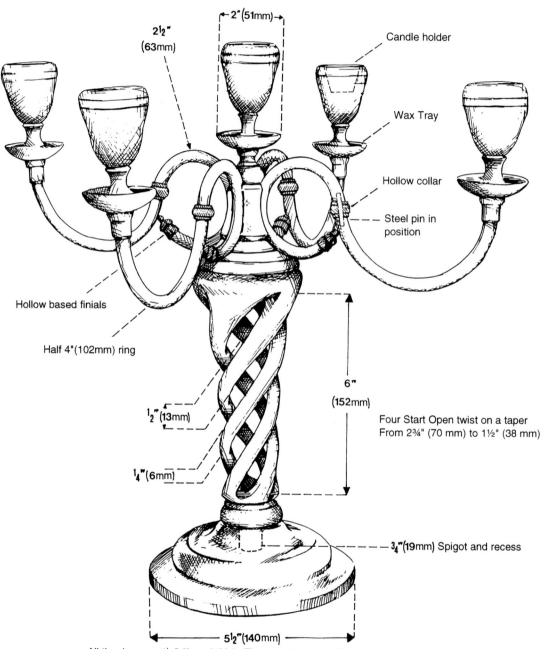

2" (51mm)

2½"
(63mm)

Candle holder

Wax Tray

Hollow collar

Steel pin in
position

Hollow based finials

Half 4"(102mm) ring

½" (13mm)

6"
(152mm)

Four Start Open twist on a taper
From 2¾" (70 mm) to 1½" (38 mm)

¼"(6mm)

¾"(19mm) Spigot and recess

5½"(140mm)

All the rings are ⁵/₁₆" (8 mm) thick. They are joined and linked with
¹/₈" (3 mm) × 1" (25 mm) steel pins.
The Open spirals taper from ½" (13 mm) to ¼" (6 mm)

Four should be drilled at the base with a $^5/_{16}$"(8 mm) drill to accept the rings. The central candle holder should be turned with a $^5/_{16}$"(8 mm) spigot.

Collars

Four ½"(13 mm) × $^3/_8$"(9 mm) collars in ebony centre drilled to $^5/_{16}$"(8 mm). These fit over the joins of the rings.

Finials

Four finials in ebony, drilled to $^5/_{16}$"(8 mm) at the base. These fit over the open end of the inner rings when cut.

After all the components have been matched in colour and polished, assemble the piece. Make sure that no stain or polish is on the spigots or the end of the rings to be glued. Assemble the candle holder supports first. For this, four 1"(25 mm) × $^1/_8$"(3 mm) steel pins are required.

Cut approximately ¾"(19 mm) from each of the inner rings. Make sure the side grain runs into the inner securing recess at the top. This will ensure maximum strength.

Drill $^1/_8$"(3 mm) holes to a depth of ½"(13 mm) at all four ends of the inner rings, and one end of the outer 4"(102 mm) rings. Fit and glue the steel pins, linking the small inner rings to the outer ones. Make sure the assemblies are pushed into place on a perfectly flat surface. When the glue has set fit the four ebony collars centrally over the join.

Fit and glue the candleholders to the arms as illustrated.

Cut the $^5/_{16}$"(8 mm) recesses, spaced exactly quarterly around the central retaining boss at the top of the stem. I recommend a sharp chisel and a ¼"(6 mm) gouge. Cut the recesses with the stem supported between centres. Use an indexer, where available, for accuracy.

Once satisfied all the components are in order, assemble the piece as follows.

1. Fit the stem into the base and make sure it is at 90 degrees.
2. Stand the piece on a flat surface. Place an elastic band quite tightly around the centre of the arm retaining boss. Set the candle holder arms in turn into the recesses. Use the elastic bands by pushing them into the inner rings to hold the arms in position. Make sure they are level by measuring from the flat surface to the top of each candle holder.

Notes: 1. The tops of the inner ring finials should touch and just support the outer rings.
2. The inner candle holder may be set a little higher than the outer ones.
3. The central boss, that supports the inner rings, may be cut separately then fitted to the stem. Employing this method, the recesses may be cut with a saw then trimmed with a gouge.

When satisfied that the components are fitted correctly and the piece is in balance, glue it together.

Detail of the assembled arm and candle. The components are quite fragile so a dense hardwood such as rosewood must be used and attention paid to grain direction

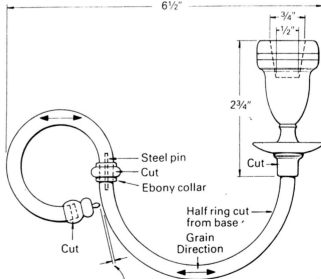

6½"
¾"
½"
2¾"
Cut
Steel pin
Cut
Ebony collar
Half ring cut from base
Grain Direction
Cut

Note $^1/_{16}$" gap to take spring in wood when pressure is placed on candle holder

Assembled arm and candle holder

14

STRETCHING A PITCH AND LENGTHENING A TWIST

STRETCHING A PITCH

I feel this is a convenient stage to introduce the procedure for stretching a pitch. I can find no reference anywhere to the method I use, but it is accurate, fast, very easy and, in my opinion the best way of doing the job. There are other methods for carrying out this work, such as using an angled tube of cardboard over the blank or a piece of string or tape. I have, in the past, tried several methods and have never found it necessary to adopt any.

In the previous section dealing with the Open 4-Start a brief mention was made to lengthening a bine. The best method in describing these procedures is by way of illustrations, so please study those below before reading on.

On a pre-prepared blank with a 10"(254 mm) cylinder centre section mark out a 9"(228 mm) twist with a 3"(76 mm) pitch. Divide the pitch three times and the result will be twenty-four segments measuring ³/₈"(9 mm)

wide. Mark out four Start Lines and number them 1 to 4.

Illustrated below are three different pitch measurements, a 1½"(38 mm), a 3"(76 mm), and a 4½"(141 mm). As you can see, taking the system to extremes, a pitch can be decided from ³/₈"(9 mm) to any length desired.

This is also the system I use when designing a twist. Remember this is only an example.

Other points to remember are:

1. Stretching a pitch is different from lengthening a twist or bine.
2. The length of a twist is decided according to the piece and regardless of the pitch length, and stretching the pitch does not alter the length of the twist.
3. Stretching a pitch is used mainly where strength is required when lighter and weaker materials are used, or to achieve a certain design effect, particularly in the case of an Open twist.

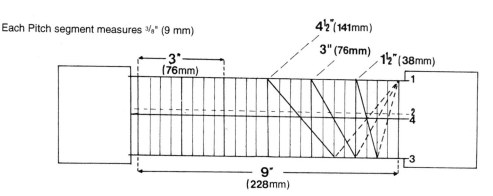

Stretching a Pitch

LENGTHENING A TWIST

A twist can be cut at any length. Once cut, with the end design finished, a twist cannot be altered. However should a situation arise where the design of the workpiece to be twisted is longer than the intended twist, then the twist may be lengthened to accommodate the design. Like all spindle work, twists can be joined together to form a larger column. This is not lengthening a twist. They are individual twists joined together.

A traditional twist is balanced in the sense that each bine should start and finish on the same Start Line. However, the twist may be lengthened without altering the pitch by cutting over one or both end Pitch Lines to a determined point.

The requirement to lengthen a twist may be where another twist has to be copied exactly. Where the traditional twist is not long enough for the blank, and in order to keep the twist traditional without stretching the pitch, a percentage of a pitch has to be added to meet the requirement.

Where the addition of a full pitch is too much, the requirement may be $1/8$, $1/4$, $1/2$ or $3/4$ of a pitch length in the case of a Single, Double etc. Or $1/6$, $1/3$, or $2/3$ in the case of a Triple, 6-Start etc. The method I use is to add the number of segments for the particular pitch as required.

The main point to remember when lengthening a twist is that any copy must be lengthened in the same manner. See the illustration below.

Note: Should you stretch the pitch in an attempt to lengthen the twist, the design will be altered. In effect you have designed a twist. A good way of illustrating this is to take a light coil or spring and from the spring position between two fixed points pull it out slowly, to almost a straight wire. Note the changes of the pitch as you do so. This will give you an idea. With each little pull the pitch and design changes and the twist is different.

The above exercise also illustrates how a bine may be stretched to give added strength when opening a twist or hollow form; the more you pull on the coil or spring the more rigid it will become giving added strength.

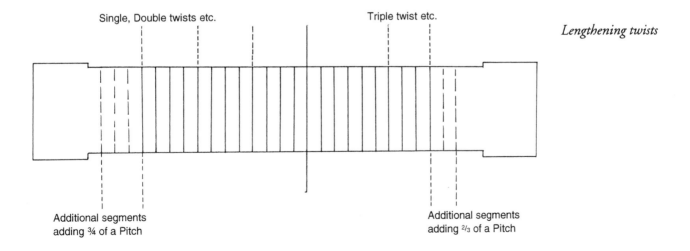

Lengthening twists

Single, Double twists etc.

Triple twist etc.

Additional segments adding ¾ of a Pitch

Additional segments adding ⅔ of a Pitch

15

CABLE, ROPE AND MULTI-START TWISTS

A Cable or Multi-Start twist may appear to be one of the easier twists to cut. In respect of cutting this is true. However, the marking out and cutting technique has to be more accurate otherwise the end result will be a 'drunk' twist. A mistake is more easily spotted on a small bine or twist.

These twists are strong with a most attractive spiral and selecting the material for the design is problem-free as any species of timber may be used.

I will start with the Cable twist, sometimes referred to as a Rope twist, aptly named because it resembles a cable or rope. Readers will by now be well aware that the pitch on a twist is critical to its design and this is justly so in the case of a Cable.

When an intended Cable twist goes wrong and does not resemble a cable or rope, the pitch is invariably too long or too short. In the case of one that is too long the bines will appear too large. It may be possible to keep the same pitch and increase the number of bines to compensate. Where the pitch is too short, stretch it. Should the completed twist fail to resemble a rope it should be referred to as a Multi-Start.

Normally the hollows or troughs on a Cable twist are not rounded at the bottom, they are V shaped and the angle of the V is dependent on the size and number of bines. However, a Cable or Rope twist with a rounded bottom looks most attractive.

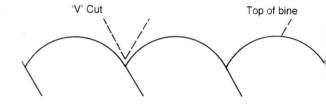

Rope twist

A Cable twist should have at least eight or nine bines on material around 2"(51 mm) wide. As the width is increased the number of bines may also be increased in order to imply a tighter cable, and this will also mean that the bine width will be narrower. Be careful not to make the bines too narrow or too wide.

As you may have guessed, the Cable twist can be marked out starting with three or four Start Lines. Should one so desire, the Start Lines can be marked out in the normal manner in pencil or after making eight or nine equal divisions with dividers or a piece of tape as previously explained. Page 68 refers.

For this exercise I will explain how to mark out a nine bine Cable twist with a 9"(228 mm) pitch. Using three Start Lines. The pitch on a Cable twist should be at least three to four times the width of the material used.

When marking out these twists I do not recommend

the Complete Marking Out as the piece becomes too cluttered. This applies to the smaller pieces rather than the large. It is a matter of room on the blank.

All measurements and marking out for cable and Multi-Starts *must* be accurate.

Stage 1:

Select a 14"(355 mm)× 2"(51 mm) × 2"(51 mm) blank, and prepare a 10"(254 mm) centre cylindrical section as before. Mark the nine Start Lines by whichever method you prefer.

The first, by using a piece of tape placed round the blank. Cut the tape to the exact size of the circumference, measure and mark the tape at eight equidistant points making nine segments. Replace the tape and mark the Start Lines from the marks on the tape, including the join. Using this method, my measurements are approximately $^{21}/_{32}$"(17 mm) between each Start Line mark on the tape.

The second is to use dividers adopting the triangulation method to find the first three Start Lines. Use the dividers again to measure and mark three equal sections between the primary Start Lines. Mark in pencil at these 6 points. There are now nine Start Lines as above.

On this second method I set the dividers at $1^{11}/_{16}$"(34 mm) to find the first three Start Lines and $^{21}/_{32}$"(17 mm) to find the remaining six Start Lines.

Stage 2:

Mark centrally to the 10"(254 mm) centre section 9"(228 mm). That is the pitch and, in this case, the full length of the twist. Divide the 9"(228 mm) section into nine equal sections measuring 1"(25 mm). There are now eight Pitch Dividing Lines.

Stage 3:

From all nine Start Lines mark in pencil the Cut Control Lines diagonally across each intersection with the Pitch Dividing Lines. This will result in nine Cut Lines.

Repeat the above marking out, this will indicate the Bine Apex Lines. You should have eighteen Start Lines and nineteen Pitch and Control Lines.

COMPLETE MARKING OUT
For the Complete Marking Out, double the Start Lines. Divide the pitch segments and complete the Width Control Lines in another colour.

As mentioned previously, marking out and cutting a twist of any description is a discipline. To maintain the proper balance the traditional pitch measurements and method of marking out must be followed. With most twists, whether Single, Double, Triple or 4-Start, they

Marking out in graph form the Cut Lines for a Cable or rope twist

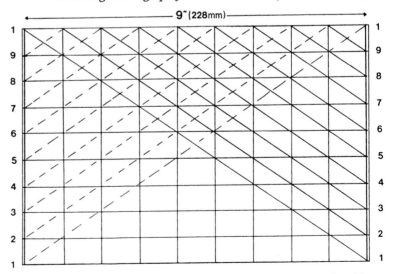

The above illustration represents one Pitch only. There are nine Start Lines, nine diagonal Cut Lines and nine Pitch segments

will retain their identity regardless of the pitch. This discipline becomes more important when cutting the Cable twist. The Cable or Rope can very quickly lose its identity as the pitch is stretched or is made shorter. If the Cable twist loses its identity, it would automatically convert to a Multi-Start of some description as previously mentioned. However, there is a fair degree of flexibility in the marking out of a Cable. The main criterion is to retain the cable effect. Whatever the width of the blank, vary the pitch to suit, add bines where necessary. For example a 3"(76 mm) blank could carry twelve bines and a 6"(152 mm) thick blank could quite easily carry twenty-four bines with a 12"(305 mm) pitch.

Another very important point to remember at this stage is, where the number of bines and the pitch have been determined for a particular width of material, lengthening the pitch will result in wider bines and shortening the pitch will obviously have the opposite effect. As you can see, we are getting very close to twist or spiral designing.

CUTTING THE CABLE OR ROPE TWIST

Stage 4:

With the tenon saw on the first pass cut very lightly and accurately along the Cut Lines. This is to make sure there are no mistakes. One wrong cut can ruin the bine. On this twist the cut should be about 3/16"(5 mm) deep.

Stage 5: Using the gouge:

Be very careful when cutting the Cable. Good control of the tool is called for as the bines are fine. One cannot afford to slip and cause damage even from the beginning. The first cut should be light and about 1/8"(3 mm) from the saw cut lines. Whether you are left- or right-handed, turn the workpiece round to cut the other side of the line. To balance the bines, two deeper cuts with the gouge should remove the saw cut lines and complete the gouge cutting process.

Stage 6:

In order to get the V shaped hollow, use a 1½" (38 mm) carpenter's chisel in the same manner as for the Single twist.

Stage 7:

It is not necessary to use the palm plane on this twist. Round the top of the bines using sandpaper only. Prepare another sanding tool from a piece of wood approximately 14"(355 mm) long, similar to the previous sanding tool (page 35 refers), only this time one side has to be almost sharp. Use the sharp edge when sanding the bottom of the hollow. Remember to count the strokes with the sanding tool and keep the workpiece rotating evenly into the sanding cut, otherwise flats will occur.

The tops of the bines can be sanded with the lathe in motion, provided the lathe speed can be reduced to around 200 r.p.m. This will regularise the top of the bines. Do not use a strip of sanding cloth, adopting the see-saw method on this type of twist, unless experienced. If the cloth jumps the bines, they can be easily damaged.

Stage 8:

To finish off the ends of this type of twist, turn the hollows at either end to the same depth as the twist hollows.

The design at the end of a Cable or Rope twist may be finished in other ways. Here are a few suggestions:

1. A spigot may be turned at the very end of the spiral to form a square end in order that the bines butt onto the piece for which it was designed.
3. The end of the spiral itself may be slightly rounded off into a cove or V according to taste. See the Illustrations right for several ideas in this area.

These designs may also be used on other twists.

An 8-Start Cable twist

*Design features for the ends of twists,
particularly the Rope and Cable twists*

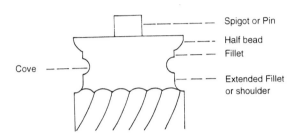

Spigot or Pin
Half bead
Fillet
Cove
Extended Fillet
or shoulder

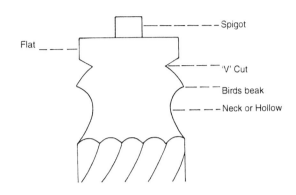

Flat
Spigot
'V' Cut
Birds beak
Neck or Hollow

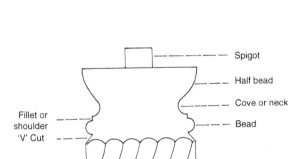

Spigot
Half bead
Cove or neck
Bead
Fillet or
shoulder
'V' Cut

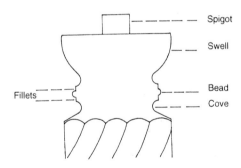

Spigot
Swell
Bead
Cove
Fillets

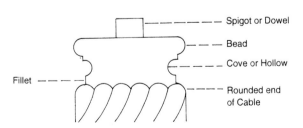

Spigot or Dowel
Bead
Cove or Hollow
Rounded end
of Cable
Fillet

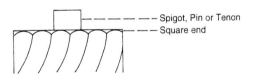

Spigot, Pin or Tenon
Square end

All the above features can be mixed provided
they balance

Note: There are different terms for particular features,
depending on which part of the country you come from

CABLE OR MULTI-START (OPEN DESIGN)

It may be perfectly obvious that the actual act of opening a Cable twist is a tricky affair, and it will also result in the twist losing its identity. I personally refer to this twist as an Open Cable or an Open Multi-Start. Any Cable or Multi-Start type of twist can be opened, however to succeed in this exercise is dependent on several points:

1. The type of material selected. It is better to be a harder, stable timber.
2. The thickness of the bine, in other words the design.
3. On softer material the bines must be thicker in order to retain strength.
4. Should the requirement be for very fine bines, the timber should ideally be dense and straight grained.

In the case of larger Open Multi-Starts, consisting of six bines or over, these can be opened regardless of the length of pitch. The explanation for this is that the thickness of the blank will only accommodate a certain number of bines at a given width. If the pitch is set too short it will be impossible to cut, and the hollows will be too narrow to permit access for cutting purposes. It follows, therefore, that the pitch is pre-determined unless it is stretched.

PROCEDURE FOR OPENING THE CABLE OR MULTI-START

The procedure for opening a Cable or a Multi-Start is much the same as for the Open 4-Start. (Chapter 13).

The only difference is that there are more bines and they are likely to be considerably thinner.

Remember to drill the central relieving hole in the blank before cutting the twist. In the case of a 2"(51 mm) thick Cable twist, I recommend a ¾"(19 mm) hole at least. Do not go over ⅞"(22 mm).

The thickness of the bines when finished will be approximately ¼"(6 mm).

Always complete the main twist and the design features at both ends before breaking through. Drill the holes at the end of the hollows in the same manner as any other open twist. Rasp and sand these holes before breaking through. Open one bine at a time. This method will keep the twist rigid until the last two bines are opened.

When rounding the tops of the bines very little planing will be required. There will be less room to work between the bines with the carpenter's chisel, therefore less access to trim the inside edges. It will be an advantage to use a narrow bladed chisel. Do not use excess pressure when cutting the bines. *Do not* lever the chisel against the bines when cutting the inside as they could break.

The best method of sanding is the use of a strip of cloth sanding material. Put very little tension on the sanding cloth around the bines; this will result in a lighter sanding action and avoid possible damage.

Once the twist is cut further turning is impossible. In unusual circumstances where it is absolutely necessary to re-turn such a piece, the twist may be taped very solidly with a splint, in order that it may be turned in safety.

16

TAPERED AND GRADUATED TWISTS

Tapered and Graduated twists have been around for a long time. They are mainly used in staircases, balconies and furniture of all descriptions. This type of twist tends to be seen on heavier types of woodwork and traditionally was applied to add elegance and design to a rather bulky column. Where a normal twist adds to the elegance of a spindle, a tapered twist increases that elegance and appeal even further on a tapered piece of work.

Any type of twist can be used on any taper, provided there is sufficient material to cut the twist and sufficient strength left in the piece to serve the purpose for which it is designed.

A Tapered or Graduated twist normally tapers inwards from the bottom up. For certain projects I have made inverted Tapered and Graduated twists. This is referred to in the Designing Twists section. The principles for cutting these twists are the same as any other, whether Single, Double or Multi-Start. The difference is in the marking out once the size of the taper and pitch have been decided. Both twists are extremely attractive when finished.

When planning the twist, make sure that the project is balanced. With experience, one can visualise the finished article. However, if you are uncertain, plan the piece on paper, make the complete project or the section where the column is to be used, turn the spigots

and fit the blank. This will give an indication regarding balance. The reason I mention this is because there is a lot of work in this type of twist, and once cut it cannot be shortened or altered successfully.

See also Chapter 21 on Pineapple twists. Page 139 refers to an occasional table, where the main central teardrop section of the column is un-cut. The piece looks quite plain in its un-cut state, but it does balance. Imagine it with a 4, 6 or 8-Start twist.

TAPERED TWIST

An ordinary Tapered twist is based on standard marking out as for any other twist whether Single, Double, Triple etc. Mark the Pitch Lines equally along the tapered section. In other words, all the pitch measurements are the same, regardless of the thickness of the material. Ignore the taper. The twist is cut in the normal manner.

For marking out, cutting and finishing, refer back to the relevant chapter for details.

A Tapered or Graduated twist *must* be cut on a true taper otherwise the imbalance will be noticeable immediately.

An ordinary twist on a taper, such as a Single, Double, Triple, etc. can look a little unbalanced to the trained eye, and the pitch may look stretched at the thinner end of the taper and tight at the thick end. This is not so obvious when tapering a Multi-Start twist, in fact, in some instances this slight imbalance can enhance the design of the Tapered twist. Some people prefer this twist to the Graduated type.

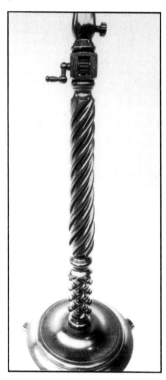

6-Start Tapered twist on a centre column

GRADUATED TWIST

For the purpose of marking out and cutting a twist, 'graduated' means to mark out in stages along the tapered section, the required pitch at a given point in relation to the width of the blank. In other words, the bines from the thickest point will reduce in size in proportion to the material as it gets thinner along the taper. Unlike the Tapered twist there are no restrictions on design or the type of twist that may be cut. There is also an added advantage for designing and mixing twists.

PREPARING FOR THE GRADUATED TWIST

Before marking out and cutting your first Graduated twist, select a good quality piece of stock to match the rest of the intended project. I recommend a piece of straight grained mahogany or similar wood.

There is a lot of work in cutting this type of twist and there is no practice run in this exercise.

The first decisions to be made are:

1. The use for the twist. Whether a small table, plant stand, candlestick, the first of a pair maybe, (left and right), or of a set for a larger table etc. This twist will usually serve a functional purpose. Should the project involve copy turning, refer to Chapter 20 for further information.

2. Designing the piece. Decide the proportions, make sure everything balances. Once this is done the column or spindle may be prepared for twisting. This will invariably determine the length and width of the twist.

3. The next decision is the type of twist best suited for the purpose. For example, the combination of the taper and cutting a Single twist can result in a weak spot at the top of the twist. This is a WARNING not to taper the material too steeply or too thin at the top. Take into consideration the amount of material that will be removed to cut a particular twist. The more bines there are the less cutting into the cross grain. Always calculate the thickness of the uncut core of the twist as the strength of the column or spindle.

From this stage onwards, the decision as to the length of the twist is for the individual. Therefore, the blank will have to be prepared in accordance with the plan of the project. There are several examples in this book to prompt ideas. (See also Chapter 14 for stretching a pitch or bine and lengthening a twist).

For this exercise I have decided to explain and illustrate the method I use to mark out and cut a Graduated Single twist approximately 12"(304 mm) long, tapering from 3"(76 mm) to 2"(51 mm). For a traditional twist the following procedure must be followed regardless of length and taper on the blank:

Stage 1:

Select an 18"(457 mm) × 3"(76 mm) × 3"(76 mm) piece of good quality straight grained mahogany. Turn a 14"(355 mm) centre section into a 3"(76 mm) cylinder, leaving the normal 2"(51 mm) square end sections. If necessary, remove the sharp edges to prevent damage to your hands. Mark centrally a 12"(304 mm) section on the blank. These two lines are the end Pitch Lines. Taper this section from 3"(76 mm) to 2"(51 mm). Note:

On large pieces the taper may run from, or towards, the headstock. It is a matter of choice. However, I always recommend that the wide end of the taper is always at the headstock end. This is common practice as it retains strength at the drive end and helps to stop vibration, particularly when turning thinner pieces.

RIGHT-HANDED PERSON: For stability and safety when cutting the twist, cut uphill with the twisting gouge, as there is less likelihood of slip. I mention safety at this point for one reason. Cutting down a tapered section of material towards the driving hand can be dangerous, particularly when cutting a twist with a long pitch or with small bines.

LEFT-HANDED PERSON: A left-handed turner may cut the taper from the other side of the lathe, or turn the workpiece around between centres so that the thick end of the taper is at the tailstock end. Some may suggest my reasons are not valid as one should always cut downhill when using a gouge. In normal turning when preparing the taper, I agree, however, when cutting a twist by hand this rule does not apply.

Stage 2:

The next stage is to establish the remaining Pitch Lines. Over the full length of the twist we are losing approximately 1/3rd of the full width of material which is 1"(25 mm). This loss must be distributed evenly along the bines. It automatically follows that the length of the pitch must be reduced in proportion to the width reduction. Forgetting the end pitch lines, there are four remaining Pitch Lines to be established. This calculation is simple, each pitch has to be reduced by ¼"(6 mm).

Measure 3"(76 mm) from the Pitch Line at the thick end. At the mid-way point measure the thickness of the material, it will be 2⁷/8"(73 mm), that is the length of the first pitch. Mark it in pencil. The next pitch will reduce by ¼"(6 mm) therefore it will be 2⁵/8"(67 mm). Calculate and mark the remaining Pitch Lines accordingly, at 2³/8"(60 mm), 2¹/8"(54 mm) and 2"(51 mm). This gives a total of 12"(304 mm) and five Pitch Segments.

Mathematically, the above measurements are based

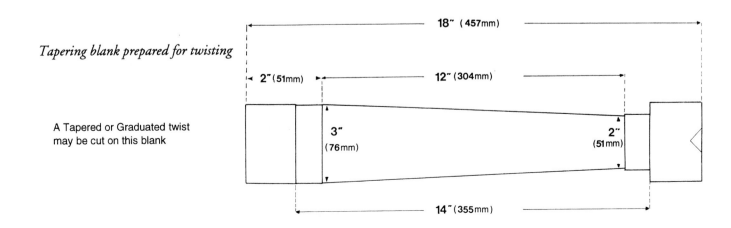

Tapering blank prepared for twisting

A Tapered or Graduated twist may be cut on this blank

on establishing the central Pitch Lines; the end Pitch Lines are excluded from the calculations as they are automatically established when the length of the twist is marked out. This calculation has resulted in the fifth pitch being the same thickness as the material at the thin end. This balances perfectly with the rest of the twist. See the illustration right.

On a Graduated twist, regardless of shape, always calculate the pitch from the thick end downwards. Any loss or gain which may occur can be easily worked in at the thin end of the twist. This may be done by stretching the twist. Hopefully this should not occur.

Stage 3:
There are now six Pitch lines and five segments along the blank. Divide each segment twice in the same manner as a normal Single twist. With the inclusion of the Pitch Dividing Lines there are now twenty Pitch Segments. See illustration right.

Stage 4:
Mark the four Start lines equally along the blank as indicated right. Set the tool rest in line with the corners of the square ends to find the correct position for these lines. Number them 1 to 4 at the thin end of the blank.

Stage 5:
From number 1 Start Line mark in pencil a diagonal line across the segments from right to left. This is the Cut Control Line.

With confidence, and a little experience, this twist may be cut quite successfully from this stage without further marking out. If necessary, for accuracy and peace of mind, mark at all four Start Lines.

Extra colours should not be necessary once you have reached this stage.

Line 1 is the Cut Line. Line 3 is the Bine Apex Line and lines 2 and 4 are the hollow and bine Width Control Lines. This is the Complete Marking Out as illustrated on p.100.

CUTTING THE GRADUATED SINGLE TWIST
When cutting any twist the use of the free hand, whether left or right, when rotating the material into the cutting tool is critical. There is no doubt that the co-ordinated action between both hands, and maintaining a smooth cut, makes the difference when cutting a twist. Without this co-ordination cutting becomes difficult and irregular. If the gouge is blunt the job is almost impossible. I find when teaching, pupils have a tendency to 'dig'. This is caused by stabbing at the material. Keep the gouge on its side and let the leading edge slice into the workpiece, link the co-ordination with this smooth cutting action. That is the main hurdle. The gouge cutting angle must always be parallel to the Cut Line. Practise the technique on any waste piece of timber, take small cuts until you get it right. Keep the tools sharp.

Stage 6:
With the tenon saw cut along the Cut Line in the same manner as before. I recommend that the cut is started from the thin end, and whilst I appreciate it is more difficult to cut into end grain, it is safer and there is less likelihood of a mistake. One word of caution, should this cut be made from the thicker end of the blank towards the thin end, care should be exercised when coming off the thick section not to cut too deep. This cut may be deeper at the thicker end of the twist where the bines will be larger.

Stage 7:
When cutting towards the thin end, the amount of waste material removed should be reduced as the taper decreases in size. When using the gouge, a nicely rounded bine top is critical to the design of this spiral. Keep the bine and hollow in proportion with the taper and cut just within the Width Control Lines at all times. This *will* result in a well-balanced Graduated twist.

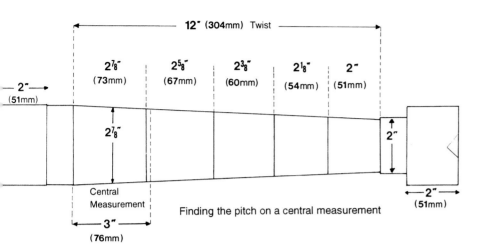

Graduated Single twist

Finding the pitch on a central measurement

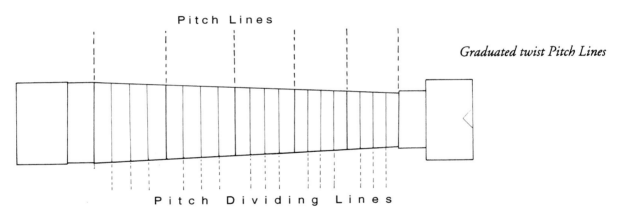

Graduated twist Pitch Lines

Note: The pitch segments reduce in size as the taper gets thinner

Graduated twist Start and Pitch Lines

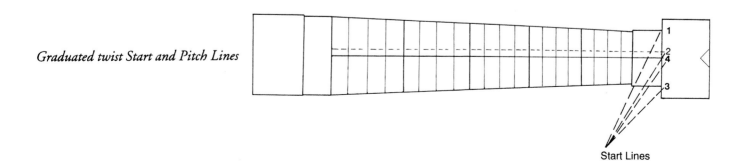

Complete Marking Out for a Graduated Single twist

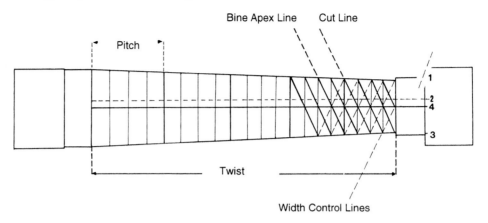

Stage 8: Palm Plane

This is where this tool is a delight to use. Make sure it is sharp and is capable of a nice long clean cut. The method to adopt when rounding the bines on this type of twist with this tool, is to plane as much as possible downhill. Count he strokes in equal numbers at corresponding segments along the length of each bine. Due to the fact that the bines reduce in size, you may find that the thin end of the bines will be rounded before the thick end. Continue planing and counting the strokes on the thicker bines until you are satisfied that they appear balanced.

A good guide for the depth of the hollow is one third the width of the material at any given point. Gauge the depth at each pitch line according to the length of pitch before the lines are removed. The hollows will obviously increase in depth as the bines increase in size.

The hollow or trough on this twist should be finished by cutting a V at the bottom with a 1½"(38 mm), carpenter's chisel in the same manner as the standard Single.

Stage 9:

Sand this twist before turning the design at either end. This will prevent any damage to the design, should heavy sanding be necessary. Otherwise, there is no difference in the sanding method from that of the standard Single twist.

Stage 10:

Finishing the ends of the Graduated twist is dependent on the purpose for which it is made. Should the full strength of the piece be required, turn the coves at either end as shallow as possible without spoiling the design. One sixth the width of material should be enough to get a crisp leading edge to the bine. Do not risk a deeper hollow if there is any doubt.

The above twist is a perfect example of a balanced Graduated Single twist. Should any variation be desired, whether longer, thicker with a shallower or steeper taper, the marking out principle remains the same. Some tapers may involve a little more calculation. Always mark out the pitch from the thick end, never the other way around. Smaller measurements are more difficult to calculate, and this can be critical to keep the piece in balance. In cases where difficulty is encountered, measure and find the approximate width of the first pitch segment, measure it at its centre point, that is the true pitch length. Do the same with the second pitch. Calculate the reduction difference between the first and second pitches. Repeat that difference in each pitch along the length of the workpiece taper.

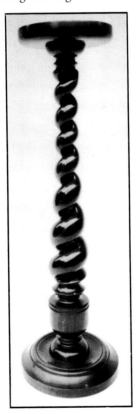

Graduated Single twist

GRADUATED DOUBLE TWIST

For the purpose of explaining the marking out for the Graduated Double twist, prepare a blank to the same specification as for the Graduated Single twist above. The twist will also be 12"(304 mm) long.

Marking out for a Graduated Single twist

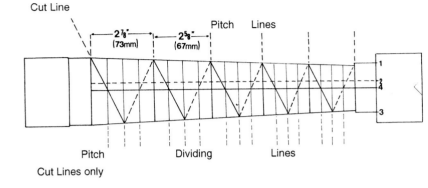

Graduated Double twist

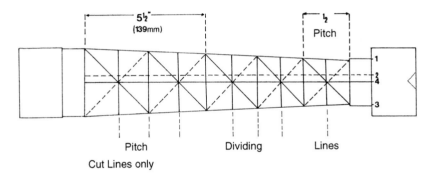

The Double pitch is based on the Single pitch marking out with only one division of the pitch segments. There will be ten pitch segments.

By using four of these segments the Double has its four pitch segments. This has, in effect, completed the marking out for the Double as far as the pitch and Pitch Dividing Lines. This particular Double will have 2½ pitches. Mark out the Cut Control Lines at Start Lines 1 and 3. Lines 2 and 4 are the Bine Apex Lines.

Should it be considered necessary, the Complete Marking Out procedure should be followed.

See illustrations above for comparable marking out for the Graduated Single and Double twists.

COMPLETE MARKING OUT

The Complete Marking Out for the Graduated Double and any other Double is exactly the same as that for the standard Double Barley twist. (See Chapter 6).

CUTTING THE GRADUATED DOUBLE TWIST

All relevant information regarding the cutting, sanding and finishing of a Graduated Double Barley twist is available in previous chapters. It is now a matter of reference. First, refer to cutting the standard Double. (Chapter 6). One may also refer to the procedure for cutting the Graduated Single twist above.

There are however, several points to take into consideration when cutting this twist:

1. The depth of the hollow should be gauged at a quarter the width of the material and should be in proportion to the width of the material at every individual Pitch Line.
2. The width of the bines and the hollows will reduce as they go down the taper. Care should be exercised not to overcut the Pitch Control Lines.
3. Before finishing the twist be sure the bines are balanced. That is, all the bines are the same width at any given point around the twist and the hollow is cut parallel to the bines.
4. The hollows, beads, etc., at either end should be in proportion to the twist and any other decorative feature on the column or spindle.

PROJECT: COOK BOOK STAND

This book stand is quite an elaborate piece. It is constructed of mahogany with rosewood fittings. It can be free standing or it can be hung up by means of brass hangers located in the two rear bun feet. For the overall dimensions see the illustration below.

All spindle work is quite straightforward and may be copied as seen.

The main uprights, base and central hollow stretcher, are made from 1¼"(32 mm) mahogany.

There are four main sections that make up the piece.

1. The base.
2. The main frame
3. The book carrier
4. A cranked hinge.

The base

The base is a square frame constructed on four 1½"(38 mm) × ½"(13 mm) bun feet. On the front of the base, located above the front two bun feet, are two trunnion supports fitted by means of ½"(13 mm) spigots. These are centrally drilled at ¾"(19 mm) to house the mounting bosses for the main frame. When gluing the base, make sure it is properly clamped and placed on a perfectly flat and level surface.

The main frame

The two main uprights feature a 7"(178 mm) standard Double Barley twist with a 2"(51 mm) pitch on a taper, from 1½"(38 mm) to 1"(25 mm) at the top of the twist. See the illustration opposite for exploded view of a main upright. The most complicated feature on this piece is the adjustable book carrier. The gearing of which is housed in the central hollow stretcher.

The stretcher carries a ³/8"(9 mm) 5-prong star drive shaft that runs clear through the hollow stretcher to locate with two rosewood adjustment knobs.

On the way through the stretcher the star drive locates with the two ridged carrier uprights, located within the two large beads seen at the left and right of centre on the stretcher. A ³/8"(9 mm) hole is drilled at ¹/3 the width of these beads to accept the geared section of the book carrier uprights.

Book stand in mahogany with rosewood fittings, featuring a tilting rise and fall book carrier.
Free standing or wall hanging

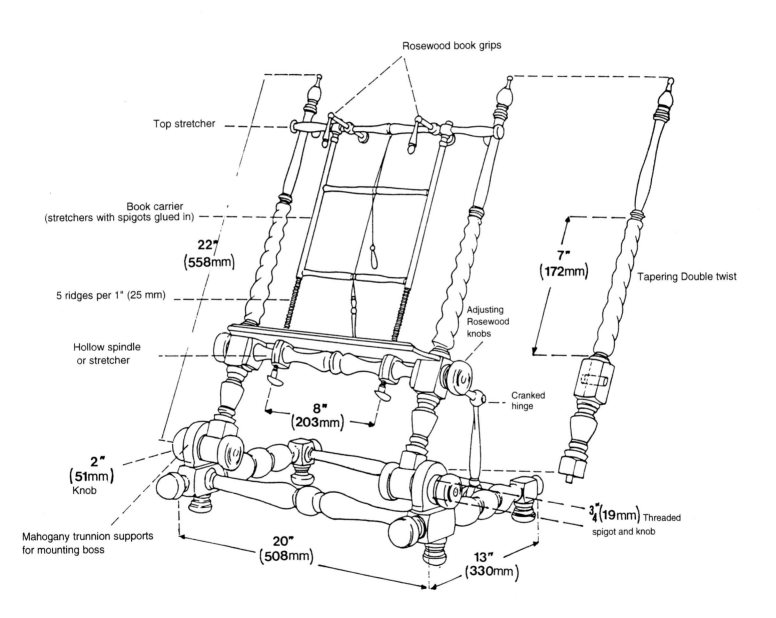

Rosewood book grips

Top stretcher

Book carrier
(stretchers with spigots glued in)

22"
(558mm)

5 ridges per 1" (25 mm)

Hollow spindle
or stretcher

2"
(51mm)
Knob

Mahogany trunnion supports
for mounting boss

8"
(203mm)

20"
(508mm)

Adjusting
Rosewood
knobs

Cranked
hinge

7"
(172mm)

Tapering Double twist

3/4"(19mm) Threaded
spigot and knob

13"
(330mm)

Note: The beads have to be accurately flattened at the top and bottom to allow for accurate drilling. Keep the two larger top pieces.

When the piece is assembled the two adjustment knobs will be glued in position. When gluing the two main uprights to the central hollow stretcher make sure it is lying on a flat surface. The uprights should be glued into the bosses last, with the bosses firmly located in the trunnions.

Main frame bosses

The main frame bosses are made in rosewood. They are fitted with ¾"(19 mm) thick by 1½"(38 mm) long threaded spigot to fit the trunnion supports. They are also drilled to accept ¾"(19 mm) spigots at the bottom of the two main uprights. When fitted, the main frame is fitted and locked in position by means of two threaded rosewood knobs to match.

The book shelf

The bookshelf is cut accurately to fit between the two main uprights. They are also resting on the flat topped sections of the two gear housing beads. The shelf is also accurately drilled to allow the geared section of the carrier uprights to pass freely through. The shelf is glued in position.

The book carrier

Turning the spindles for the book carrier is straightforward. The top stretcher is made from ½"(13 mm) and the rest from ³/₈"(9 mm) mahogany.

Note: There are retaining knobs at either end of the top stretcher, they locate over a plain section of the main uprights. The two inner beads house the rosewood book grips, and the two remaining beads are fixing points for the carrier uprights.

At the bottom of the carrier uprights there is a 5"(127 mm) adjustable section with five small beads and coves to every 1"(25 mm). These sections run through the ³/₈"(9 mm) hole drilled in the two gear location beads on the central hollow stretcher.

Note: The two boat features are glued by means of a small spigot to the bottom of the carrier uprights. These two pieces are cut from the top of the beads in order that the bookshelf lies flat on the beads. The bottom of these beads are also flattened to allow for accurate drilling. With the carrier fully extended these small boat features complete the profile of the beads at the bottom.

Located on the top stretcher there are two book retaining grips. These are made from ¼"(6 mm) rosewood. The shafts of the grips are turned to ³/₁₆"(4 mm). They are set into ³/₁₆"(4 mm) holes drilled horizontally at 90 degrees through the two inner beads on the stretcher. These shafts are a tight sliding fit and are retained on the stretcher by two ½"(13 mm) buttons on the back end. Note the two teardrop shaped page grips dangling from the front end of these retainers and the two rosewood bookmarks on a string centred on a 'V' at the centre of the top stretcher.

The cranked hinge

The cranked hinge is necessary, giving extra security, to lock the mainframe at the desired angle when loaded with a book. It is fitted to the right-hand side of the right main upright.

The top arm of the hinge has a ring that fits over a collar on the carrier adjustment knob. The opposite end of the hinge also has a collar, through which a threaded spigot, on a knob, locks the hinge into a threaded recess (female) on the inside of the base stretcher. The rings mentioned are made by cutting the sides off a ball at the end of both arms, leaving a ¼"(6 mm) disc section. The disc is centrally drilled to suit as required.

The centre point of the hinge is two half balls. The opposing halves are pulled together and swivel on a ¹/₈"(3 mm) rosewood securing pin. This pin is secured by two ¼"(6 mm) buttons with ¹/₁₆"(1.5 mm) spigots. Only the small spigots are glued.

Make sure you are satisfied with the design and that they are matching in colour. Before gluing the components together, finish to the desired standard with a good water resistant finish, and make sure that all the moving parts are working correctly.

See the illustration on p. 103 for spindle identification and the assembled piece.

Gearing

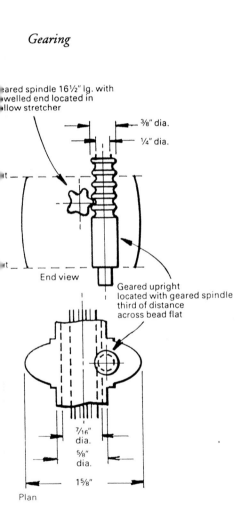

eared spindle 16½" lg. with welled end located in llow stretcher

⅜" dia.
¼" dia.

End view

Geared upright located with geared spindle third of distance across bead flat

⁷/₁₆" dia.
⅝" dia.
1⅝"

Plan

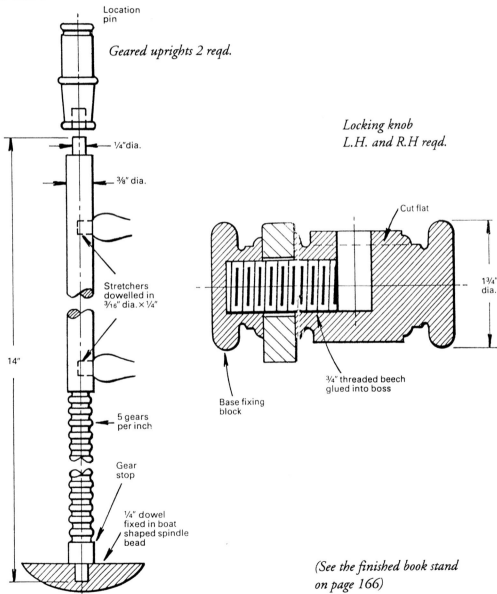

Location pin

Geared uprights 2 reqd.

¼"dia.
⅜" dia.

Stretchers dowelled in ³/₁₆" dia. × ¼"

14"

5 gears per inch

Gear stop

¼" dowel fixed in boat shaped spindle bead

Locking knob L.H. and R.H reqd.

Cut flat

1¾" dia.

¾" threaded beech glued into boss

Base fixing block

(See the finished book stand on page 166)

17

TEARDROP TWIST

For centuries the teardrop has been a popular shape in woodturning and it can be seen mainly on spindle work, columns for tables, lamp standards, jardinieres, candlesticks, etc. Smaller pieces, such as vases, hollow vessels and so on, are often designed in a ballooned or bellied teardrop style. An inverted teardrop designed properly into any piece is a very attractive form and one of my favourites.

In woodturning, the teardrop in all its varying lengths and thicknesses, is not the straightforward shape it appears. It is quite easy to turn a teardrop shape from new, it is a different matter when copying one. The profile must flow, be regular and pleasing to the eye. When copying a teardrop for twisting, as for any other reason, it must be accurate, otherwise variations in the profile will reflect in the twist.

Should a number of teardrop twists of the same size be required, all the workpieces should be copy turned accurately before twisting. All the pieces should be marked out together for twisting, before cutting is commenced.

Apart from the standard copying procedures I adopt, the following method ensures that all the profiles are the same: lay the master horizontally on a flat surface in order that it may be viewed comfortably, at eye level. Lay the copy perfectly parallel behind the master, line up the profiles to find any discrepancies. There will be no problem if the copy is oversize. If it is over cut, bring the copy to the front of the master to see how much damage has been done. You may get away with a little variation here and there.

Before explaining the method of marking out and cutting a 4-Start Graduated Teardrop, the following brief marking out notes should be noted for other teardrop twists.

SINGLE TEARDROP

1. This twist can be marked out and cut in the same manner as a standard Tapered Single, regardless of shape.
2. The Single Teardrop may also be marked out in the same manner as the Graduated and Tapered twist, with variations which will be explained in the marking out of the 4-Start, illustrated right.

DOUBLE TEARDROP

1. For a standard Double Teardrop twist mark out as for the standard Tapered Single, use two of the Single pitch segments to establish a Double pitch. The centre line will indicate the first dividing line. Divide once again, to produce all the Pitch Dividing Lines. Mark the Cut and Bine Control Lines as normal for the Double.

2. For the Double Graduated Teardrop twist, mark out as for a Double Graduated Tapered twist, with variations, as explained in marking out the 4-Start below.

TRIPLE TEARDROP

The same principle as above applies to the Triple, except for the number of Start Lines. Whether a Standard, Tapered, or Graduated twist it again is based on the Single Pitch Dividing Lines. Add three Single pitch segments together to get the Triple. However, a complete Single pitch will mean the Triple may be too long, therefore shorten the initial Single pitch to ⁷/₈ or ¾ of its traditional length or width of material. This will produce a shorter Triple pitch.

MULTI-START TEARDROP. 8-BINE

The reason I refer to an 8 bine or 8-Start, is purely to give an indication as to how easy it is to develop this twist from one with four Start Lines, or a 6-Start from three Start Lines, etc.

The method of marking out this Multi-Start Teardrop successfully is to mark out the 4-Start Graduated twist Start, Pitch, Pitch Control, Cut and Bine Lines as illustrated. (See also the section below regarding Start Lines.) Double the number of Start Lines to eight, then divide the pitch segments. Mark out the Cut Control Lines at all eight Start Lines. The pitch may be decided according to the number of pitch segments crossed between intersection.

On larger pieces cut and finish the twist as normal. On small or thin twists of this nature, use the correct size of rasps or files to suit the size of the hollows. Should the proposed bines appear to be too tight, (very close together) it may be necessary to lengthen the pitch. (See Chapter 14 regarding lengthening a pitch or twist).

Illustrated above is an example of a 4-Start Teardrop twist.

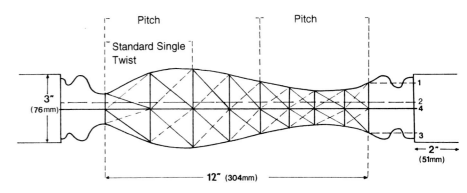

4 -Start Teardrop twist

To set the four Cut Lines, the blank has set out with a graduated Single twist. the pitch segments of the Single pitch have been divided once

CRITICAL POINTS

In the case of copy turning a twist or making a pair, always remember when marking out any piece to be copied, the twist may have been lengthened on the original when it was produced. Identify the end or ends where the addition was made before marking out and add the extra length accordingly. The twist may have been lengthened where it has been cut over the end pitch lines. This could occur automatically where the person making the twist has used a different marking out and cutting method. As previously explained, a twist can be lengthened by adding pitch segments.

Another point to note: The pitch may not be a traditional length, it may have been stretched to suit a particular piece. When producing a new piece, either end can be lengthened or stretched. It is a matter of choice.

START LINES

I make reference to possible permutations regarding Start Lines to clear up any questions which may arise regarding other spiral work not mentioned in this book.

Regardless of the number of bines, all twists start with one, two, three or four Start Lines.

The reason I refer to one Start Line is to clear up any ambiguity, one Start Line is necessary only for five, seven, ten, etc., bine twists. For these twists, the blank can be divided equally from one Start Line. Once you have five Start Lines divide once to get ten and so on. I use two Start Lines where I am using a two prong drive as a guide, I then divide the workpiece into four or six Start Lines or as required. There is nothing to stop one marking out a twist with as many hollows and bines they wish, provided the piece is large enough to carry the number of starts. I conclude on Start Lines at this point, the variation and escalation is obvious and may probably never be required.

OPENING A TAPERED, GRADUATED OR TEARDROP TWIST

Before turning the square blank, drill a hole down the centre on the lathe, pillar drill or by any other means as previously discussed. Normally the piece will be quite large. The size of the hole will depend on the thickness of the material to be twisted and the thickness of the intended bine. There must be sufficient material left after drilling to accommodate the bine. Should the hole be drilled too large the inside of the bine will be concave. The only way to overcome this is to make the bine thinner.

Before attempting to open one of the above mentioned twists, experience should be gained by opening a normal straight Double Barley twist.

The procedure for opening the standard Double is the same for opening the Tapered or Teardrop twists.

POINTS TO NOTE WHEN CUTTING ON A TAPER

1. The bines on Tapered and Graduated twists reduce in size evenly as the material gets thinner. In the case of the Teardrop twist the bine will vary according to the shape of the teardrop and width of material.
2. Once the bines have been opened on any of the above twists, the bines may be trimmed down to any thickness desired.

Drilling procedure for a tapering or graduated Open twist

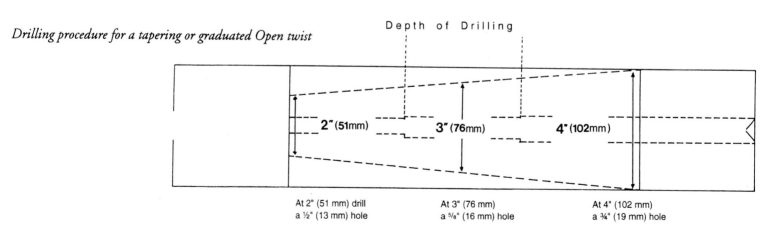

Depth of Drilling

2" (51mm)   3" (76mm)   4" (102mm)

At 2" (51 mm) drill a ½" (13 mm) hole

At 3" (76 mm) a ⁵⁄₈" (16 mm) hole

At 4" (102 mm) a ¾" (19 mm) hole

Note: The size of hole depends on the proposed thickness of the bine at a particular point. There must be sufficient material to form the bine or spirals

In the case of a steep Tapered, or any Teardrop twist the following drilling procedure may be adopted. This method reduces the necessity for a lot of heavy chisel work when removing waste material from the inside of larger pieces. See illustration left.

The method I recommend for drilling large pieces up to 1½"(38 mm) on the lathe is as follows:

Mount the workpiece between centres, turn the spigot at either end. Make sure it is larger than the required hole. Re-mount the workpiece in a jaw chuck between centres. At the tailstock end use a substantial, properly constructed steady, fitted into the tool rest to support the piece at the spigot. When properly mounted, remove the tailstock for access when drilling by hand. With the appropriate size of extended drill, complete the drilling procedure. Do not exceed 200 r.p.m.

Proper tools must be used. I personally use extended engineer's drills. *Do not* improvise. Do not use too much force. The drills must be sharp. The workpiece must be perfectly balanced when drilling. Should it start to wobble or bind, stop the lathe. reset the work and wax the drill bit. A hole 24"(610 mm) deep may be drilled quite comfortably.

18

TWISTING OR OPENING A HOLLOW FORM OR VESSEL PROJECT

Any shape of hollow form or vessel can be twisted and opened.

The main points to remember are:-

1. The form to be twisted is turned to the correct thickness for the bines. Unless this is done correctly it can be very hard work trimming the inside of the bines. This is obviously dependent on the species of timber used.
2. The form cannot be re-turned after the twist has been opened.
3. The thickness and number of bines must suit the design of the piece.
4. There is no restriction, except the size of the piece, as to the number of bines or starts.
5. In the case of a solid twist remember to leave sufficient material to accommodate the hollow, otherwise you may break through and open the twist accidentally.

A twisted hollow form can be any design: a lamp, candlesticks, pot-pourri container, decorative vase or similar item. The shape and size can vary from a small egg shape to a large open cylinder.

For this particular exercise, I allow for a good deal of licence by illustrating with a medium sized piece in a very simple form. A balloon shaped vase approximately 12"(304 mm) tall and 8"(203 mm) wide, including the base.

This may be a very simple form. However, for a first attempt at twisting a hollow form, it will be a nice challenge and, hopefully, with a very pleasing result.

SELECTING TIMBER FOR HOLLOW FORM TWISTING

For this project, follow one of the recommended methods of mounting the material. Some may wish to twist their own design. In this event the marking out will differ according to height and width although the principle remains the same.

Select a 14"(356 mm) × 8½"(216 mm) blank in yew or other medium density species of timber and mount it between centres. I have selected yew, because it is strong and attractive and can be cut quite easily.

Turn the blank into an 8"(203 mm) cylinder. Square both ends, select and prepare the end for mounting.

There are several very safe methods of securing such a piece, some are old, some new. Probably the oldest is to use a home made wooden jam chuck, or a face plate and securing screws. Most of the new methods have been developed with the introduction of modern woodturning chucks or old engineering chucks which have been modified.

See the illustration top right for a few of the most common methods of mounting this type of work. It also shows the profile of the workpiece.

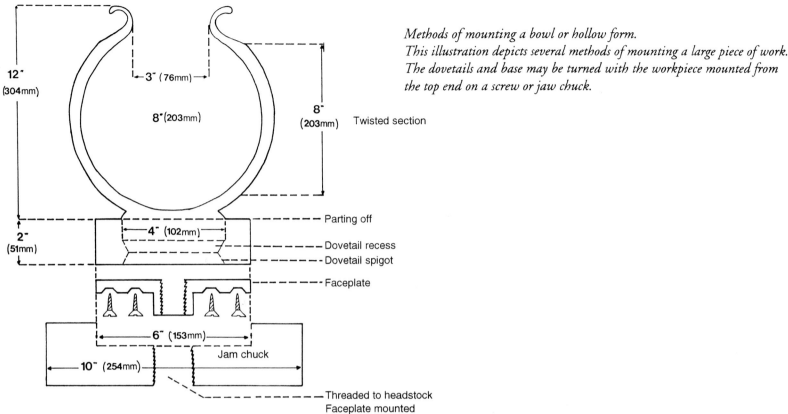

12"
(304mm)

3" (76mm)

8"(203mm)

8"
(203mm) Twisted section

Methods of mounting a bowl or hollow form.
This illustration depicts several methods of mounting a large piece of work.
The dovetails and base may be turned with the workpiece mounted from
the top end on a screw or jaw chuck.

2"
(51mm)

4" (102mm)

——— Parting off

——— Dovetail recess

——— Dovetail spigot

——— Faceplate

6" (153mm)

10" (254mm)

Jam chuck

——— Threaded to headstock
Faceplate mounted

The illustration right shows an alternative
shaped vessel (also shown as a finished
piece on page 117).

When satisfied with the workpiece mounting turn it to the desired shape, finish the outside completely including the base, and any internal plain turning. Regardless of the design, make sure the wall is a regular ½"(13 mm) thickness throughout the area to be twisted.

Make sure you are satisfied with the design. Once the inside has been turned out, the twist has to be cut. Re-shaping is not possible.

Turn the top and neck above the intended twisted section to the required thickness. Note: Make sure, when marking out, the twisted area does not overlap into this thinner neck area. The piece illustrated right is prepared for twisting.

The dovetails may be turned with the workpiece mounted between centres or from the top end on a screw chuck before hollowing out.

I have decided to mark out the 8½"(216 mm) global section of the piece. This will mean the twist will round off dramatically at both ends, in the same way as a very steep taper. It will also mean that the bines, initially, will be quite thick at the widest point of the globe. The thickness of the bines may be reduced to suit the design. Make sure they are in proportion to the rest of the piece.

Although I have decided to twist an 8½"(216 mm) section of the piece, the twist will have eight starts on a 10"(254 mm) pitch. (Refer to the illustration right). This means I am not using the full length of the pitch and, therefore, the bines will be cut 1½"(38 mm) short of a full circumference of the piece. This will result in a very strong twist. See Stage 2 below regarding 'Cutting the bine short'.

CUTTING A BINE SHORT

With reference to the points above: one, the thickness of the bines and two, a bine falling short of a complete circumference, keep these points in mind and imagine the bines being trimmed down to ¼"(6 mm) thick. The

bines, although a great deal weaker in themselves, will retain a good supporting strength because they are short of a full circumference. However, should the bines complete the full circumference, the twist would, to a degree, act similar to a spring. Cutting the bine short is a method of strengthening a twist. To retain the length of the twist, the pitch may be stretched. It can be used and designed into all types of work.

The design I have illustrated is a suggestion only and need not be followed slavishly. Obviously the pitch and the number of bines can also be altered. Whatever shape and thickness have been decided, run through the intended marking out on paper or lightly in pencil on the workpiece itself. Any mistakes can be sanded out.

Once the marking out has been completed in pencil, visualise the finished product. If you are not satisfied, sand it out and start again. Increase or decrease the number of bines and alter the length of the pitch until the desired style is achieved.

This will give readers a good opportunity to have a go at designing an open twist.

Stage 1:
Mark four Start Lines in pencil using the tool rest as a straight edge guide along the profile of the piece. Use an indexer, or line up on the four dovetailed jaws, or use dividers to quarter the blank. Divide these Start Lines once to make eight.

Stage 2:
This is an 8-Start with a 10"(254 mm) pitch. Each bine will require eight equal segments measuring 1¼"(32 mm) to complete the circumference of the piece. Remember, however, that this twist will only be 8½"(216 mm) long. Measure 8½"(216 mm) towards the base, from the point at the neck where the intended twist will start. This is the area to be twisted. From the same end measure and mark 2½"(63 mm) three times. Divide

these segments once to give six 1¼"(32 mm) segments and one 1"(25 mm) segment along the 8½"(216 mm) twist section. The shorter 1"(25 mm) segment will give a tightening effect at the base of the twist.

Had I intended to cut the full length of the 10"(254 mm) pitch there would have been eight segments measuring 1¼"(32 mm). However this particular twist can be faded out into the hollow at the base. For 'fading out' see the designing section in Chapter 20.

Note: On a 10"(254 mm) pitch the first dividing line should have been at 5"(127 mm). The reason I went straight to the second dividing line is that the base half of the twist is only 3½"(89 mm) long and therefore cannot be divided into 1¼"(32 mm) segments.

Stage 3:
Mark all the Cut Control Lines from all eight Start Lines. You will discover on the last 1"(25 mm) pitch

segments are smaller. There is a slight tightening of the bines on this small section. However, as the material gets thinner towards the neck and base, the angle of the Control Lines across the segments are not as steep. From a central point on the marked out area, the segments get smaller towards the neck and base. This means the pitch is automatically stretching in relation to the width of material. Unless the pitch is graduated, the pitch will remain the same length regardless of the thickness of material — the longer pitch at these points will strengthen the bines. This twist should be cut without further marking out.

COMPLETE MARKING OUT
In the case of a very large piece, or where confidence is lacking, follow the Complete Marking Out procedure which is explained for a 4-Start or Multi-Start. (See Chapter 12). This will deal with bine thickness at the

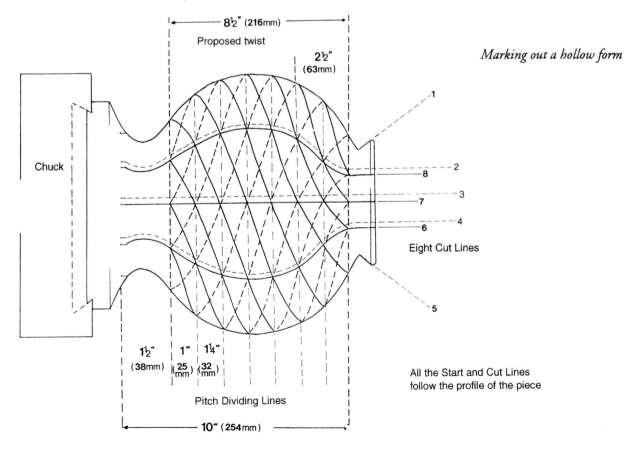

Marking out a hollow form

neck and base areas, but will still leave the bines wider in the middle. This method of marking out can be employed if it has been decided to taper the bines at either ends. To regularise the bines, mark a parallel line ¼"(6 mm) from either side of the Cut Line along the full length of the twist. This procedure will widen the openings between the bines on the thicker section of the workpiece.

CUTTING A TWIST ON A HOLLOW FORM

There is no fast and easy way of cutting this type of twist. It is hard but very rewarding work.

There are various hand tools on the market, such as rifflers and rasps of various types, which help to speed up this process of cutting. There are also drill/rasps, rotary rasps and cutters which can be used in a hand drill. Some are very effective and are made of quite expensive and durable materials such as tungsten carbide.

Do not be tempted to use certain types of high speed tools with unguarded cutting edges, or one-handed type of routers. They can be very dangerous in inexperienced hands. The cutting methods for this type of work depend on the density of the material. On soft materials normal cutting with the tenon saw, twisting gouge, etc. should be used. On very hard materials I employ engineering drills and a combination of cutting procedures previously mentioned.

METHOD OF CUTTING THE PIECE

Before starting the cutting procedure disconnect the electric power to the lathe.

Until experienced, the safest way to cut this piece is to cut one or two bines at a time. Trim each bine as another is opened. Using this method will mean that the strength of the piece will be retained until the last two or three bines remain uncut. Before breaking through the last two bines, trim and finish the complete piece.

Stage 4:

With a ⅜"(9 mm) drill or bit, centring on the Pitch Line and Cut Lines at both ends of the twist, drill holes all the way through into the hollow centre. There should be eight holes at either end of the area to be twisted, they should be perfectly in line around the circumference of the vase. These lines indicate the ends of the openings.

With a tenon or other suitable small saw, cut into the hollow form along two of the initial Cut Lines, cut into the neck and base drill hole openings. It does not matter if the cut is short of these drill holes. The intention is to expose one bine at a time.

Use the saw to cut along both cut lines at either side of the initial Cut Line, cut all the way through into the hollow form. Cutting the bulbous central section will be quite easy. However, be careful when cutting the ends at the neck and base. Use a thinner bladed saw or the tip of the tenon saw blade. Cut gently, taking care not to slip or jerk into the drill hole. I sometimes use a good quality medium duty hacksaw blade to cut the ends. Repeat this cutting procedure according to the Complete Marking Out. With these six cuts, three per hollow, the waste material will drop out or be easily removed with a small chisel. This will expose the first roughly cut bine. Round off the drill holes at either end with a round file.

In certain cases one may be able to remove the waste material by cutting at the ¼"(6 mm) Cut Lines only, and miss out the initial or central Cut Line.

Once two or three bines have been cut use the palm plane to trim the tops of the bines. At the base and neck ends where there is no access for the plane, use the 1½"(38 mm) flat carpenter's chisel to round off the bine tops.

Use the ½"(13 mm) carpenter's chisel, as before, to trim the inside edges of the bines.

Should the requirement be to taper the neck end of

the bines in order to make the piece more elegant, trim them to suit as you progress round the workpiece. It may well be the intention to taper the bines at both or one end of the work. Should this be the case, make sure everything balances all the way round.

When breaking through the last two or three bines, the piece at this stage will be considerably weak. If excess pressure is applied damage could occur. A safeguard against this is to tape all the completed bines together with masking tape. This will give support and added strength to the piece when cutting through and finishing the remaining bines.

Taping up is particularly important when cutting very thin bines and other types of open twisting.

To regularise and trim off any bumps, knots etc. along the length of the bine use a small flat rasp or file, making sure that the bines and hollows are properly trimmed and balanced before sanding. Use heavy grade sandpaper at first with the grain along the bines. This will ensure the bines are regular.

SANDING A TWISTED OPEN FORM
The procedure for sanding a twisted or open hollow form is the same as for any other solid or open twist (Chapters 6 & 7 refer). *Except for one important point.* The piece is supported at one end only. The tailstock end must be supported otherwise there is a good chance the piece could be damaged during sanding, particularly when using a strip of sanding cloth. Make a jig to fit the end of the piece so that it can be supported by the tailstock. Do not apply too much pressure with the tailstock otherwise the spiral could be contracted and this could also cause damage. *Never* attempt to hand sand an Open twist with the lathe in motion.

In the case of thin or long open bines it is always advisable to tape the bines at their centre points to give support to one another whilst sanding. The centre sections can then be sanded by removing the tape as you progress round the piece. Make sure you are satisfied with the finish on the inside of the piece before going any further. Finish and polish the piece before parting off.

In order to safeguard the piece during parting off, tape up all the bines with low contact masking tape. This will give the whole piece strength before putting the lathe in motion. Should the piece require further sanding or polishing to the non-twisted areas now is the time to do it. Support the open top end of the vase with a large cork, jig or other suitable bung in the tailstock. Start the lathe on a slow speed, say 400 to 500 r.p.m. Finish the piece very carefully as necessary.

PARTING OFF A LARGE OPEN FORM
Parting off a twisted hollow form is virtually the same as parting off any normal hollow form, provided the bines are taped up properly.

Always use a good wide solid type of parting tool at this stage and not one with a narrow blade, as binding could occur. Any vibration must be avoided when parting off, otherwise the base will be rippled and rough. Vibration tells you that the speed is too quick, the parting tool may be blunt and/or too much pressure is being applied. In the case of larger pieces it may be necessary, if possible, to reduce the lathe speed even further.

With the workpiece properly supported at the tailstock end, use a parting tool to part off at the base leaving at least a 1"(25 mm) dowel section in the middle. Make sure there is ample room for the tool to operate to prevent binding and burning. If there is sufficient waste material, remove as much material as possible between the chuck and the base, to permit access in order that the base may be cleanly cut.

Increase or reduce the speed of the lathe in order to obtain a nice clean cut with a skew or a small spindle gouge across the base towards the dowel.

Make sure the base is slightly concave to ensure that the piece will sit properly. Before parting through the final 1"(25 mm) or so, reduce the lathe to 200 r.p.m. and relax the pressure on the workpiece from the tailstock end, leaving sufficient pressure to lightly support the end of the piece. To check this, touch the revolving centre with your finger. A little pressure should stop it. With the pressure off and a wide enough gap at the base, parting off can be completed. Just in case the piece drops off the lathe during the final parting off, lay a heavy blanket on the bed of the lathe to prevent damage to the piece. Finish the final parting in stages of approximately ⅛"(3 mm) with a narrow slightly skewed parting tool. Clean up the base as you progress with the sharp skew side of the parting tool. You should be able to reduce the size of the supporting spigot to ¼"(6 mm) dependent on the weight of the piece. When parting off the last ¼"(6 mm) support the base end with your free hand and very lightly finish off the parting with the sharp skew corner of the parting tool next to the base.

I have used this method of parting off larger pieces for years and, except for the odd exceptional case, have always been satisfied with the final result. In cases where the lathe speed cannot be reduced sufficiently, it may be necessary for the final parting off to be carried out by hand with a saw on or off the lathe.

Be careful when removing the masking tape, otherwise damage could occur, particularly where the bines are very fine. *Do not* attempt to re-mount an open twisted vessel for any reason once complete.

ALTERNATIVE METHODS OF CUTTING A TWIST ON HOLLOW FORMS

Large forms

On heavier hollow forms where the bines are thicker, one of the quickest methods of opening this type of twist is to use the appropriate size of bit to drill a series of holes closely together along the Cut Lines.

An alternative method is to drill the end holes to gain access with a padsaw to cut along the Width Control Lines. The bines can then be parted with the use of a hand held round rasp or heavy-duty file.

Caution must be exercised if you use a powered rotary rasp, these may jam resulting in damaged or broken bines.

Once the twist has been opened, trim the bines using chisels as before.

Small forms

On small or thin pieces where the intended bines will be close together or fragile, drill the holes at the end of the Cut Lines as above.

Use a small saw to open the Cut Lines, then open the saw cuts using slightly wider files in stages until the desired width of opening has been attained.

Round off the bines with a small carpenter's chisel.

Thin bines should be sanded by hand along the grain of the wood to remove any high spots and to regularise the bines. See the far right photograph showing the inverted egg-shaped small open form, set within the ebony candlestick.

*Twisted hollow form
or vessel in yew*

*Ebony candlestick
with open form*

19

THIN TWISTING

TOOLS REQUIRED

Before any explanation, see the photograph below showing the type of tools required for this delicate work. They range from small files measuring $1/16$"(1.5 mm) to $3/8$"(9 mm), and include rifflers, rasps, engineer's files, flat and rat-tail files of several designs and brands. All can be found in large hardware and tool stores.

A selection of small tools for thin twist work

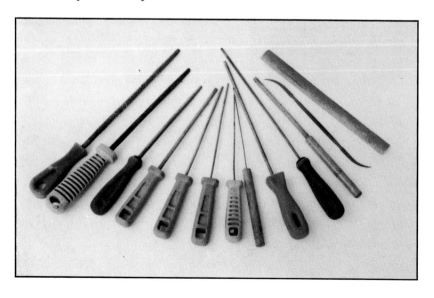

This chapter deals essentially with thin twisting and the procedures are covered in three sections. These should be completed in order. The first section is to complete a goblet with a Double twist. The remaining two to combine and produce an Open twisted goblet, the stem of which, is a Twist within a Twist.

Section 1 deals with twisting where the material is large enough to be marked out, but too thin for the normal cutting tools to be used. Section 2 deals with material which is so small that marking out is impossible. This type of twist has to be cut free hand. And Section 3, explains the method of opening a thin Open twist and, where the bines are very fragile, deals with the method I recommend for supporting the workpiece throughout the opening process.

THIN STEMMED GOBLET PROJECT

SECTION 1

This section illustrates the preparation of a 4"(102 mm) × ¼"(6 mm) thick section of a goblet stem, in a light coloured straight grained wood.

The reason I advise a light coloured wood is because it is very confusing and difficult to see the marking out on thin dark material.

Be careful when selecting wood for this type of project. It must be very dry, straight grained and free from knots and shakes particularly in the proposed twist area.

This piece will have a Double Barley twist with the pitch stretched to 1"(25 mm). Note that the stem is ¼"(6 mm) thick. On this thickness the pitch on a traditional Double should be approximately ½"(13 mm). Here in fact we are stretching the pitch to twice its traditional length. The main reason for this is to retain as much strength as possible in the stem by lengthening the cut along the grain. On a thin twist, lengthening the bine to this degree also adds to the elegance of the work.

When turning a short goblet or any thin stemmed piece, the procedure I use and recommend is illustrated below. Note that I prepare the piece in a sequence of stages as shaded areas in numerical order, depicted as S1, S2, etc. from right to left.

Mount a 9"(228 mm) × 2½"(63 mm) × 2½"(63 mm) blank in a 3 or 4 jaw, cup or jam chuck. The intention is to turn the goblet with a 4"(102 mm) × ¼"(6 mm) central section on a 5"(127 mm) stem using the sequence of stages described.

Stage 1:

Round off the blank and turn the outside profile of the goblet top only to the desired shape, sand and finish accordingly. When turning soft material do not cut the neck at the base of the top to less than ¾"(19 mm), also leave the decoration at the base of the bowl until **stage 3**. Any thinner may result in vibration when hollowing the bowl of the goblet.

Stage 2:

Hollow the bowl of the goblet, sand and finish the top completely. Ensure that the finish is satisfactory, because once the stem is turned, further tooling is not advised.

Stage 3:

Before starting on Stage 3, support the goblet at the tailstock end. Where the goblet is thin walled, either use a jig over the end of the bowl or a small cloth pad inside at the bottom of the goblet. This prevents the possibility of splitting or causing internal friction damage when turning the rest of the piece. A piece of carefully rolled up rag or a cork may also be used within the bowl of the goblet. Be careful when applying pressure with the tailstock not to over-tighten otherwise the bowl may burst. Tighten just sufficiently to give support and keep the piece in line whilst turning and twisting is in progress.

On softer material, where the base of the bowl has not been completed from Stage 1, finish and sand the design. When you are satisfied with the finish turn the section of the stem to ¼"(6 mm). Turn the small cove or hollow at either end of the 4"(102 mm) twist area. The cove should be no deeper than a quarter of the width of material. From this stage care must be taken not to exert too much downward pressure on the stem.

Stages of preparing a thin stemmed goblet for twisting

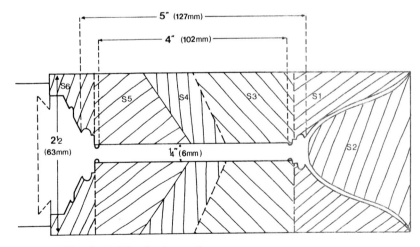

Note: The dovetail for chuck mounting

Stages 4 and 5:

Complete and finish Stages 4 and 5 shown in the drawing, ensure the stem is parallel, regular and free from shakes etc.

Stage 6:

Design and finish the base to balance with the top of the goblet.

Remember to cut the small cove at the base end of the twist. The basic turning of the goblet should now be complete and ready to accept the twist.

MARKING OUT AND CUTTING THE STEM FOR THE DOUBLE BARLEY

Stage 1:

Use dividers or the chuck jaws as a guide, mark the four Start Lines along the length of the 4"(102 mm) twist section. Number the lines 1 to 4 if considered necessary. With practice these lines may be marked free-hand.

Stage 2:

Mark the 2"(51 mm) pitch central line. Divide once to get the four 1"(25 mm) pitches. Divide the pitch segments twice for the Pitch Dividing Lines.

Stage 3:

Mark the Cut Control Lines at 1 and 3 as illustrated below. In the case of thin twisting there is normally insufficient room for the Complete Marking Out procedure. Cut the twist from this stage.

Stage 4:

The tools required to cut this particular twist, are the ⅛"(3 mm) and ³/₁₆"(5 mm) round rasps and ³/₁₆"(5 mm) engineer's file. To round off the tops of the bines a ½"(13 mm) rat-tail file is used.

Before starting the twist, make sure the tailstock is still securing the end of the goblet. Tighten slightly without putting too much pressure on the stem. The reason for this is, during cutting, a fair degree of bending will occur as pressure is applied with the cutting rasp. This bending will shorten the piece between centres and it may slip off the jig at the tailstock end.

Stage 5: Cutting the stem

It is obvious that a cut with a tenon saw is not practical on such a small piece.

Using the small ⅛"(3 mm) rasp, cut a very light groove along the first Cut Control Line from right to left. Once satisfied, make this same cut slightly deeper,

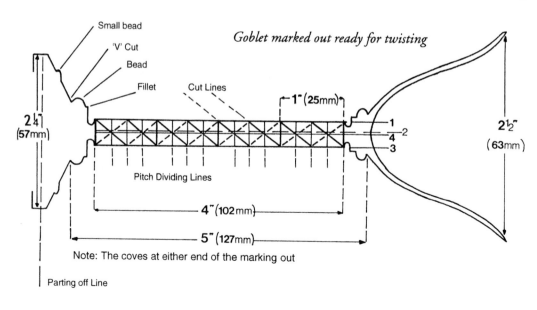

Goblet marked out ready for twisting

Small bead
'V' Cut
Bead
Fillet
Cut Lines
1" (25mm)
Pitch Dividing Lines
2¼" (57mm)
2½" (63mm)
4" (102mm)
5" (127mm)
Note: The coves at either end of the marking out
Parting off Line

sufficient to be a good guide for the next tool. Repeat this process at Cut Line 2. At this stage you will know the cut lines are balanced and in the correct positions. Even at this stage the cuts should balance. The second cut should be central to the first and vice-versa as they spiral around the workpiece. Remember to rotate the workpiece into the forward cutting action of the rasp with your free hand, just as one would with the saw, this will ensure a smooth and even cutting action.

When satisfied that the shallow cuts are in the correct position, the hollows may be cut to their full depth using the ³/₁₆"(5 mm) rasp. Cut them to approximately a quarter to a third of the depth of the material. That will be approximately half the depth of the rasp.

Note: The piece could lose two thirds of its original strength. Flexing will increase dramatically as cutting progresses. Care must be exercised. *Do not apply too much pressure, particularly at the centre of the stem.*

When satisfied with the depth use the engineer's file to clean up the hollows.

Take care when using this tool. If it is new it will tend to bite and possibly bind in the hollow. Do not clean out the teeth when full, as there will be sufficient teeth exposed to cut, and this will stop it biting too hard. A slight tap on the lathe from time to time will get rid of sufficient waste to keep it cutting. Support the back of the twist with your free hand to prevent excess flexing.

Stage 6:

The bines are obviously too small to be rounded with a palm plane. With a ½"(13 mm) rat-tail file, use it to bridge the hollows to cut on the left and right inner edges of the bines.

Use the file very lightly in long even strokes. Keep the workpiece moving with the free hand into the file cut in a co-ordinated manner, taking care not to create any flat areas. Keep checking the result of each stroke behind the

cut to ensure the bine has been properly trimmed. See illustration below.

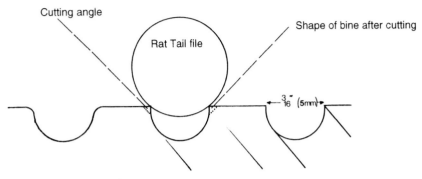

Stage 7: Sanding a thin twist

With the main waste removed from the bines it is quite easy for them to be rounded off by sanding. Use a length of emery cloth about ¼"(6 mm) wide to finish the rounding. Use the abrasive horizontally along the bines with the workpiece in a stationary position. Turn the twist round in quarter stages and repeat the process. four or five passes should complete the rough sanding.

To regularise and finish the sanding, use a length of fine cloth abrasive, turned into a tube or cord and use the method described before. Be careful when using this method as one could, without realising quickly cut too deeply and ruin the twist. Apply polish with a thin strip of cloth in the same manner for the desired finish.

Stage 8: Parting off fine turnings

With the piece supported between centres, and the lathe speed at approximately 2000 r.p.m. partially part off the goblet leaving approximately ¼"(6 mm) remaining.

The piece is ready for the final parting off. You will find that the twist area is fragile. Stop the lathe and support the top of the goblet with your free hand. Remove the tailstock and very carefully remove the jig, cork or rag from the goblet. *Do not* attempt to remove the rag or cork with the lathe in motion or run the lathe without supporting the top of the piece, It *will* break.

With the parting tool in your predominant hand, the free hand will cradle the top of the goblet very lightly so that it is just being supported. Start the lathe, clean the bottom of the base with the parting tool and slowly part off at the same time. Parting off a thin twist in this manner is a matter of confidence. A twist may flap about and appear very fragile on the lathe, once off the lathe it is surprisingly strong. Be positive when supporting the piece. Do not move your stance or twitch during the process.

Sand the base with the grain by hand.

WIRE TURNING AND TWISTING

SECTION 2

This section deals with very thin turning, but only as thin as necessary to accommodate a twist $1/8$"(3 mm) thick.

There are several methods of thin turning, but the one I favour requires the use of a hollow headstock and tailstock and a 3 or 4 jaw chuck with the facility to grip a $1/4$"(6 mm) square blank. Also required will be a cork

Double Barley in ebony and holly

centrally drilled to $1/8$"(3 mm) which will fit tightly into the tapered end of the hollow tailstock recess.

Preparing the blank for thin turning

Bandsaw an 18"(457 mm) × $1/4$"(6 mm) × $1/4$"(6 mm) piece of ebony or similar hard exotic species of timber. Feed the blank through the chuck into the hollow headstock leaving approximately 3"(76 mm) overhanging the chuck between centres. See the illustration below.

Turn a 2"(51 mm) section of the overhang to $1/8$"(3 mm) at the tailstock end.

Bring up the headstock and feed the $1/8$"(3 mm) turned section into the cork located in the tailstock. This will support the workpiece as it is turned.

Using this method one should be able to turn 4" to 6"(102–153 mm) lengths of $1/8$"(3 mm) material between centres with ease. The beauty of this method is that there is no pressure between centres, therefore flexing is at a minimum.

Pull a 4"(102 mm) long section of the blank through the chuck from the headstock, and turn this section to

Square blank mounted through headstock into chuck

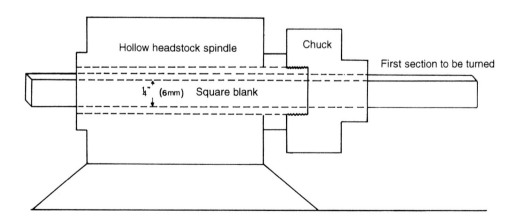

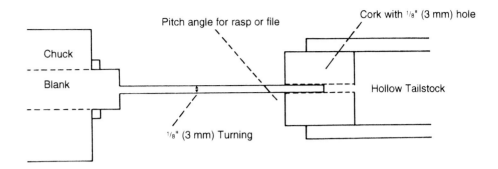

¹/₈"(3 mm) between centres. This section is ready for twisting. Using this method lengths of up to 3'(914 mm) and over may be twisted.

Should the turned material start to judder during turning, tighten the cork in the tailstock. It, in turn, will grip the workpiece. Wax the workpiece if there is squeaking or other signs of friction. (Smoke or flames maybe !).

Because the finished product is very thin and resembles wire, I refer to these thin turnings as 'Wire Turnings' and 'Wire Twisting'.

WIRE TWISTING
With the end of the ebony wire supported in the cork, take a ¹/₁₆"(1.5 mm) rasp or file and judge the pitch at approximately 1¼ times the width of material.

Start to cut the twist against the cork end, retaining the angle. Use the free hand to turn the workpiece as the hollow is cut to depth around the circumference of the

material. Once the first two or three pitches have been completed you should be better able to judge the width of the bine and balance the twist. (See the above illustration for the angle of cut).

The depth of the hollow should be a third of the width of the material. Once satisfied with the first twisted section continue on to the next 4"(102 mm) section and repeat the process.

Feed the completed twist through the cork as another section is released from the headstock. Carry out this procedure until the required length of twist is completed.

The only type of twist that can be successfully cut from ¹/₈"(3 mm) material is a Single. However, certainly have a go at a Double under a microscope!

Should the cut twist appear to be very flexible and weak, do not attempt to twist too long a section at one time. Complete a 1"(25 mm) section at a time then feed the finished piece into the cork. Cut the twist as close to

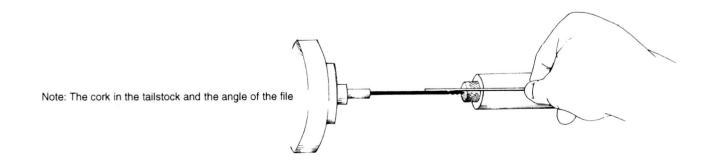

Note: The cork in the tailstock and the angle of the file

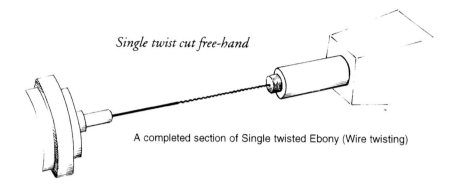

Single twist cut free-hand

A completed section of Single twisted Ebony (Wire twisting)

the cork as possible as this will give added support.

Round off the top edges of the bine with a ¼"(6 mm) file in the same manner as described and illustrated in Section 1. This should be done before feeding the work through the cork. This also applies to sanding.

Sand the piece very lightly otherwise it will break.

Long lengths of dowelling may be turned and twisted using this method.

Material may also be supported at the headstock end with the aid of a cork on the outboard side of the lathe. This prevents the workpiece from rattling around in the headstock whilst turning is in progress. There are some lathes with a hollow headstock up to ¾"(19 mm). This is a very useful facility for turning a dowel. In the case of longer and thicker twists using the same method, the blank may have to be supported beyond the headstock in a suspended tube.

When using this method, it may also be necessary to support the finished work as it progresses through and beyond the support of the tailstock, and this can be achieved by placing a tube over the threaded end of the tailstock. This, in turn, can be supported by a block of wood on the lathe bed. Some may not be familiar with this method, but it works and the results are fast. See illustration below.

It can also be used to produce other projects. Thickness is governed by the size of the headstock recess.

There are the normal methods of thin turning between centres, using all sorts of supporting 'steadies' and other ingenious innovations. I mention this as the above is not the only method which can be adopted.

Before moving on to the next section, see the photograph right showing a set of six goblets with Single Twists measuring from 1"(25 mm) to 5½"(140 mm) tall; the twist on the smallest is ¹/₁₆"(1.5 mm) thick and largest is ³/₁₆"(5 mm).

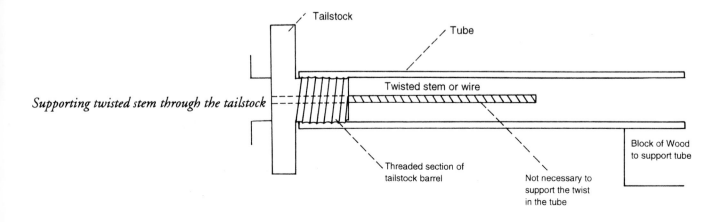

Supporting twisted stem through the tailstock

Tailstock

Tube

Twisted stem or wire

Threaded section of tailstock barrel

Not necessary to support the twist in the tube

Block of Wood to support tube

Set of six rosewood goblets with Single twist

OPEN TWISTED GOBLET PROJECT (TWIST WITHIN A TWIST STEM)

SECTION 3

The third section deals with thin Open twisting.

Whatever style of twist has been decided, particularly in the case of thin twisting, the choice of material is most important. In the case of thin Open twisting this choice is even more critical. The material must be very strong and straight grained. Such work can be used for candlesticks, cakestands (where several of the same type may be used as supports), goblets and other decorative work.

The twist illustrated here is a 4"(102 mm) × ³/₈" (9 mm) Double Open with a 2"(51 mm) pitch on a goblet stem.

Select a 9"(228 mm) × 1¾"(45 mm) × 1¾"(45 mm) piece of ebony, African blackwood, rosewood or similar hard species of timber.

Mount the piece in a chuck and drill an ¹/₈"(3 mm) hole centrally to a depth of 5½"(140 mm) from the intended base end.

Turn the workpiece round in the chuck and turn a goblet as in Section 1, with a 3"(76 mm) top and a

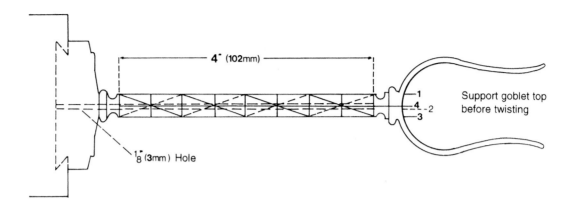

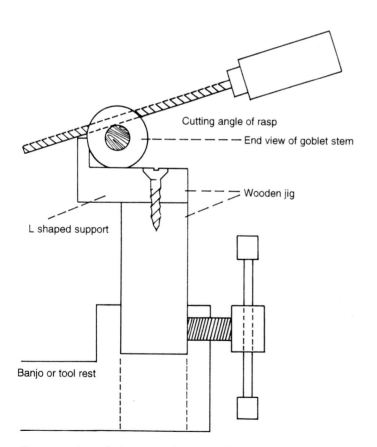

Cutaway view of a home-made support for the thin stemmed goblet

5"(127 mm) × ³⁄₈"(9 mm) stem. Support the goblet at the tailstock end as before. Measure a 4"(102 mm) central section on the stem. This will be the twist. Turn the desired designs at either end of this section before proceeding further.

Stage 1: Marking out

Mark out the four Start Lines using the jaws of the chuck or dividers.

Measure and mark the central line on the 4"(102 mm) section. There are now two pitch segments. Divide the 2"(51 mm) segments twice making a total of eight segments. These are the Pitch and Pitch Dividing Lines. There is no need for further marking out.

Stage 2:

Mark the diagonal Cut Lines from lines 1 and 3. Lines 2 and 4 will be the bines. See illustration above.

Stage 3: Cutting a thin Open Double twist

Cutting this type of twist can be particularly delicate and during cutting it will be necessary to give the workpiece support. For this make up a jig which will fit snugly under the stem. A simple method is to prepare a 4"(102 mm) long 'L' shaped rest which can be fitted on a pillar and supported in the tool rest banjo in the same manner as the tool rest itself. The 'L' section should be placed under the stem and adjusted to give support. The upright of the 'L' should be low enough to permit cutting the twist over the top. See illustration left.

Stage 4:

With a ¹/₈"(3 mm) rasp or file remove waste material along both Cut Lines to a depth of approximately ¹/₁₆"(1.5 mm) after which satisfy yourself the twist will be balanced. These two cuts are a guide for the larger rasp which will cut the hollows to the required width.

The main point to remember when cutting this type of twist is that there is a ¹/₈"(3 mm) hole down the centre. In a solid twist this is where the strength lies. When breaking into the hole flexing will increase dramatically, so great care *must* be exercised in order not to break the piece. Another point to consider is that the bines will only be ¹/₈"(3 mm) thick.

Once you are satisfied with the balance of the proposed bines, start opening the twist from the tailstock end, but only 1"(25 mm) at a time. When rasping keep the rasp as flat as possible, cut through one hollow at a time and just enough to see breakthrough very slightly at the bottom.

Do not go through all the depth of the rasp, as it will bind and the piece could be damaged. There should be sufficient room to get a small chisel or blade through the recess, to round the inside of the bines.

Complete the second hollow in the same manner as the first. When breaking through this time the piece will become very flexible, so much so that one may lose confidence and consider it impossible to complete the piece. This is *not* the case.

In order to lend a fair degree of support and security when opening and cutting this twist, take a length of ¹/₈"(3 mm) fencing wire. It is available practically anywhere, or even a length of 'wire turning' described in Section 2. Place it through the centre of the twist. This,

in effect, is returning the piece almost to the strength of a Double.

Withdraw the 'wire' as each 1"(25 mm) section is opened to clear that section in order that the inside edge of the bines may be trimmed.

As the first section of the twist is finished, push a ¹/₈"(3 mm) round file gently through the openings between both bines. Round off the end of hollows to leave a clean, nicely rounded end to both openings.

This process will have to be repeated when the twist is opened at the other end.

It may be that the bines at this stage will be irregular and too wide. Trim the sides only to the intended width, not the inside or the top.

Round off the top of the bines using the same method in Section 1. A small flat file may also be used. Trim the inside corners with a small chisel or knife.

Sand the 1"(25 mm) section to the desired standard with a ¼"(6 mm) width of cloth abrasive as previously described. Finish the sanding by hand along the bine with the grain. You will be able to 'feel' the wood and regularise the bines. Complete this procedure in 1"(25 mm) stages until the twist is complete.

Note: the following are alternative methods of supporting a fragile piece:

1. As the work is completed in 1"(25 mm) stages, tape each finished stage with masking tape before proceeding to the next.
2. On longer pieces, make up a cardboard tube and slide it over the stages as they are completed.
3. When parting off a very fine Open stem keep the piece of thin wooden wire or dowelling in place through the centre of the piece.
4. A fine piece of work can also be supported for parting off by taping a pair of splints along the stem.

Polish and part off the goblet in the same manner as in Section 1, adopting one of the above supporting methods if necessary.

TWIST WITHIN A TWIST

The concept of a twist within a twist, or within an inverted turning is rare. Any pieces I have seen personally have been built into antique staircase newel posts in large houses. I have not seen, to date, a thin or finely turned piece. Obviously the outer twist has to be an open one, whilst the inner is normally a solid type.

A good reason for such a design is to add strength to the outer Open twist and give the piece a very striking and attractive appearance.

An Open twist may also be placed within another Open, or inverted form.

The process of putting a twist inside the other is simple enough. The central twist is pushed into the centrally drilled hole on the Open twist, normally from below.

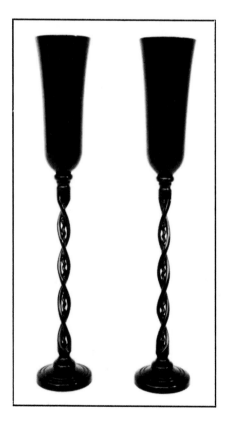

When preparing the central twist, only twist the area which will be seen through the openings. Both ends should be turned spigots to fit tightly into the drill hole. Should it be decided to fit a larger twist, the bottom drill hole may be opened further to allow access.

Any Open twist can be used on the outside and the same applies to the centre. One of my favourites is a Ribbon twist inside an Open 4-Start in mahogany.

Example of a twist within a twist
As an example I refer back to Sections 2 and 3 on Thin Twisting.

Take the open twisted goblet in Section 3. Note that the central hole was drilled out at $\frac{1}{8}$"(3 mm). In Section 2 a 'wire twist' measuring $\frac{1}{8}$"(3 mm) thick was prepared. Take a 5"(127 mm) length of this pre-prepared wire twist and push it all the way up through the hole at the base of the goblet until it seats firmly at the top of the Open twist. Glue the inner twist into position and trim the end. The result is a very elegant goblet.

When I made my first goblet in this style I was so pleased with the result that I immediately made a partner for it, in its 'mirror image'.

There are many turners who may think there is too much time and work involved to produce such an item of a purely decorative nature. However, with practice it need not take an overly long time considering the individuality of the project. I produced the pair shown in the photograph left in under 5 hours.

See Chapters 12 and 20 for producing a left- and right-hand twist and copying.

Ebony goblets with $\frac{3}{8}$" (9 mm) Double Open twist on a 2" (51 mm) pitch with an $\frac{1}{8}$" (3 mm) wire Single twist within

20

COPY TWISTING

Copy turning and twisting is a very important area in spindle turning. To produce a duplicate or batch from an original in any turning is always difficult.

To produce a duplicate twist — whether a left, right, thick or thin, solid or open and varying design pitch lengths — the procedures for copying must remain the same and must be strictly followed.

In the first section of this chapter we shall be dealing with copying a twist from newly created work, whether a traditional design or otherwise. In the following part, copying existing work, such as an antique twist. Identifying the twist in the planning stage is critical. Thereafter, follows a section on design.

COPY TWISTING FROM NEW

When preparing a piece to be twisted, reproduce the piece exactly up to the stage ready for copying the twist. When you are satisfied that both workpieces are exact, mark the required number of Start Lines, (four for a Single or Double and three for a Triple and 6-Start etc.). Mark the Pitch and Pitch Dividing Lines. Mark the Cut and Pitch Control Lines, one for the Single, two for the Double and three for the Triple and Ribbon etc. Decide whether the Complete Marking Out procedure is required.

If in doubt regarding a particular twist refer to previous chapters for the marking out procedure.

When satisfied with the marking out, transfer the same marking out measurements to the second workpiece or pieces. Before starting the cutting, lay the pieces side by side to ensure they are marked out the same and that the Pitch Lines are exactly in line. Any number of copies can be made using this procedure.

Cut the particular twist using the procedure previously described.

Note: Should a left-hand copy be required, Refer to Chapter 9 and the following paragraphs and illustration.

Copying a left-hand twist

In order to have a 'correct' pair of twists there must be a left- and a right-hand twist. In other words a mirror image of the other.

To copy a left-hand from a right, or vice versa, the marking out procedure must be followed exactly through the Start, Pitch and Pitch Control Lines. Marking out the Cut Control Lines is what makes the difference between the two. For a right-hand twist the Cut Control Lines are marked diagonally from right to left across the pitch segments. For the left-hand twist the Cut Control Lines are marked diagonally from left to right across the pitch segments.

See illustration over page for the comparison.

Copying a Double Barley left or right twist

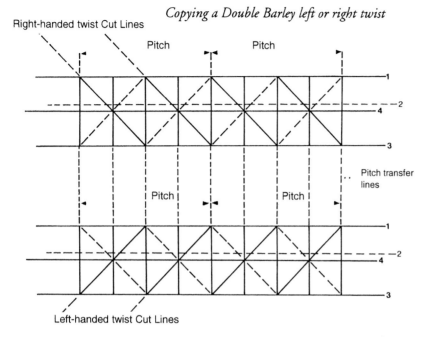

Right-handed twist Cut Lines

Pitch   Pitch

1
2
4

3

Pitch transfer
lines

Pitch   Pitch

1
2
4

3

Left-handed twist Cut Lines

COPY TWISTING FROM AN EXISTING TWIST

As with the new work, first copy the original workpiece to its basic shape, prior to it being twisted.

Then check the original piece stage by stage to establish its identity in the following way:

1. Establish whether the twist to be copied is a Single or Double etc., to determine the number of Start Lines.

2. The next process is to find the pitch and length of the twist. On a regular twist this is not too difficult as you can measure apex to apex along the top of the bines, and normally that should be sufficient to determine the pitch.

3. Also check to ensure it is a true twist, for example the bines start and finish on the same Start Line. If it is a true twist, say a Single measuring 12"(305 mm) long by 3"(76 mm) wide, it is quite likely that there will be four 3"(76 mm) pitch segments.

4. If the twist has been lengthened, add segments as necessary to the desired length, also check if segments have been added at both ends. See the section referring to stretching a pitch and lengthening a twist. (Chapter 14)

5. Another important point to check is the width of the bines and hollows. It does not necessarily follow that the hollows are the same width as the bines. Should the sizes differ this will mean that the Complete Marking Out procedure will have to be followed. The Cut Control Lines will have to be adjusted to suit and the width of the hollow cut accordingly.

Once the above points have been established, mark the required number of Start Lines and set the Pitch and Pitch Control Lines. Before marking out the Cut Control Lines etc., lay the piece alongside the original piece and check that the Pitch Lines are in line with the original bine apexes. When satisfied, mark out the Cut Control Lines. Before cutting the twist lay the workpiece along side the original once again and check by eye if the Cut Lines are parallel to the original bine profiles. When satisfied, cut the twist as normal.

An original and new blank marked up ready for copy twisting

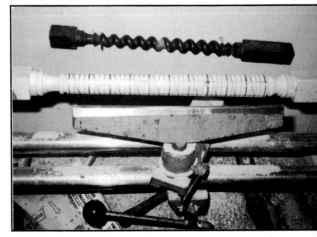

The procedure is the same for a left-hand twist except, as mentioned previously, the Cut Lines are marked from left to right.

To copy a Graduated or Teardrop twist, each pitch has to be measured individually and transferred on to the blank for copying. The copy can be a left or right according to the requirement.

DESIGNING TWISTS

It is important to have a section on designing as it allows for clearing up any points of ambiguity which may have arisen throughout the book and also allows the opportunity to put twisting in physical perspective to turning.

As in all woodturning, the permutations in design are many and varied. In designing twists, it obviously follows that the controlling factor for the final shape of the twist is controlled by the design of the blank. Unless you are satisfied with the blank you will not be satisfied with the twist.

The process of designing a twist itself relates to:

1. The length of the area to be twisted.
2. Thickness and shape of the twist.
3. The pitch in relation to the thickness of the material and whether it should be stretched or shortened according to the required design. In most cases this is the most important feature as the finished product can only be seen in the mind's eye.
4. Design is also dependent on the thickness and shape of the bines, whether solid or open. They must harmonise with the pitch, otherwise mistakes will creep in, such as the twist being too springy, the bines too thick or thin for the piece. The worst thing that can happen is for the twist to look out of balance when built into the final project. The design at either end of the twist must balance with the twist itself and together form an integral part of the whole piece for which it is intended.

In short, the finished product must balance. The method to adopt when designing complicated pieces is to commit the design to paper or memory then decide where the appropriate twists should be built in. *Never* do it the other way round unless you are experienced in twisting and have a flair for design or you are a professional production turner with the knowledge. For the inexperienced, the best method for developing a sense of design in spiral work is to produce a pleasing shape from a traditional or original piece and complete all the features around the area to be twisted. Once satisfied, decide on a twist that will balance to enhance the finished product. You can then be certain of a very satisfying result.

It would be pointless to suggest any particular design or pitch etc. As mentioned above the variations in design are endless, and all that is intended in this section is to encourage readers to develop their own ideas in this area. There are, however, numerous twisted features and profiles not previously featured which are well worthy of consideration when designing, and some are listed below.

1. Cutting a twist, solid or open, on a *waisted* blank.
2. Twisting a *knob or ball*
3. Twisting a *cup* shape, e.g. the base of an acorn or bowl.
4. *Cross bine twisting,* where the twist is cut in the same manner as for a pineapple, but not necessarily pineapple shaped.
5. Where the bine itself is a *teardrop shaped bine* on an open or tapered twist.
6. *Fading out* where, on a solid or open twist whether a complete pitch or otherwise, instead of stopping the twist short of the hollow and tapering the cut outwards as normal, continue the cut through and into the hollow, fading it out as you go. This process is more effective on larger work with a neck or large recess at the base. It can also be used

to twist a *pointed dome* feature at the top of a column.

7. *Splitting or gathering bines* applies to the process of dividing a bine, normally into two. However, there are permutations of this process.

8. *Cutting the bine short,* normally relates to a twist where the length is shorter than a complete pitch.

Design features seen on traditional spindle work

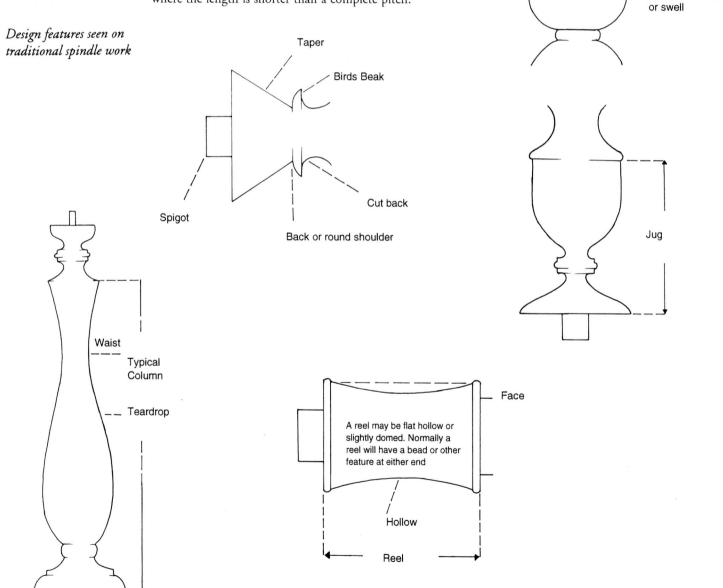

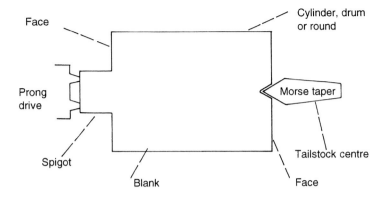

Face
Cylinder, drum or round
Prong drive
Morse taper
Spigot
Blank
Tailstock centre
Face

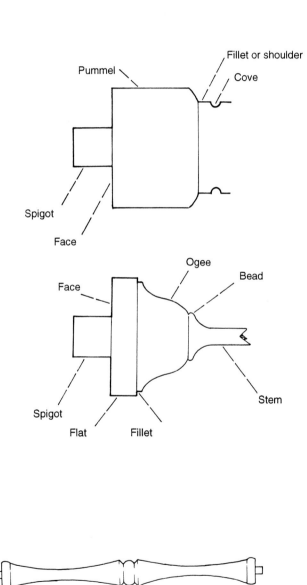

Pummel
Fillet or shoulder
Cove
Spigot
Face

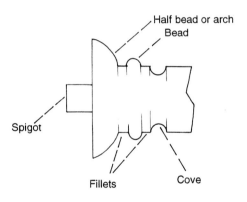

Half bead or arch
Bead
Spigot
Fillets
Cove

Face
Ogee
Bead
Spigot
Flat
Fillet
Stem

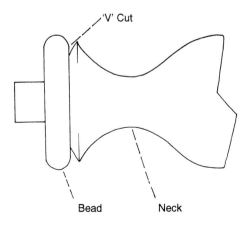

'V' Cut
Bead
Neck

Typical spindle or stretcher

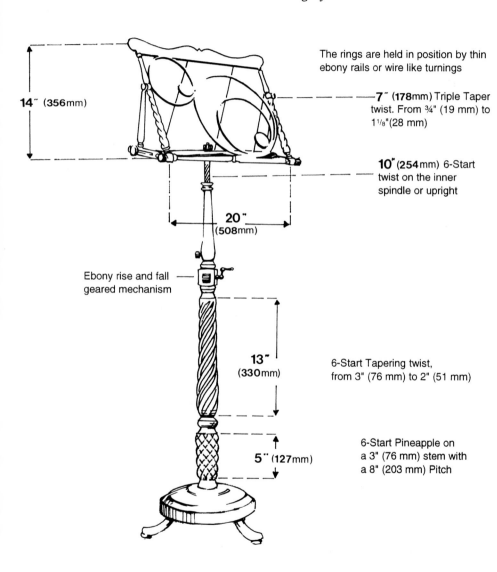

Music stand in mahogany

14˝ (356mm)

The rings are held in position by thin ebony rails or wire like turnings

7˝ (178mm) Triple Taper twist. From ¾˝ (19 mm) to 1⅛˝(28 mm)

10˝ (254mm) 6-Start twist on the inner spindle or upright

20˝ (508mm)

Ebony rise and fall geared mechanism

13˝ (330mm)

6-Start Tapering twist, from 3˝ (76 mm) to 2˝ (51 mm)

6-Start Pineapple on a 3˝ (76 mm) stem with a 8˝ (203 mm) Pitch

5˝ (127mm)

The mahogany base is 12˝ (305 mm) × 3˝ (76 mm) with short legs and 2˝ (51 mm) ebony bun feet

PROJECT: MUSIC STAND

The music stand illustrated is constructed in mahogar with ebony fittings.

To duplicate this piece will involve some advance turning, particularly on the music sheet support. It w also involve a degree of engineering in wood. I ref particularly to the geared mechanism for the rise ar fall facility and the angle adjustment on the support.

It is not intended to go into great detail in respect the spindle work, the illustrations should be sufficie to give a good understanding on design and balance.

There are four twists involved in decorating th piece.

1. On the music sheet support uprights there is a l and right Triple twist with a 3˝(76 mm) pitch or taper, measuring 1⅛˝(28 mm) at the bottom ar ¾˝(19 mm) at the top.
2. On the visible area of the adjustable inner stem a Start twist with a 4˝(102 mm) pitch adds to t elegance of the main column.
3. The main column features a 6-Start twist with 9˝(228 mm) pitch on a taper. The twist tapers fro 3˝(76 mm) at the bottom to 2˝(51 mm) at the to
4. The base of the main column is dominated by a Start Pineapple twist measuring 5˝(127 mm) × (76 mm) with an 8˝(203 mm) pitch.

Reference may be made to the appropriate Chapt for the above defined twists.

All necessary components required for t construction of this piece are listed below.

Music support frame

1. Top rail is designed as shown.
2. Three mahogany rings measuring,
   (a) 11˝ (279 mm) × ³⁄₁₆˝ (5 mm) × ¼˝ (6 mm)
   (b) 7¾˝ (196 mm) × ³⁄₁₆˝ (5 mm) × ¼˝ (6 mm

(c) 6¼" (159 mm) × ³⁄₁₆" (5 mm) × ¼" (6 mm)

3. Two 2" (51 mm) × ¼" (6 mm) ebony discs.

4. Three 18" (457 mm) and one 12" (304 mm) lengths of ¹⁄₈"(3 mm) ebony.

5. Two 12½"(317 mm) × 1"(25 mm) mahogany uprights, featuring left and right Triple Tapering twists.

6. Two 7" (178 mm) stays that locate in the end pummels of the main horizontal support bar, to the uprights at 5 above.

7. Four 1" (25 mm) × ³⁄₈"(9 mm) retaining pins with ebony knobs. Two for the top of the stays at the centre of the uprights, and two for the front end of the sliding hinges located on the bottom corners of the frame.

8. One main horizontal supporting stretcher, 1" (25 mm) thick with a 1" (25 mm) ball in the middle. The ball is drilled to ½" (13 mm) to fit the threaded end of the inner upright support stem.

9. The front stretcher in ¾" (19 mm) mahogany, turned with a pummel at either end. The pummels are drilled to accept the main upright spigots.

10. Two mahogany sliding stays 7" (178 mm) long, with a 4" (101 mm) × ¼" (6 mm) sliding and retaining slot. The front of the stays are turned with a ¾" (19 mm) knob. The knob is drilled at ³⁄₈" (9 mm) to accept the retaining pins at 7 above.

11. Two 1½"(38 mm) × ½" (13 mm) threaded ebony pins, located into the pummel ends of the main supporting stretcher.

12. Six 1¾" (44 mm) × ¹⁄₈" (3 mm) turnings in ebony with a ¼" (6 mm) ball on one end. These balls are centrally drilled at ¹⁄₈" (3 mm). These holes are used to retain the 18" (457 mm) length of ¹⁄₈" (3 mm) ebony. The six pieces are fitted along the front of the front stretcher at 90 degrees to the main uprights. Once in position, the ebony wire can be threaded through the holes to form the music sheet support.

13. Two ¾"(19 mm) × ¼"(6 mm) finials drilled to ¹⁄₈" (3 mm) to accept the thin wire-like ebony rail. finials are glued on the ends of the rail to retain it in position once it has been fitted to the stretcher.

14. Three 1¼" (32 mm) × ½" (13 mm) knobs, serrated at the edge for grip. These are centrally drilled and threaded to match the threaded ebony pins that secure the sliding section of the stays. The third knob is used to secure the music support to the inner supporting and geared stem, at 8 above.

Setting out and fixing the music support

Note: The position of the mahogany rings and ebony discs on the music sheet support. The rings and discs are drilled at varying angles to accept the ¹⁄₈" (3 mm) ebony rails or wire.

Main Frame uprights – two required

Ball drilled to ³⁄₈" (9 mm)for securing the top of the stays

Triple taper twist

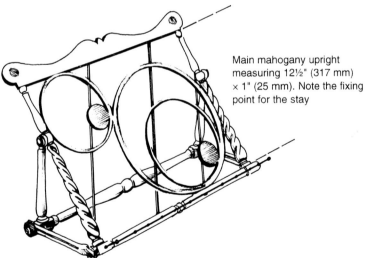

Main mahogany upright measuring 12½" (317 mm) × 1" (25 mm). Note the fixing point for the stay

Points to Note: The angle of the ebony rails or wire running through the rings.
The touching points of the rings on the frame, on one another and the discs. These points are all pinned and glued.
On the front stretcher at the bottom, set at 90 degrees to the uprights is the music sheet shelf made of ebony wire like turnings.
The mahogany slide hinges at either side of the frame. The knobs at the back of these hinges locks the piece at the desired angle.
The main frame pivots at the two knobs at the top of the stay.

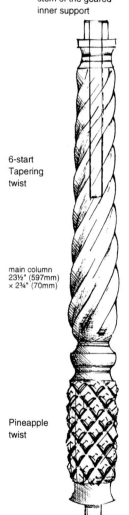

Note the 12" (234 mm) × ¾" (19 mm) drilled recess for housing the stem of the geared inner support

6-start Tapering twist

main column 23½" (597mm) × 2¾" (70mm)

Pineapple twist

To find the correct angle for drilling

Lay the front of the frame on a flat surface and position the rings and discs in position. Mark out where the ebony wire will pass through the rings and discs with a straight edge. Also mark on the main frame where it is to be drilled to accept the ends of the wire. Once satisfied that the ebony wire will be parallel, carefully drill the holes free-hand.

Before setting the design into the frame. Drill the rings and discs at all six points where they touch one another and the main frame, with a ⅛"(3 mm) drill. Once fitted within the frame, the ends of the ebony wire can be glued in position. Fit and glue six securing pins on the rings and discs where previously drilled.

Column components

1. One 23" (584 mm) × ¾" (19 mm) upright inner support stem with a 10" (254 mm) 6-Start twist section at the top. At the bottom of this stem, out of view, and housed within the upper hollow spindle work and geared housing, is a 13"(330 mm) geared section. This section has 4 teeth to the 1" (25 mm) turned to a depth of ⅛" (3 mm). This section will locate through the ¾" (19 mm) hole in the gear housing with the two flanged cogs.

2. Set into the top is a ½" (13 mm) threaded retaining spigot. This spigot fits through the ½" (13 mm) hole, located centrally on the main supporting stretcher of the main frame. The piece is then secured by means of the third threaded knob previously referred to.

3. One 10" (254 mm) × 2" (51 mm) spindle hollow bored to ¾" (19 mm) to accept the above mentioned inner support stem. Note: On the illustration, located on the left side of this hollow spindle, there is a ½"(13 mm) threaded locking spigot with a knob. The spigot is slightly pointed to locate with the geared section of the inner stem.

4. The main supporting column measures 23½"(597 mm) × 2¾" (70 mm) in mahogany. It features a 6-Start twist, tapering from 2¾"(70 mm) at the bottom to 2" (51 mm) at the top. Also featured is a 5" (127 mm) Pineapple twist at the bottom. This column is centrally drilled to ¾" (19 mm) to a depth of 12" (305 mm), to house the inner support stem when at rest.

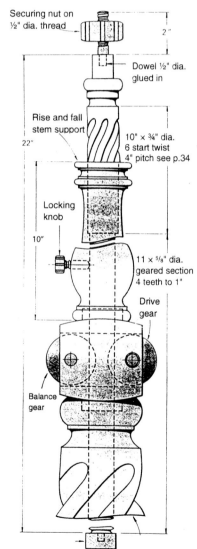

Securing nut on ½" dia. thread

2"

Dowel ½" dia. glued in

Rise and fall stem support

10" × ¾" dia. 6 start twist 4" pitch see p.34

22"

Locking knob

10"

11 × ⅝" dia. geared section 4 teeth to 1"

Drive gear

Balance gear

Gearing stop ¾" dia. glued on ¼" dia. dowel

Main column hollowed out to ¾" dia. to house rise and fall stem

Base and legs

The base is Georgian in style, measuring 12" (305 mm) across and 2½" (63 mm) thick.

The legs are made from 1½"(38 mm) × ¾" (19 mm) ring turned with a design on the inner side. The ring is then quartered, only 3 of the quarters are used.

Each leg is fitted by means of two 2" (51 mm) × ⅛" (3 mm) steel pins. These pins are set into the legs to a depth of 1" (25 mm) and the same into the base exactly 1½" (38 mm) from the outside edge.

Bun feet measuring 1½" (38 mm) × ½" (13 mm) are fitted to the legs by means of a ½"(13 mm) spigot.

Geared mechanism

A geared mechanism is not necessarily required to complete the stand. A threaded spigot may be fitted through the upper hollow spindle. This could be used to lock a plain rise and fall central stem. However, for those who wish to make this gearing the following is a list of the components required:

1. Gear housing: One 2" (51 mm) × 2" (51 mm) mahogany housing with a centrally drilled ¾" (19 mm) hole with the grain. This hole is also drilled through a 1" (25 mm) spigot at either end of the housing. The housing is then mortise drilled to 1¼"(32 mm) × ⅞"(22 mm), centrally and completely through two sides of the housing. On the opposing blank sides of the housing, drill a ⅜"(9 mm) hole, ¼" (6 mm) from the edge and central on the block, drill all the way through, across the mortise recess and through the other side. This hole will house the lay shaft.

   A second hole the same size is drilled in the same position at the other side of the block, only this time the hole will be ⅜" (9 mm) from the edge. This hole will house the drive shaft.

   Great care must be exercised when drilling the gear

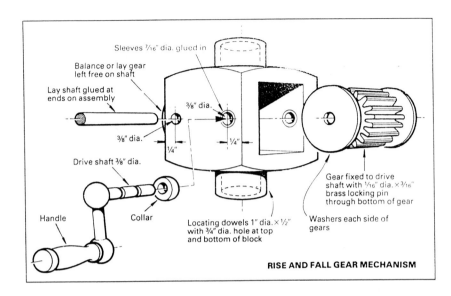

Sleeves ⁷⁄₁₆" dia. glued in

Balance or lay gear left free on shaft

Lay shaft glued at ends on assembly

⅜" dia.

⅜" dia.

¼"

¼"

Drive shaft ⅜" dia.

Handle

Collar

Locating dowels 1" dia. × ½" with ¾" dia. hole at top and bottom of block

Gear fixed to drive shaft with ¹⁄₁₆" dia. × ³⁄₁₆" brass locking pin through bottom of gear

Washers each side of gears

RISE AND FALL GEAR MECHANISM

housing, to avoid breakout (This is where a drill or mortise pushes and breaks out the material on breakthrough.)

2. Two ebony cogs measuring ⅝"(16 mm) wide and 1"(25 mm) in diameter. Eleven teeth measuring ⅛"(3 mm) deep are cut around the circumference of the cogs. Both cogs are centrally drilled to ⅜"(9 mm). The teeth of these cogs must be cut along side grain, in other words, along the grain. Cross grain teeth break off. I used a small hacksaw and a smooth file to cut the teeth.

3. Four 1¼" (32 mm) × ¹⁄₁₆"(1.5 mm) ebony washers also centrally drilled to ⅜" (9 mm). These act as guards and shims for the sides of both cogs when fitted in the housing.

4. Two ebony shafts. One drive shaft 2½" (63 mm) × ⅜" (9 mm) and one lay shaft 2" (51 mm) × ⅜" (9 mm).

5. Two 1½" (38 mm) × ½" (13 mm) spindles turned and fixed with a spigot to form an 'L' turning handle. The fixing and driving end of the handle should feature a ½" (13 mm) knob, drilled to ⅜" (9 mm) for securing the drive shaft.

The completed music stand

Assembling the gear mechanism

Before assembling the mechanism, make sure all the components fit and run smoothly.

1. Insert the geared inner stem through the gear housing.
2. Locate both cogs with their washers into the housing at either side of the geared inner stem. Make sure the cogs mesh with the gears on the stem.
3. Push both shafts through the holes in the housing, they should locate with the centre holes in the cogs. Once in position, both cogs should turn and run freely when the inner stem is drawn backwards and forwards.
4. Fit the ' L' shaped handle to the longer shaft. When satisfied all the components are fitted correctly and the mechanism is working properly, glue at the following points:
   (a) The drive cog on its shaft. It may be necessary to drill a very small hole through the centre of the cog into the shaft, to insert the glue and fit a securing pin.
   (b) Glue the handle on to the drive shaft.
   (c) Both ends of the lay shaft into the housing. Take care not to glue the cog on to the shaft. It must run freely.

Before assembling the piece, make sure all the components are colour matched, sealed and finished to the required standard.

Assemble the base, legs and bun feet first.

Glue the main column upright into the base.

Fit the geared mechanism into the column.

Fit the hollow spindle over the geared stem.

Fit the locking spigot.

Fit the music support frame on to the top of the inner stem and lock it on with the threaded ebony knob.

21

PINEAPPLE TWIST

A Pineapple twist is a most attractive feature. It is invariably used on top of a newel post in the shape of a pineapple or at the base of a column incorporating another twist. However, the twisting process may be considered for virtually any piece except for an open twist. It is particularly attractive on a drum shape or decorating a complete column. It may also be used on a jug, bowl, or in a column at the bottom of another feature.

The size is not restrictive as it can be cut to any shape or size. A traditional size is approximately 6"(152 mm) × 4"(102 mm) × 4"(102 mm), and to explain and illustrate this very attractive form and to put the finished product to good use, the pineapple will be built into a column for a mahogany occasional table.

This project is in a typical traditional style with a 20"(508 mm) × 1"(25 mm) table top, 6"(152 mm) × 1"(25 mm) support plate, with 14"(355 mm) × 2"(51 mm) base with bun feet.

Prepare a 24"(610 mm) × 4"(102 mm) × 4"(102 mm) blank in mahogany and turn it to the proposed design, including two 2"(51 mm) spigots at either end. See the illustration right and note that the 6"(152 mm) section is to accommodate the Pineapple twist.

Prepare the table top, support plate, the base and the bun feet as illustrated. (For those wishing to design their own piece, prepare the workpiece to incorporate the 6"(152 mm) section illustrated.)

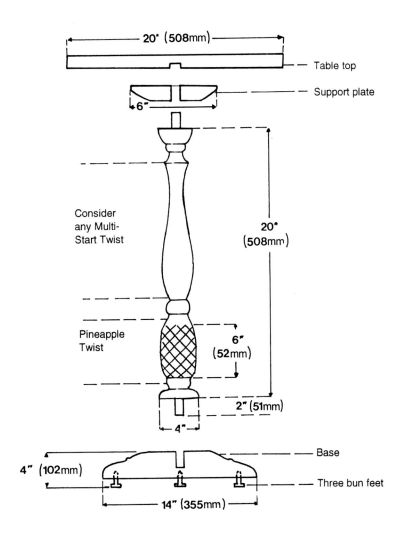

The centre column has two main features: a teardrop Multi-Start twist, (which by this stage in the book, should no longer be a problem to readers), and a Pineapple twist at the base. Note that the Pineapple twist in this case is slightly tapered at both ends.

With all the table components made and the column prepared with the Teardrop twist cut, it is time to mark out the pineapple.

Stage 1: Marking out the Pineapple twist

Keep the workpiece on the lathe. Mark four Start Lines using dividers, tape or ruler using the centring ' X ' across the base of the blank. Divide the four Start Lines once to give eight Dividing Lines. There is no need to number these lines. Both the twist and the length of the pitch are 6"(152 mm), therefore the twist will be an 8 bines start with one pitch. A true twist with the bines and hollows starting and finishing on the same Start Lines. See the illustration below which shows how to mark out the Pitch and Pitch Dividing Lines. As an exercise, mark out the Cut Control Lines very lightly before reading Stage 2.

Pineapple Start and Pitch Lines

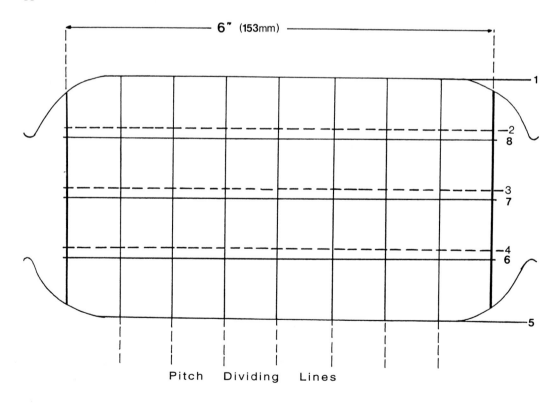

Stage 2: Pineapple pitch and Pitch Dividing Lines
On the 6"(152 mm) blank mark a central dividing line. Divide the two segments twice. There should now be eight segments measuring ¾"(19 mm) wide.

I hope you got it right. Remember, regardless of the length of the pitch the number of Start Lines or bines on a Multi-Start dictates the number of segments along each pitch.

Stage 3: Pineapple Cut Control Lines
To attain the pineapple look, the Cut Control Lines have to be marked out from both left and right, and this will give a criss-cross effect at the intersections with the Pitch Lines.

Mark out all eight Cut Control Lines from the left and right as illustrated below.

CUTTING THE PINEAPPLE TWIST
Before cutting the twist there are points to consider: the depth and width of the cuts will determine the size of each pineapple segment; consider whether the hollows should be 'V' shaped or slightly rounded at the bottom. See illustration p. 142. To determine the width of the hollows it may be necessary to use the Complete Marking Out procedure described in the earlier chapters. Should this be considered unnecessary cut the twist free hand. It is not necessary for the cutting of a pineapple to be very accurate otherwise it will have little character.

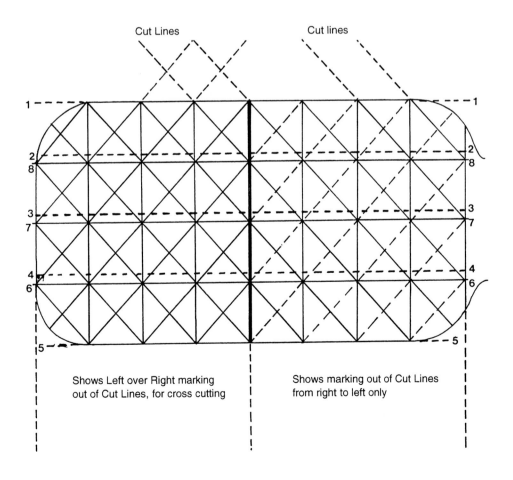

Shows Left over Right marking
out of Cut Lines, for cross cutting

Shows marking out of Cut Lines
from right to left only

To achieve large or small pineapple segments is dependent on the size of the hollows. Wider hollows will result in smaller segments and vice versa.

In the illustration the continuous lines are the Cut Control Lines, and the dotted lines are the Complete Marking Out lines.

The illustration left shows the variations on the design of the segments and the illustration below shows how the segment top is made smaller.

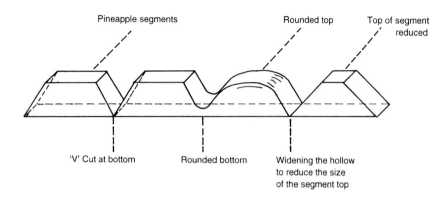

Pineapple segments

Rounded top

Top of segment reduced

'V' Cut at bottom

Rounded bottom

Widening the hollow to reduce the size of the segment top

Method of sizing the pineapple segments

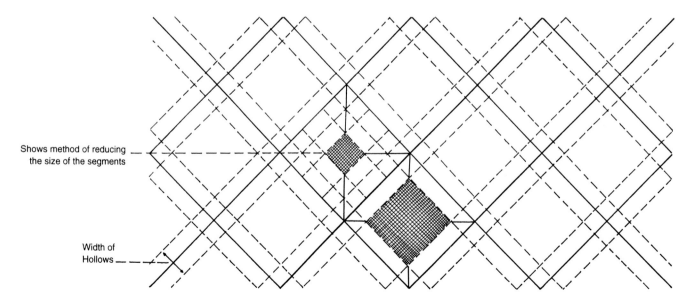

Shows method of reducing the size of the segments

Width of Hollows

The continuous lines are the Cut Lines, the broken lines are the Control Lines

Use the tenon saw to cut along the Cut Lines as in other cases, count the saw cuts to three across each segment before moving on to the next. Use the left hand, as before, to turn the workpiece into the forward cutting action of the saw.

Cut the right Control Lines first. Do *not* cut the left lines until the first hollow has been finished completely. The reason for this is that chunks can be broken off the segments when cross cutting.

The first hollow can be cut with the gouge as normal, or cut a 'V' along the Cut Line with the saw. Do *not* cut too tightly against the segments otherwise they may end up too small. Where the hollow is rounded at the bottom use a round file or rasp to round off the bottom of the hollows as necessary. Finish off with the wooden sandpaper tool. Do not round off the top of the bines at this stage.

Cut the left Control Line with the saw to cut the 'V'

at each segment. Don't attempt to use the gouge as it will only jerk across the first hollow and cause damage. When cutting with the tenon saw use it very lightly, particularly when cutting the left hollow, as you will be cutting across the bines and hollows, and try not to cut too deeply otherwise the segment hollows will get damaged. A flat chisel may be used in a downward cutting action to cut the 'V' or to trim the sides of each segment as illustrated below.

At this stage the pineapple is a series of flat topped pyramids. Round off the bines with a smooth flat rasp or file, (do *not* attempt to use a palm plane) then sandpaper. Take care not to sand the tops of the segments too much.

Sand the whole column with fine sandpaper until the correct finish is achieved. Glue the table together, clean off excess glue and allow to dry. Stain and polish to the required finish.

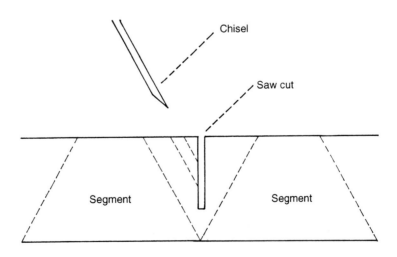

The hollow or 'V' Cut between the segments may be cut with a saw or carpenter's chisel

22

LAMINATED WORK

Laminating different timbers in woodturning is common enough and widely practised. Perhaps more novel is using this design device in twisted work. Contrasting colours of material gains maximum effect once a twist has been cut and many carefully selected species will blend to give a subtle, enriching appearance

Listed below are several laminations that have proved very workable.

1. Ebony and holly or boxwood. Black and white.
2. Piquia-amarello with padauk, pink ivory or bloodwood. Yellow, dark red and pink.
3. Mahogany and yellow pine. Brown and creamy yellow.
4. Padauk and African blackwood. Dark red and black.
5. Rosewood and ebony. Rich brown and black.

There are numerous species of timber that may be used in this method and there will be readers who have access to fantastic colours in wood. Try laminating some, and cut a twist. I am certain the results will be very striking, maybe even fantastic. Shown on pages 145 and 146 are a few results of such work.

There are three methods of laminating I use for the purpose of twisting. The first is to drill a very accurate hole centrally through the length of the timber along the grain. Turn a length of contrasting dowel to fit the hole exactly. Slide and glue the dowel into the hole along the full length of the piece. When dry re-turn the piece, use the centre dowel turning points to make sure it is centred. Turn the piece to the desired thickness. There should be an even thickness of laminated material around the central dowel.

The second method is prepare perfectly square and equal in size, lengths of contrasting timber and glue them alternately into a blank for turning and twisting.

The third is to plane all four sides of a length of material, then glue four lengths of a contrasting colour or colours to each of the sides. Allow to dry, turn the blank to leave the desired thickness of strips along the cylinder. Cut the twist as required.

A combination of all three methods may be used.

There are other methods of laminating timber and the adventurous turner may well like to experiment further.

GOBLET PROJECT

As an example and project, I explain here how to prepare a goblet with a laminated stem for twisting.

The stem of the goblet is made up of thin laminations and the twist is, of necessity, small in diameter. It is therefore a difficult piece to do well. If you feel worried about your ability to work in this small scale practise on larger dimensioned pieces until you are confident to give this a try. (The thicker the laminate the easier the task).

The thickness may vary a little in such a piece, e.g. $1/8$"(3 mm) dowel into a $1/4$"(6 mm) laminate up to a $3/16$"(5 mm) dowel into a $5/16$"(8 mm) laminate.

1. Turn the top of a goblet in ebony and turn or drill

a ¼"(6 mm) hole at the base to accept the stem.

2. Drill a ³⁄₁₆"(5 mm) hole along a 6"(152 mm) × ½" (13 mm) × ½"(13 mm) blank of ebony. Use an extended engineer's drill for this purpose for accuracy.

3. Turn a ³⁄₁₆"(5 mm) × 6"(152 mm) long stem of holly. The holly must be turned accurately to fit snugly into the barrel of the ebony. When satisfied with the fit, glue the holly in position and allow to dry.

4. Turn the stem to ¼"(6 mm) using the centre points on the holly to ensure an even laminate of ebony over holly.

5. Turn the base of the goblet in a jaw chuck. With the base still in the chuck drill a ¼"(6 mm) hole centrally to fit the stem. Use the tailstock to centre the stem whilst fitting and gluing.

6. Use masking tape around the rim of the goblet bowl, mount the goblet bowl in a jaw chuck. Make sure it is running perfectly true. Centre the base in the tailstock centre, fit and glue the top end of the stem into the bottom of the bowl. Allow the glue to dry. The piece is ready for twisting.

7. To twist the stem, re-mount the base in a jaw chuck and support the goblet top with the tailstock using a jig or other preferred method.

8. Cut a Double Barley twist with a 1"(25 mm) pitch. This twist is twice the traditional pitch length, and will help to retain as much strength as possible.

9. Before starting the lathe to complete the base and part off the goblet, make sure there is no drag at the tailstock end, otherwise the inertia of starting the lathe may break the stem. It may be necessary to reduce the speed of the lathe or rotate the lathe sharply by hand before pressing the start button. Complete the base of the goblet.

10. To part off the piece, remove the tailstock. Hold the top of the goblet very lightly in the free hand whilst parting off. The same procedure applies as in Chapter 19.

Ebony and holly laminated goblet

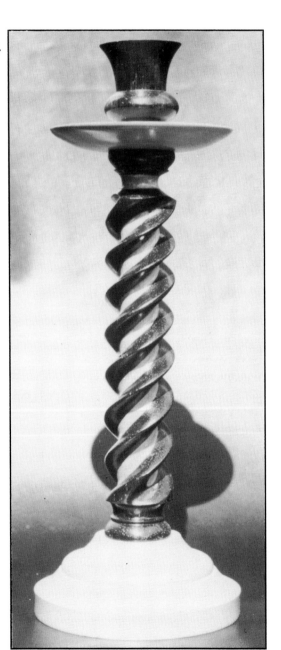

Laminated candlestick

Goblets with laminated stems

23

TWISTING A RING OR HOOP

One of the main problems when twisting a ring or hoop is the strength and stability of timber and how the ring is constructed. Regardless of the species, when it is turned into a ring it is very weak in the areas across the grain. When twisted it becomes very fragile. With a small ring this is not so critical.

The only method of overcoming this is to laminate the timber. The larger pieces and hoops need to be laminated in two or three layers to gain the necessary strength for twisting and to be of any practical or decorative use. The best method of laminating for this purpose is to prepare a blank the size of the piece to be twisted. The timber should be dry and free from shakes, knots, etc.

The following example will show how to prepare a blank and mark up and cut a 10"(254 mm) dia. × 1"(25 mm) ring in yew.

Select a straight grained piece of yew and turn a 10"(254 mm) × 1¼"(32 mm) blank. Bandsaw or part the blank into three discs and plane them perfectly flat to approximately ³/₈"(9 mm) thick for gluing.

Arrange the three blanks in order so that the grain on the top and bottom discs is running in the same direction and the grain of the middle disc is running at right angles to both. The discs can also be arranged with the grain of the three discs set separately at 45, 90 and 180 degrees. The main purpose is to gain

maximum strength in the areas of cross grain.

Glue the three discs together with 'Cascamite' or other similar UF (urea formaldehyde) type of glue. Do not use a PVA (polyvinyl acetate) glue as it has a degree of elasticity which can affect the twist. Clamp the three discs together very firmly until completely dry.

See the illustration below.

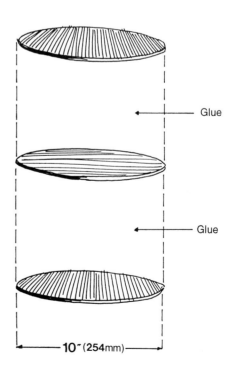

Shaded areas show direction of grain

Glue

Glue

10″(254mm)

Mount the prepared blank on a screw chuck and turn a 1" (25 mm) thick ring. From this blank you should be able to get at least five rings reducing in diameter size, should they be required for another project.

It is not important if the ring is a little rough at this stage, however the bine must be cylindrical. The intention is to cut a Double Barley twist with a traditional double pitch. The pitch should be approximately 2" (51 mm). However, the pitch has to be set in order that all the bines balance around the ring.

Stage 1: Marking out the pitch on a ring
The outside circumference of the ring is approximately 31½" (800 mm).

Place the ring on a flat surface and quarter it at 7⅞" (200 mm). Divide again twice. Each pitch segment is now just under 2" (50 mm). These are the Pitch Lines. Divide twice again for the Pitch Control Lines.

Note: All the Pitch Lines should be marked directly towards the centre of the ring. This takes care of the

reduction in size of the inside edge of the ring. See the illustration below left.

Stage 2: Marking out the Start Lines on a ring
The circumference of a 1"(25 mm) thick ring is approximately 3¼"(83 mm).

Divide the circumference by four or use dividers. Measure and mark the Start Lines around the ring at ¹³/₁₆"(21 mm). See the illustration below.

Stage 3: Ring Cut Control Lines
With the ring still on a flat surface, begin from the first Start Line on the outside and mark from right to left clockwise over the ring to the second line at the top, then to the centre and so on. Complete both Cut Control Lines at Start Lines 1 and 3. The piece is ready to cut.

Stage 4: Saw cutting a ring twist
With the ring on a flat surface, with one stroke only of

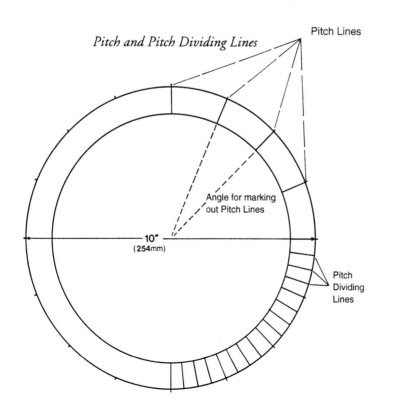

Pitch and Pitch Dividing Lines

Pitch Lines

Angle for marking out Pitch Lines

10" (254mm)

Pitch Dividing Lines

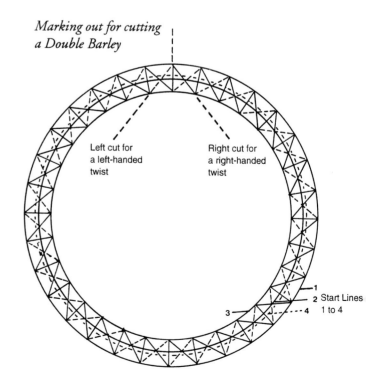

Marking out for cutting a Double Barley

Left cut for a left-handed twist

Right cut for a right-handed twist

1
2 Start Lines
3
4 1 to 4

the tenon saw, cut across the second start line. Do not go too deep as this cut is only a guide for a rasp. On completion of the first circumference turn the ring over and cut the other side in the same manner.

To cut the inside edge, lift the ring to 90 degrees with your free hand and lightly cut across the inside. Rock the ring a little to link the saw cuts.

To complete the sawing and cutting make up a 5"(127 mm) blank on the lathe with a recess to accept approximately a third of the depth of the ring. Leave the blank on the lathe, hang the ring on the blank in the recess and hold it in position with your free hand. Cut the outside section with the saw.

Cutting a left-handed twist on a ring

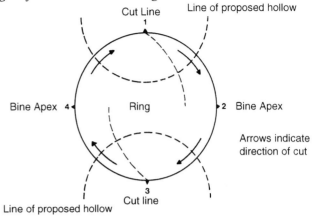

Cutting a right-handed twist on a ring

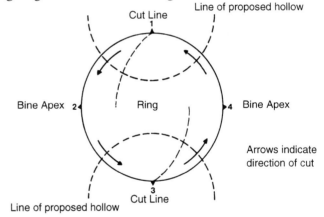

Method of cutting a ring twist

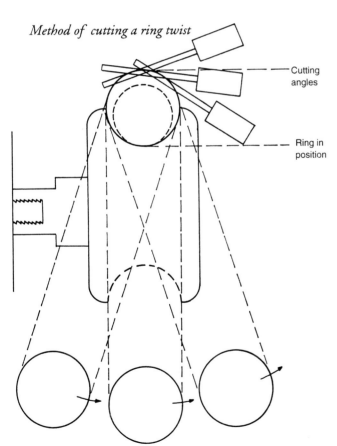

Direction of ring during cutting.
Swing the ring in the direction of the arrows all the way over to rest on the headstock.

Method of using a jig to cut a ring twist

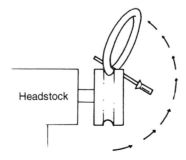

Swing towards headstock when cutting.
Note the rasp cutting the inside of the ring

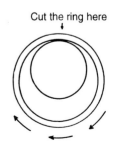

Rotate ring to cut a right-handed and in the opposite diirection for a left-handed one. (It is possible to cut both ways for either)

Stage 5: Cutting the bines

With the ring still in the jig, cut the hollows with a ³/₈" (9 mm) rasp. Do *not* attempt to cut the bines with a gouge. Follow the angle of the saw cut with the rasp. Count the cuts with the rasp in threes. This will ensure an even cut hollow. To gain maximum cutting at the top of the ring, push the ring under the jig as close to the headstock of the lathe as possible. Cut the hollow to the required depth (approximately a quarter of the thickness of the material). Slowly pull the bottom of the ring towards yourself with the free hand, continue the cutting with the rasp. This cutting process can be continued until the ring is virtually upright. Turn the ring round to complete the cut. Repeat the process for the second hollow.

With this method the ring can be cut section by section, moving the ring around on the jig until the complete circumference is cut. The bines can be rounded with a flat rasp or file using the same cutting process. Sand in the same manner with the wooden sanding tool.

Bowl with a twisted gallery rail

A ring twist may be a Single, Double, Triple, Ribbon or a 4-Start. To increase the bines beyond this point is tricky. As the inside of the ring is smaller the cutting area gets less and the bines start to distort.

A ring twist cannot be Opened!

BOWL WITH A TWISTED GALLERY RAIL PROJECT

This project is mainly to illustrate the use for twisted ring or hoop for decorative purposes.

Any type of twist, other than an Open one, can be cut on a ring or hoop.

As mentioned in the early stages of this book. a twist should be cut to suit a project and not the other way round. This rule still applies. However, in this case, provided the size and design have been decided, the twist may be cut before the main piece is turned.

The assembly of such a piece is self explanatory from the illustration.

In the case of this bowl, the twist is a Double Barley with a 3½"(89 mm) pitch. The twisted ring is larger than the bowl itself. This means the supports will have to be a determined length in order that the bowl line flows. To do this lower the ring towards the bowl to find its position in relation to the profile. When satisfied, measure the gap to establish the length of the supports.

The length of the pitch and the number of times the bines go round the ring will determine the number of supports. In this case there are 12 pitches, the twist is a Double Barley, therefore 24 supports are required.

Turn 24 supports to the exact design and length with ³/₁₆"(5 mm) spigots at either end.

Mark out all 24 drilling points around the bowl rim. Also mark out all the drilling points on the ring, at the top of the bines on the side to be mounted.

The drilling angle for the holes in relation to the length of the supports has to be decided. To do this, place four blocks the length of the supports between the rim of the bowl and the ring. Draw a pencil line across one of the blocks between the centre of the ring and the rim at the proposed angle of drilling. Drill a $^3/_{16}$" (5 mm) hole in the block at the angle decided. Use the block as a jig to drill four quarterly holes the same size around the rim of the bowl. Drill all the holes to the same depth. To check that the angle is correct, measure and fit four pins to emulate the supports.

To drill the ring lay it on a flat surface, with the side to be drilled facing upwards. Use the jig to drill four holes the same size, at the same through angle as the bowl. These must be drilled on top of the bines which will be directly opposite the holes on the bowl. Mount the ring on the four test pillars. If satisfied drill all the holes using the same method.

An alternative and easy way to drill these holes is to find the angle and set the table of a pillar drill as required. With a stop on the pillar drill table, drill all the holes on the bowl first. Use the same principle to drill the holes on the ring.

Before fitting the ring to the bowl, flatten off the top of the holes on the ring very slightly. This will allow the supports to seat properly at the top.

With all the pieces properly prepared, fit and glue the supports into the ring. Immediately after, glue the bottom of the supports into the bowl.

The method I suggest to clamp the piece whilst the glue is drying is to place a blanket on a flat surface, position the bowl ring side down on the blanket. Pad the upturned base and place a board on top. Weight the bowl sufficiently to clamp it firmly in position. I recommend about 80 pounds.

Yew bowl with 1" (25 mm) thick Double Barley twist with a 4" (102 mm) pitch

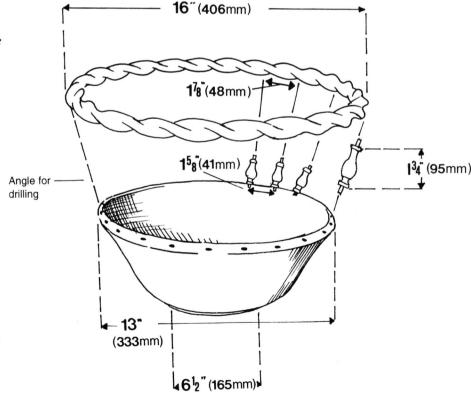

1. Bowl overall height 7" (158 mm).
2. 24 small spigot pillars 1¾" (70 mm) × ¾" (19 mm).
3. Set pillars into the ring first.
4. The angle of drilling is set in accordance with the length of pillars and angle of bowl rim.

24

COMBINED TWISTS & CONVERTED TWISTS

A Combined twist is where two compatible twists are mixed on the same column or spindle. This is not to be confused with Converted twists which is explained in the next section.

The best method of explaining this is to give examples by way of cut through profile illustrations.

1. A Double Barley twist combined with a Double Ribbon twist.(See below).
   This twist is really a 4-Start with two differently shaped bines. It may be necessary to use the Complete marking Out procedure on the Ribbon bines only.

Cut this twist in the same manner as normal, taking care to shape the bines during the course of cutting. When sanding take care not to round the top of the Ribbon bines. It is possible that two different methods of sanding may have to be adopted. The method used for over the top sanding for rounded bines and the sanding tool together with the strip of sanding cloth for the Ribbon twist.

2. A combination of a Triple and Ribbon twists. The marking out and cutting of this twist is the same as for a Multi-Start twist, only this is a 6-Start. See illustration below.

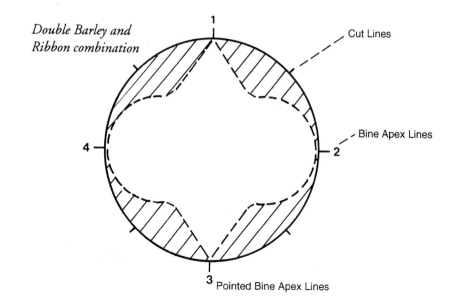

Double Barley and Ribbon combination

Cut Lines

Bine Apex Lines

3 Pointed Bine Apex Lines

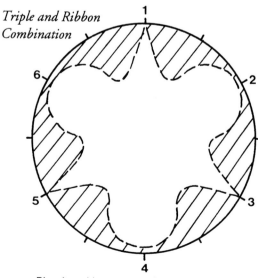

Triple and Ribbon Combination

Bine Apex Lines are numbered.
The Cut Lines are indicated by a –.

Marking out

Mark out three Start Lines as for the Triple (Chapter 11 refers). Divide the start lines making a total of six. Decide the pitch and mark out the Pitch and Pitch Dividing Lines. Complete the Cut and Bine Control Lines.

There is only one point to remember: there must be sufficient room on the material to accommodate the bines, so it may be necessary to stretch the pitch sufficiently to ensure this.

3. The next illustration shows an 8-Start with one set of bines with a hollow top. This type of twist gives an indication of how a twist can be modified to any shape desired.

   The marking out of this twist begins with four Start Lines. Divide twice to get sixteen, the result is eight Cut and eight Bine Apex Lines.

   The marking out for a Combined twist appears complicated. However, with the knowledge of previous marking out procedures most readers will discover the simplicity of it all. The Complete Marking Out procedure is not necessary.

Any Multi-Start, subject to size limitations, can be easily cut with good quality rasps and files. To get the desired profile, this type of twist can be a very rewarding challenge

Note: The hollow topped bine is a new feature and it is very easily cut. All that is required is to saw a very light cut along the top of the *larger* alternating bines as a guide for a smooth round rasp. Sand as before, taking care not to damage the sharp top edges of the bines.

4. The last illustration shown is a combination of the same type of twist, but with a variation on thickness of the bines.

   The variation on the shape of a bine is limited. However, the thickness may be varied considerably as they alternate around the twist. This leads into another important factor when designing this type of twist. The twist itself may be **Graduated** or **Tapered** as well as the bine.

Readers who have worked logically through the text and mastered the various aspects of the work involved would now have reached a stage of thinking ahead to

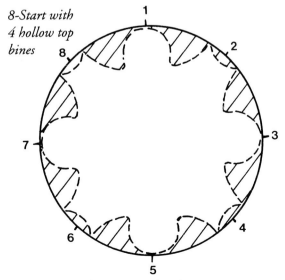

8-Start with 4 hollow top bines

Bine Apex Lines are numbered.
Note the alternating hollow topped bines

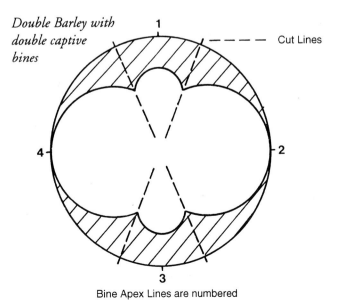

Double Barley with double captive bines

Cut Lines

Bine Apex Lines are numbered

new designs and styles of twists and to thinking ahead of the text. With this twist, for example, it should be apparent that additional features can be added. It may be cut into the shape of a Teardrop, Opened and, according to the next section, which we are shortly to discuss, it can also be Converted.

For this type of twist mark out for the Double. There should be four Start Lines. Instead of cutting with the saw on the Cut Lines, mark out additional Cut Lines at either side and parallel to the original Cut Line, these lines should be measured to suit the desired width of 'captive' or smaller bine. There are now four Cut Lines.

Cut along the four Cut Lines with the tenon saw, use the twisting gouge and palm plane as normal. In order to get the 'V' effect at the bottom of the hollows use the 1½"(38 mm) wide carpenter's chisel in the same manner as for the Single. (Chapter 5 refers). Sand and finish as before.

CONVERTING TWISTS

Converting a twist from one form to another is unusual.

However, the process of marking out such a twist is not so different. The difficulty arises in the area of conversion. The area of conversion is where the bines of one twist divide or gather from one to the other. For example, where the bines of a Double twist divide into a 4-Start or the 4-Start opens into an Open twist.

A Converted twist may be used for the same purposes as any other, but this is obviously dependent on its size, and strength. As with any other twist, its purpose is mainly decorative. With this process the results can be exceptional. The first example, by way of illustration, will be a Double Barley converting to a 4-Start on a 3"(76 mm) × 3"(76 mm) blank.

Prepare a column measuring 24"(610 mm) × 3"(76 mm) × 3"(76 mm) for a plant stand or small table. Turn the necessary fixing spigots at either end and a 12"(305 mm) section for twisting.

Stage 1: Marking out

With the prepared blank between centres mark out four Start Lines along the 12"(305 mm) section. Mark one central dividing Line on the 12"(305 mm) section and two end Pitch Lines. The central dividing line will be where the Cut Lines convert from 2 to 4.

Before moving on to Stage 2, which will be the Pitch Lines, the decision on pitch angles for each section must be made. The pitch angle should not be too long otherwise the twist will look out of balance.

Traditional marking out for this type of twist may be disregarded. This is an opportunity to design a twist.

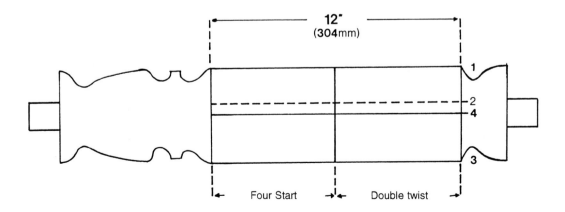

Double and Ribbon plant stand

*Double and Ribbon conversion
(Detail)*

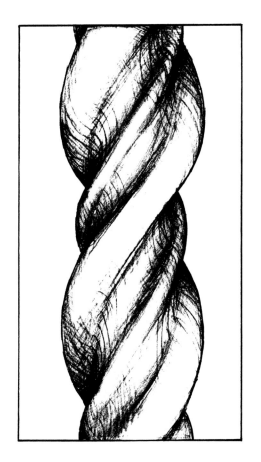

Solid laminated twist in ebony and holly converting an Open twist at one end

There are 3 conversions on this piece. Double to 4-Start to Pineapple and on to an Open 4-Start. The Pineapple and the Open are split by a bead with coves at either side.

There are three sections to this twist: 1. The Double twist area, 2. The 4-Start and 3. The conversion area in the middle.

For this twist the Double will have a short pitch, in fact half the traditional pitch and the same as a Single. The blank is 3"(76 mm) therefore the pitch will be 3"(76 mm). The 4-Start section will have a 6"(153 mm) pitch which is the pitch for a traditional Double on this thickness of material. The central conversion area will accommodate the bines where they split from 2 to 4.

It has to be decided how quickly the conversion is to be made. In other words, the length of material to be used for this purpose will depend on the angle of cut into the Double bine before true separation has been established.

In this case the conversion will take place over one width of the material, which is 3"(76 mm). A perfect Double will enter and, hopefully, a 4-Start of equal quality will exit. Within the 3"(76 mm) section the Double bines will automatically widen, this will give sufficient material to accommodate the splitting of the bines.

Stage 2:
See the illustration above for the Pitch, Pitch Dividing Lines and Control Lines for all three areas.

Mark out the Double along the length of the blank as normal.

Note: In the illustration, the pitch has changed to twice its length at the centre line. The Cut Lines will be at 1 and 3 for the Double and will continue the full length of the twist, although the pitch has changed at the centre point. Starting from the centre line, all four Start Lines will become Cut Lines. Also note that the conversion area consists of two Double pitch segments and one 4-Start segment.

(This twist may be opened, as illustrated. For the Opening procedure refer to Chapters 7 and 12.)

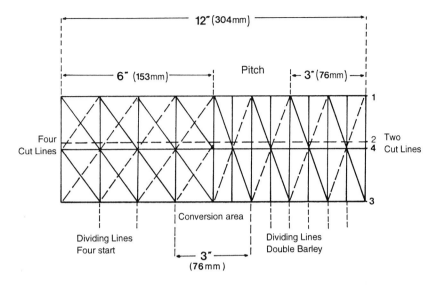

Illustration shows Cut lines only

Stage 3: Cutting a Converted twist
Cutting this type of twist is the same as any other, the only difference is the manner in which the conversion area is dealt with. The cutting methods are dependent on the size of the twist which will, in turn, decide the type of tools used.

The twist illustrated will be cut with a tenon saw, gouge, palm plane and sandpaper as normal. Remember when cutting this twist, the pitch changes quite dramatically at the centre point. When cutting the Double cut lines, continue past the centre point to the end of the twist. The extra two cuts for the 4-Start begin at this centre point.

When using the gouge, cut the true twist areas first. They are the Double and the 4-Start sections. Leave the conversion area until last. This will allow for blending in the two twists to ensure that the conversion balances.

The ends of the two extra hollows that form the 4-Start will split the Double bines. They have to be tapered out and backwards towards the Double. This must be done equally within the 3"(76 mm) conversion area.

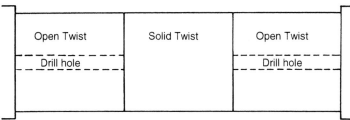

The blank should be centre drilled to suit the designs of twist:

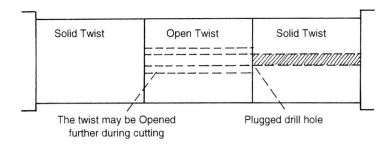

The twist may be Opened further during cutting   Plugged drill hole

Use a gouge or rasp to cut the hollow or trough tapers. Take care not to distort the tapered cut when sanding.

For an example of a Triple converting to a 6-Start on a teardrop, see the photograph on p. 155.

Any Converted twist can be opened or partially opened. However, care must be exercised when opening a Converted twist where the bines are a Ribbon or are irregular in shape. A smaller twist may also be set inside to form a twist within an Open Converted twist.

CONVERTING A SOLID TWIST TO AN OPEN

Regardless of the design, virtually any twist can be converted or partially opened, and this can be at one or both ends, leaving a solid twisted section in the middle, or vice-versa, an Open twist in the middle with a solid section at either or both ends.

Drill the correct size of hole to the required depth, centrally in the blank at either or both ends to suit the particular design. The drilled section, or sections, will be the Open twist areas. See the top illustration.

The depth of the drill holes may be varied to open any percentage of the twist. The open sections may also differ in length and type of twist.

In the case of a twist with an open centre section, drill the hole to the depth required from one end. This will mean that part of the solid section will have a hole down the centre. In this case it is better to drill a hole slightly smaller than normally required, as this will give insurance that 'break through' will not occur accidentally when cutting the solid sections of the twist.

The unwanted drill hole may be plugged with a dowel of the same material. See the illustration left.

Open Double Barley twist converting to an Open 4-Start twist, or vice versa

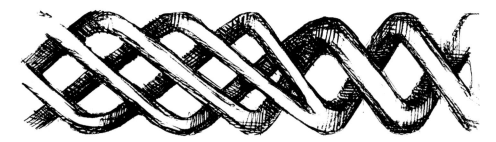

Note: In the centre conversion area the Double Twist bines split to form a double bine resulting in four thinner ones. The 'V' cut of the 'Y' should be slightly tapered and rounded at the bottom.

Care should be exercised when cutting the conversions, as the Double bines are significantly stronger than the 4-Start ones.

25

CUTTING OR STRIKING THREADS

Thread cutting in wood has been around for a long time. Threading sections of spindle work is a traditional method of joining shorter pieces to form a column, such as lamp standards, candlesticks, snooker cue stands, etc. 'striking', 'chasing', 'laying' and 'tapping' are terms used for cutting threads whether by machine or free hand. Tools such as taps, dies, chasers, thread cutting boxes and a 'V' chisels are the main tools used.

There are several machines and devices which have come onto the market in recent years, and some of these can be fitted on to any standard lathe.

There are also automatic traverse thread cutting machines, but these are normally for mass production and are expensive. The thread cutting systems mostly seen in D.I.Y. workshops are thread boxes and taps.

The thread box houses a 'V' cutter which projects into a recess the circumference of the dowel or spigot to be threaded. There is normally a sizing block on the entry side of the box, which also sets the spigot before thread cutting takes place. At the other side of the cutter there is a thread guide, this accepts the lead thread as it passes the cutter.

A tap, the same size as the thread box, is used to thread the recess which will accept the threaded dowel. These thread boxes and taps normally range from ½"(13 mm) to 1½"(38 mm) in size and are available in most large woodworking stores or sometimes through mail order catalogues. Larger sizes can be obtained from specialist tool stores.

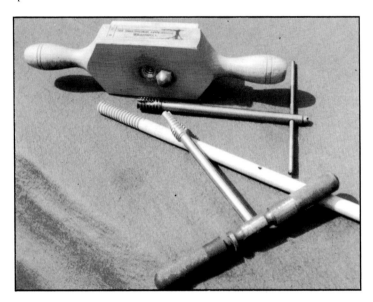

Thread box and taps

CUTTING THREADS WITH A BOX AND TAP
Using a thread box is relatively easy, dependent on the size of box. On smaller sizes, prepare the dowel or spigot the size of the box recess. Hold the box in your free hand, introduce the spigot with the other and push it gently against the cutter. Turn the spigot clockwise into

the cutter, look through the waste relief recess to see the cutter bite into the material. After approximately half turn the new thread will bite on the thread guide. Continue turning and the spigot will be automatically pulled through the box with the thread guide. When threading dowelling there is no limit to the length of thread that can be cut. When threading a spigot, it may be necessary to withdraw the workpiece before completion, by reversing the twisting action. Remove the sizing block from the side of the box, this will permit the spigot to be threaded up to the shoulder of the workpiece.

When threading larger pieces, hold the workpiece upright in a vice. Place the sizing block over the spigot or dowel, exert a little downward pressure. Use both hands to turn the box around the workpiece.

Threading the Recess with a Tap

Drill a hole the desired depth and the size of the tap. (not including threads). Sizing is normally done by measuring the shank of the tap. Some taps have fitted 'T' handles, others require an adjustable tap handle. Push the tap firmly into the recess and turn clockwise, keep the pressure on until the required depth is reached. From time to time remove the tap and clean out the debris.

There are traditional freehand methods of thread cutting. These are explained in the following paragraphs.

The first method, is to use 'chasers'. These are used to cut threads in steel as well as timber.

CHASERS

Chasers are hand held blades with a series of sharpened 'V's, like teeth along the cutting edge of a flat scraper type of tool. The 'V's are set at a specific pitch with the heel ground away at a slight angle to permit cutting with the sharp upper edge. They come in matching pairs, one for external cutting (male), and one for internal cutting (female). The cutters vary in size according to the pitch and number of threads to the inch.

Chasers are normally used from right to left to cut right-handed threads, but may also be used to cut left-handed threads by cutting left to right.

The external chaser (male) cutting edge is at the end of the tool at 90 degrees to the handle. The internal chaser (female) is on a cranked extension at the end of the tool. The teeth are normally set to cut between 0 and 15 degrees to the handle, as illustrated below.

Preparation for using chasers

When preparing the spigot care must be taken that the spigot or dowel is larger than the recess, the spigot size must include the depth of the threads. This means it is better to cut the recess, including the threads, before the spigot.

Threading soft timber internally across the grain is very difficult. The threads tend to flake and break off. This is called stripping the thread. It is better to thread soft materials with the grain, this means cutting end grain as well. It is better to select a harder species of timber until experienced.

Select a hard, tight grained, piece of wood. Prepare the recess to be threaded, ensuring that it is parallel and of the correct depth and size. Make sure that a relief hollow is cut correctly at the bottom of the recess so as to allow for clearance when extracting the tool from the threads on the inward stroke. It is most important to get the recess and spigot the correct sizes in relation to one another.

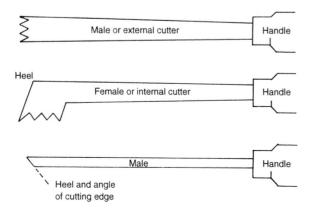

Male or external cutter | Handle

Heel
Female or internal cutter | Handle

Male | Handle
Heel and angle
of cutting edge

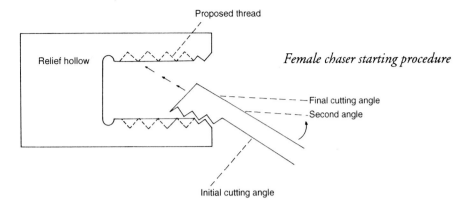

Female chaser starting procedure

When cutting threads of differing sizes, the traverse speed will change according to the size and pitch of the threads. On coarse threads the speed is fast because the pitch is long. With fine threads or larger material the speed is slower.

The most important factors of all are timing, and the angle of the tool with eye and hand co-ordination.

CUTTING A FEMALE THREAD

Using the cranked chaser (internal cutting)

With the tool rest slightly below centres, set the lathe speed as slow as possible. With practice, the correct cutting speed for each individual will be found. Hold the tool level on the tool rest and at an angle of approximately 30 degrees to the inside edge of the recess to be threaded. Using the heel of the tool to control the depth of cut, make a light pass or stroke, pushing the tool into the recess retaining the 30 degree angle of cut. The timing and pace of the tool in relation to the revolving material is critical. After the first stroke, a light thread should start to develop on the inside edge of the recess. It is important to time the passes in order that the cutters drop into the grooves made by the first stroke. Continue this action until a thread is clearly cut, which is normally after two or three passes. The cutter from this point onwards must always be placed in this 'leading' thread, but must not be allowed to cut any deeper at the entry point. Use the 'leading' thread as a guide to cutting but do not exert further pressure in this area. Continue the cutting action, at the same time reducing the entry angle slightly on each stroke. As the cutter drops into the lead thread and the angle of cut is reduced, exert firmer pressure and turn the tool slightly in a clockwise direction to introduce more of the cutting edge. This will lengthen and deepen the thread. Continue this action until the tool is parallel to the inside edge of the recess. Timing the tooling action as it

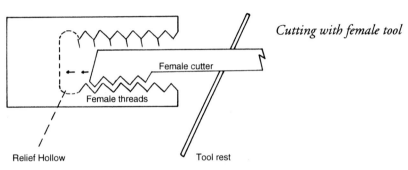

Cutting with female tool

traverses across the blank is critical in forming a thread. Practise this until satisfied with the result.

Take care to set the tool cutting edge very slightly at an angle and hold it firmly in that position until each stroke is complete. On reaching the relief hollow lift the

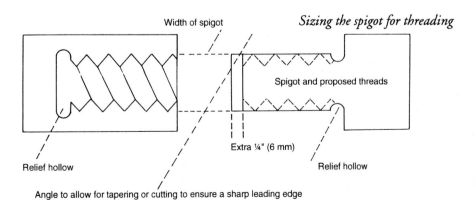

Sizing the spigot for threading

tool sharply out of the threads. Take care not to catch the threads on the way out. Repeat this action with very light cuts to clean the threads. To get a good result the chasers must be sharp.

At first do not attempt to cut too much at one time. Cut in gradual stages taking very thin shavings. Get the timing right to 'catch' that 'leading' edge of the thread and there will be no problem. However, get it wrong and the threads will be stripped.

CUTTING A MALE THREAD

Using the straight chaser (external cutting)

Before using this chaser, make sure the spigot is the correct size for the internal thread. The spigot must at least be the full width of the recess plus the depth of the thread. On the first attempts make the spigot slightly larger than necessary, this is to give a little insurance against minor mistakes and will allow for a re-cut if necessary. Always make the spigot about ¼" longer than required, making sure a relief hollow is cut as illustrated on page 161.

Cutting an external thread is easier than cutting the internal one.

When preparing the spigot, make sure there is sufficient material to allow for ¼"(6 mm) waste at the end. This will be explained later. Set the tool rest just below centres, and about ½"(13 mm) clear of the workpiece. On standard lathes set the speed on the lowest possible which is about 250 r.p.m., the speed may be increased for larger pieces. Each person may work at a different speed. Hold the tool 'set' at an angle of approximately 30 degrees with its cutting edge central to the corner of the spigot, its left corner should be clear of the spigot. Lift the hand hold -ing the tool to introduce the cutting edge, move the tool from right to left retaining the 'set' angle as you do so. Again, timing and pace is essential to strike a thread. Follow through with the tool at the same

angle until the tool is completely clear of the spigot. Lift the tool clear of the spigot in a circular action and time the stroke to re-enter the thread at the extreme end of the spigot. Continue this action until a thread has been cut on the corner of the spigot. Use this lead thread as a guide to cutting the rest of the spigot.

On each stroke reduce the cutting angle of the tool until the relief hollow has been reached and the thread has been completely cut.

Take care not to over cut the thread by exerting too much pressure; the thread will be stripped or the diameter may be reduced, thus making a loose thread. The male threads must be cut parallel to the female ones, otherwise they will jam or lock. It is very important to get the timing right. The cutting action must flow as any hesitation or jerking will destroy the threads.

Problems:

The main problem encountered when using chasers is that the timing may not be synchronised resulting in damage to the threads. This is called stripping. The threads may also be split. This indicates that the tool has been traversed too slowly or quickly and the thread line has not been accurately struck.

Crumbling at the apex of the thread is caused by cutting too deeply with the chasers; the apex is being dragged off when it reaches the base of the cutters. To avoid this cut less deeply, this will leave a slight flat on the apexes.

Practice:

Practise by using the tools on their heels only. Do not allow the tool to cut. Where the heel of the tool has been rubbing on the surface of the spigot or recess marks will appear, these will indicate where the threads will be cut. Practise this until sufficient confidence is gained to try the real thing.

Reference was made earlier to an extra ¼"(6 mm) on the spigot, this is a form of insurance when thread cutting. It can be difficult, particularly for a beginner, to successfully cut a thread freehand from the very edge of the spigot. If the leading edge is damaged, cut off the extra ¼"(6 mm), a new sharp leading edge will result.

Try fitting the threads. If too tight, repeat a few light strokes with the external chaser to reduce the size of thread a little. It may be necessary to trim the apex of the threads on the spigot. Do this with a skew or sandpaper. This will also prevent future damage occurring to the tips of the thread.

Should the mechanism be too tight, it is advisable to reduce the size of the spigot threads for fitting purposes rather than opening the more tricky internal threads.

Threads cut on softer materials can easily be chipped or broken. These may be stabilised by soaking with sanding sealer or certain types of glue overnight. Lightly re-cut the threads when dry. Wax the threads to ensure a smooth action.

CUTTING THREADS WITH A WOODCARVER'S V GOUGE

Isolate the lathe from the electricity before cutting threads in this manner.

The second method of thread cutting is to use a woodcarver's V gouge. It is obvious that this tool cannot be used to cut an internal thread (female) within a recess and it must be cut with a chaser or a tap. Only the spigot can be cut with the V gouge.

(N.B. There is a very old method of internal thread cutting. A cranked V tool like a hook, rather than a gouge, is used. This tool is not available to-day, however, one could be specially made up.)

The V of the gouge must be the same size as the chaser or tap used to cut the female thread. The thread must also be cut with the V tool at the same angle and depth as the female thread, or they will not match.

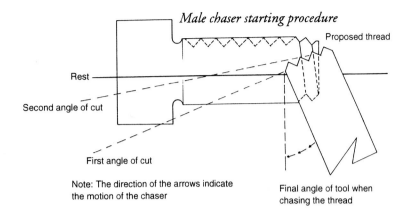

Male chaser starting procedure

Proposed thread

Rest

Second angle of cut

First angle of cut

Note: The direction of the arrows indicate the motion of the chaser

Final angle of tool when chasing the thread

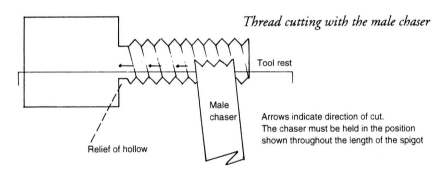

Thread cutting with the male chaser

Tool rest

Male chaser

Relief of hollow

Arrows indicate direction of cut. The chaser must be held in the position shown throughout the length of the spigot

Use the free hand to rotate the workpiece into the cutting edge of the gouge. As for any other spiral work, timing, uniformity and pace are essential.

Get the width and depth correct in one pass. Do not try to get a sharp point to the thread, it should have a very small flat at its apex. Should you over cut and pinch a piece of the thread, this will reduce its height and width. The thread will be 'drunk'. This is bad, throw it away. The theory is, cut the correct width and depth to form a regular, perfectly shaped thread around the material. You will discover that the angle of pitch will automatically follow. The leading cutting edge of the right fork on the V should cut evenly and closely to the last cut, leaving a regular apex. A perfectly formed thread will result. The width of the spigot between opposing apexes should not alter.

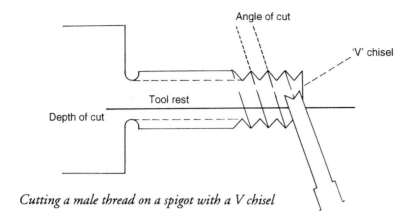

Cutting a male thread on a spigot with a V chisel

Problems:

With this method of cutting the main problems are the depth and angle of cut. Get either wrong and the threads will be 'drunk'. (All over the place). Remember you are cutting with one 'V' only. Tight and accurate control is called for.

Practise on a prepared blank before tackling anything seriously. It will surprise most people to discover how easily thread cutting can be achieved. This method is enjoyable and it works. During these trial cuts, run out of true by deliberately changing the angle of the tool, and you will soon discover what not to do.

With a threaded recess prepared, the spigot can be turned to size. Set the tool rest centrally between centres. The main difficulty at first is starting the thread at the beginning of the spigot. Every thread has a leading edge that starts as a sharp edge and widens into a full thread which tapers into the material at the correct pitch. This angle of pitch has to be set at the very beginning. To overcome this, start the cut with the V tip on solid ground just inside the extreme edge of the spigot, take care that the tool does not slip outwards. Set the angle by pointing the tool slightly to the left, start cutting from that point, push the tool into the material to reach the correct depth immediately. When the correct depth is reached, drop the right hand to raise the

cutting edge to retain the correct depth. Angle the tool at the intended pitch. On one circumference of the spigot with the free hand the V cut should have moved sufficiently to the left to allow for the width of the thread.

Once the correct angle and depth has been established, the tool should be held very firmly in that position, I use the expression, 'locked in with the body.' Once this is achieved, with the feet properly placed, move the body from right to left along the full length of the thread. With this action and firm control with the left hand rotating the workpiece, a regular thread will be made. On each preceding revolution of the work another circumference of thread is added, each one should be exactly the same size as the one before. Continue the cutting until the relief hollow is reached. Use the information above to guide the tool at the correct depth, rotate the workpiece with the free hand into the cutting edge, to control the depth, push the tool into the material and raise or lower the cutting hand. If the correct angle of cut is not achieved immediately, *do not* continue. Stop, go back to the point where the error was made and correct the angle.

When the tool starts to wander it will be noticed immediately. A small mistake can be made and go unnoticed. However, a nasty wobble on the thread will always be there. Throw it away and start again.

To obtain a clean sharp leading edge to the thread, taper the end of the spigot or cut off ¼"(6 mm).

CUTTING A THREAD FREEHAND

This method of cutting a thread is probably the oldest and most labour intensive. It can involve marking out where large threads have to be cut.

Small threads were seldom cut in this manner. If they were, it was purely guess work and was probably achieved through experience.

There is no internal thread in the recess. The method

of retaining the threaded spigot, is one or two pins at one or both sides of the recess, set to locate with the thread on the spigot.

Cut the recess and spigot to a tight fit. The thread on the spigot is cut with a saw, triangular file or chisel. The guide for cutting and using these tools is normal marking out and the best method of explaining this procedure is to refer back to Chapter 5 and the marking out for the Single twist. The threads on the illustration are large and set at two revolutions per 1"(25 mm), therefore the pitch for each thread is ½"(13 mm).

Prepare a 2"(51 mm) wide by 1½"(38 mm) deep recess. Turn the spigot or dowel to match tightly. Mark the four Start Lines and three Pitch Lines, divide the pitch segments twice and complete the single Cut Control Line.

Use a tenon saw very lightly to cut the Cut Line. Use a triangular rasp or file to cut the thread. Cut until the thread apex is almost pointed. Do not remove material from the top of the thread.

Another method of cutting this V thread is to use a wide carpenter's chisel.

Once satisfied with the spigot, lay the shoulder of the threaded spigot tightly against the end of the spigot with the thread alongside the outside of the recess. Mark the outside of the recess at ½"(13 mm) and 1"(25 mm) from the outer edge exactly opposite the bottom of the thread hollow.

Drill a ¼"(6 mm) hole at both points indicated into the recess. Push the spigot into the recess, taking care that it is properly seated. Look or feel through these holes to locate the bottom of the threads by rotating the spigot.

Make up two ¼"(6 mm) pins with conical tips and insert them tightly into the bottom of the threads. Unscrew the spigot. Once satisfied all is in working order, glue the pins in position.

In some cases these thread location pins need not be permanent. They may be threaded and the recesses tapped, so that they can be screwed into position. In these circumstances they may be turned with decorative knobs.

If the location pins are slightly out of line, it means that the thread needs to be opened a little. They can be adjusted by re-cutting slightly.

This unique type of threading is very old and probably made when 'taps' and female 'chasers' were difficult to acquire or did not exist. The method is quite crude but very interesting when used in the right circumstances.

Examples where this type of thread may be used: where a large lid is too big for threads to be cut; to fit a very heavy spigot, where it has to be regularly undone and replaced. Only one pitch need be cut and one location pin fitted. This type of thread is in effect a quick fit fitting.

Method of threading and retaining a lid

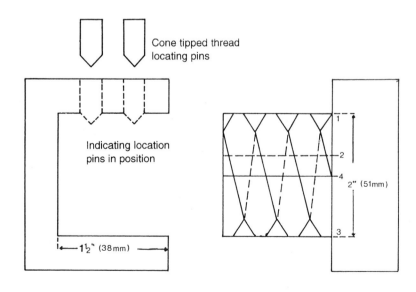

Multi-Start Open twist lamp base; 3-tier cocktail tray with twisted centre column; yew goblet with twisted stem.

Cook book stand with tapered twist uprights.

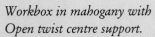

*Workbox in mahogany with
Open twist centre support.*

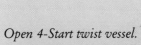

Open 4-Start twist vessel.

*Cake tray or fruit dish in padauk with
4-Start Open twist stem.*

Vessel with a centre twisted gallery.

Umbrella or walking stick stand with Double Barley twist legs.

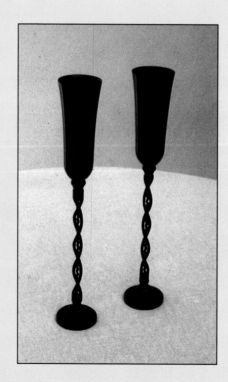

Pair of goblets with twist within a twist stems.

Twist exercise pieces: Double Open twist with thin spindle turning insert; laminated Double Barley twist.

A variety of twists on music stands and plant stands.

Rosewood trinket box with spiral stem top.

A collection of twistwork

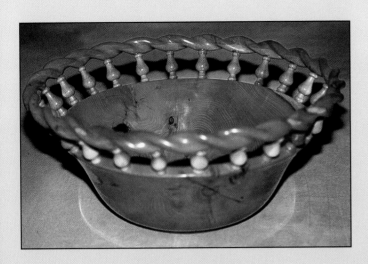

Yew bowl with ring twist gallery.

Open twist yew lamp.

Walking stick blanks with (L to R) Triple Ribbon twist, stretched Double twist, and standard Double twist, all on a narrow taper.

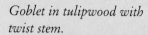
4-Start Open twist candlesticks.

Goblet in tulipwood with twist stem.

Fruit bowl with twist feature.

GLOSSARY

Whenever possible, known traditional terms are used in this publication and will be familiar to most woodworkers. There will also be some which may conjure up argument as to their authenticity. This may be the case, however the fact is that little has been documented regarding standard traditional terminology for spiral work in wood. The knowledge of spiral work has been handed down by craftsmen in spindle work for generations, mainly to their apprentices. In some cases terms change or vary throughout the country, just as do accents. Here, it is not the intention to raise argument or controversy, but to enhance the understanding and readability of this book.

APEX.   The top of an arch, ridge or thread. Reference is made to the top of a bine as its apex. The measurement from the top of one bine to another will be referred to as apex to apex.

BACK.   Refers to the back of a gouge. The front is the flute, the back is the opposite side.

BALL.   A ball shaped feature on a spindle, column or any other turning.

BANJO.   The tool rest support with a barrel to house the tool rest. It slides along the bed of the lathe to position the tool rest. It is also called a saddle.

BEAD.   In this book beads are an arched or round topped feature on a turning, they may also be pointed.

BETWEEN CENTRES.   The point to point distance between the headstock drive and the tailstock centres.

BEVEL.   The area of a chisel or turning tool, that lies between the 'cutting edge' and the heel. The bevel may be flat, concave or convex. Flat means flat ground, concave is sometimes referred to as hollow ground. Convex is referred to as rounded. Normally in turning, this type of grinding should be avoided as it may involve two or three bevels. However in *some cases* a slightly rounded bevel can allow for better control of the tool.

BINE.   Is the term used to describe the bead or bine that spirals around and runs the length of a twist. A Single twist has one bine and a Double has two, etc. An Open twist has Open bines or spirals.

BINE CONTROL LINES.   Or Bine Apex Lines. Are the diagonal lines that indicate the cut lines and apexes of the bines along the length of a blank. Bine Control Lines are the Cut and Bine Lines combined.

BIRD'S BEAK.   A half bead or a small swell with an arched cut back from the face.

BLANK.   The prepared area of the workpiece on which a twist may be cut. A blank is also a partially prepared piece of stock or turning.

BREAK THROUGH.   This is the term used for Opening a twist. An Open twist is where the bines have been separated by means of cutting through the bottom of the hollows to a centrally drilled hole in the blank. Opening is where the hollow is Opened into the centre hole in order to attain a rounded spiral.

CABLE TWIST.   A twist with eight or nine bines; traditionally the hollows or troughs should be 'V' shaped at the bottom. In some cases I have personally rounded off the hollows at the bottom. The main criterion is that the twist must resemble a cable or rope.

CATCH.   Also referred to as CRAB in the East End of London, this is where an accident occurs when tooling and damage is caused to the workpiece. The damage can range from a small unwanted cut, to a very large error with disastrous results. See DIG-INS.

CENTRES.   See Between Centres. Centres in woodturning are the tools which form part of a lathe when in use. They support and drive the stock or workpiece between the head and tailstock in their respective morse taper. In some cases they may screw on or fit in a chuck

CHASERS.   Tools used for cutting threads freehand. The external thread cutter is sometimes referred as the 'male', and the internal cutter as the 'female'.

CHASING A THREAD.   Means to cut the thread properly after it had been struck. See Striking a Thread and Laying a Thread.

COMBINED TWIST.   This is where two or three different twists run parallel along the length of the same column or spindle.

CONVERTING TWISTS.   This is where a twist converts, without a break, from one pattern into another, on the same column. The twist must be compatible, e.g. a Double into a 4-Start or a Triple into a 6-Start, and so on.

COVE.   A cove is a small, well-balanced, rounded hollow feature, normally cut with a spindle gouge around the workpiece.

COMPLETE MARKING OUT.   Is a full set of Start, Pitch, Pitch Dividing and Pitch Control Lines repeated (normally in a different colour) to attain Width Control Lines for accurate twist cutting. When cutting certain twists these lines are not considered necessary.

CROSS BINE TWISTING.   Means to cut a right- and left-hand hollow across one another on the same blank to produce a pineapple effect.

CUT CONTROL LINES.   Are the diagonal lines that are marked out from the Start Lines to the intersections with the Pitch and Pitch Dividing Lines. They indicate the angle of cut.

DEAD CENTRE.   A solid steel, cone-shaped centre with a point, that fits into the tailstock. It centres and supports the workpiece at the tailstock end of the lathe. In the production of very small turnings a dead centre may be used as a slipping drive in the headstock, this allows for loading between centres without stopping the lathe.

DIES. Circular steel blocks that fit into a handled housing. They have central cutters for cutting a 'male' thread on a spigot or pin. Dies may be used to cut threads on very hard species of timber. this is completely different from Thread Chasing. Every die has a matching tap. See Tap.

DIG-IN. This is where a tool is introduced wrongly into the material. It can happen in several ways: 1. Introducing the tool at the wrong angle. 2. Trying to cut with an unsupported area of cutting edge. 3. Bad or loose control of the tool on the rest. 4. Careless withdrawal of the tool from a workpiece. 5. Waving the tool around when chatting or after being distracted. 6. Using the wrong tool for the job, and 7. Trying or attempting something new or something you shouldn't be doing without thinking. It can do minor damage to a workpiece or completely destroy it. It can also cause injury to a turner. See Catch.

DOUBLE BARLEY TWIST. A twist with two bines and two hollows or troughs.

DOUBLE OPEN TWIST A Double twist with two Open spirals or bines leaving it hollow in the centre. It is sometimes referred to as a Hollow twist.

DRIVE CENTRE. This is a pronged drive that fits into the headstock taper to support and drive the stock or workpiece during cutting on the lathe. Drive centres normally have 2 or 4 prongs and a centring pin.

EDGE. Indicates the degree of sharpness on the cutting edge of a tool, e.g. 'Has a nice edge' means it is sharp or keen (Keen edge).

FACE. A cut right angles to the revolving stock, or a flat surface at right angles to the bed of the lathe.

FACEPLATE. A face plate (normally steel), is for securing work to the headstock. It is sometimes not possible to support the workpiece by the tailstock. This type of work is faceplate work and can be inboard or outboard.

FADING OUT. Means to taper out a cut or hollow gradually at a given angle until the tool is no longer cutting. A good example of this is to look at the flute on a gouge, it 'fades out' at the handle end.

FILLET. A fillet is also called a shoulder. It is a flat topped ridge, normally seen at the side of a pummel, bead, cove or hollow.

FLAT. A flat topped feature on a turning, may be seen at the end of a column, spindle or the edge of a base.

FLUTE. A recess that runs along the inside edge of the gouge family, referred to as fluted. When ground, the inside edge of the flute is the cutting edge.

FOUR START TWIST.   (or, 4-Start) A twist with four bines and four hollows or troughs. It may also be Opened.

GRADUATED. This is the method used to describe and explain the marking out of a twist, that is measured and cut in accordance with the width of material at a particular point. A twist is normally graduated on a taper or irregular shape.

HEADSTOCK. The headstock houses the drive shaft, which is normally hollow, thus, the term hollow headstock. The drive shaft has an inboard threaded mandrel. The end of the shaft on most lathes is tapered internally to accept a 1, 2, or 3 morse taper. The 3 is the largest. The shaft is, in the main, driven by a 'cone' of opposing pulleys to the motor. This allows for adjusting the speed of the lathe. The headstock end of the lathe is often referred to as the business end. In some cases it may be swivelled to allow for outboard turning.

HEEL. In this context the heel is the ridge at the opposite end from the cutting edge of a gouge after grinding. The bevel is between the cutting edge and the heel.

HOLLOW. Within this book a hollow is referred to as the trough or hollow that runs between the bines on a twist. When the hollow is cut the bines are automatically formed. A hollow is also a larger version of a cove and may vary in shape. It can also be shallow or deep.

INBOARD. This means to turn from the inside of the headstock, over the bed of the lathe with no tailstock support. Not between centres.

INDEXER. A device fitted to a lathe, used for dividing or measuring equal distances around a workpiece. Usually a wheel or collar drilled at equal distances with a location pin fitted to the lathe to lock the shaft in position.

JUG. An old term, used to describe a combination of several features, that may be 'jug' shaped.

LATHE BED. The base of the lathe on which the headstock, tailstock, banjo and tool rest are fitted. On modern lathes the 'bed' may be constructed of cast iron, tubular or bars in steel. One of the most important features of a lathe is that it must have a rigid bed.

LAYING A THREAD. This means to cut a thread along a piece of work.

LEFT-HAND TWIST. This is where the hollows are cut from left to right. When placed on end the bines point upwards and to the left.

LIVE CENTRE. A live centre serves the same purpose as a dead centre, except that it is fitted with a bearing. It revolves without friction when pressure is applied by the tailstock. This is a great advance on the dead centre. A live centre is also referred to as a Revolving Centre.

MIRROR IMAGE. A mirror image is exactly what it implies. It is an exact copy of a left- or right-hand twist, cut in the opposite direction to make a true pair.

MORSE TAPER. The name given to 'male' and 'female' tapers at the end of a shaft or barrel for the introduction of drives, drills, chucks, mandrels, etc. with a matching taper. Pillar drills have the same system.

MULTI-START. Describes twists and spirals with numerous bines, where there is no traditional name.

NECK. A long tapering hollow, where the extreme bottom is not necessarily in the middle.

OGEE. An ogee is an attractive feature. It is an 'S' shaped form or cut, usually on a taper. It is a swell developing into a cove or hollow.

OPEN. To Open, means to separate the bines, and carve a balanced opening or gap between the spirals. The term 'Open the Face' refers to the angling of a tool, to employ more of the cutting edge.

OPEN TWIST. An Open twist is a hollow twist, the bines have been separated. This creates a see-through effect with individual spirals.

OUTBOARD. Outboard turning is where work is turned on the outside of the headstock. This means the headstock shaft has a threaded mandrel at either end. See Inboard.

PAIR. Is a left- and right-hand twist in exact proportion to one another, a true pair in twisting terms. See Mirror Image.

PINEAPPLE TWIST. Before this twist is cut the blank must resemble a pineapple shape. The hollows are cut from both left and right. This, in effect, cross cuts the bines to form pineapple segment shaped lozenges on the surface of the blank.

PITCH. The pitch is the distance between apex on the bine, in relation to the material.

PITCH ANGLE. This is the angle set diagonally when cutting the hollow to create the bine. The Pitch Angle is calculated and set in proportion to the width of material.

PITCH CONTROL LINES. Is a combined name for the Cut Lines, Bine Apex Lines and the Width Control Lines.

PITCH LINES. These are vertical lines around the blank. They indicate the length of the Pitch, in relation to the thickness of material.

PITCH DIVIDING LINES. These lines divide the Pitch into the number of Pitch Segments required for a particular twist. They also intersect with the Start Lines to give control when marking out the Pitch Control Lines.

PITCH SEGMENTS. Are the areas of the blank between the Start Lines, the Pitch and Pitch Dividing lines. The marking out is similar to a graph.

PRONGED DRIVE. See Drive Centre.

PUMMEL. A square section on a workpiece. They can be slightly rounded or squared off on one or both faces.

REVOLVING CENTRE. See Live Centre.

REEL. A long hollow, flat or swell with a bead at either end. They are a strong and attractive feature at the top or base of a column or spindle.

RIBBON TWIST. This twist has traditionally three bines and three hollows. It should resemble a ribbon. The bines should be pointed or slightly rounded off.

RIGHT-HAND TWIST. A right-hand twist is cut from right to left. When placed on end the bines point upwards and to the right.

ROPE TWIST. See Cable Twist.

SADDLE. A mechanism that slides along the bed of a lathe for holding cutting or boring tools or a tool rest; a saddle can be hand or gear operated. See Banjo.

SINGLE BARLEY TWIST. This twist has a single bine and hollow. It is referred to as a Single.

SPIGOT. Can also be referred to as a tenon or pin or even a dowel at the end of a column or spindle.

SPIRAL. A twist is often referred to as a Spiral. It is also an individual bine, open or solid, that spirals along the length of a workpiece.

SPIRAL WORK. A general term for all twisting. It can also be defined as a single bine on an Open twist. For example, a 4-Start has four bines or spirals. See Spiral.

START OR HORIZONTAL LINES. Start Lines are those marked horizontally on a blank. They indicate the number and starting position of the hollows and bines. They also intersect with the Pitch and Pitch Dividing Lines to establish the position of the Pitch Control Lines. A Double has two hollows and two bines. It therefore needs at least four Start Lines.

STOCK. A general term for a piece of raw or unprepared timber. Partially turned blanks are referred to as prepared stock.

STRIKING A THREAD. This means to partially cut a thread; once struck it can be chased. See Chasing a Thread.

SWELL. A long gradual bulge, normally between two features and very often on a taper.

TAILSTOCK. An assembly that houses the hollow tailstock barrel which in turn accommodates a dead or live centre. The barrel is lockable and can be adjusted by means of a threaded hand wheel. The complete assembly can slide along the bed of the lathe to support a piece of stock between centres.

TAPERING. Where a prepared section of a column or spindle is thinner at one end than the other. A true taper must be straight edged.

TAPERED TWIST. A standard twist of any description cut on a tapered column or spindle.

TAP. A male thread cutter for threading a recess. See Thread Box and Dies.

TAPPING. Tapping a thread refers to cutting an internal or 'female' thread.

TEARDROP. Is named such because of its resemblance to a teardrop. It may be more bulbous or slimmer at the bottom. The design is dependent on taste.

THREAD BOX. A split wooden block drilled to accommodate a specific size of dowel or spigot. It houses a 'V' cutter, that is set to cut a thread on the dowel. There is always a matching tap to make the internal 'female' thread. See Tapping.

THIN TURNING AND TWISTING. Work where conventional tools are too large for cutting a twist. Smaller tools such as small rasps and files have to be used. Anything under ½" (13mm) in diameter could be considered thin. See also Wire Turning and Twisting.

TOOL REST. A 'T' shaped rest that fits into the banjo or saddle barrel where it can be moved and locked in position to support and guide the tool when cutting.

TRIPLE. A twist with three bines and three hollows.

TRUNNION. Supporting cylindrical projections (in this case appertaining to the supports in the cookbook project).

TWIST. A twist refers to an individual piece of spiral work regardless of the type or style. Twisting is the process of cutting a spiral.

'V' CUT. This is a 'V' shaped cut that can be cut on a square or round blank. It can be a feature on its own. It is also used to set another feature such as a bead, ball or pummel etc.

WAISTED. As defined in the dictionary. It is a feature on a column or spindle that is thinner in the middle than at both ends. A waisted section is a long flowing hollow.

WIRE TURNING AND TWISTING. Is the term used for producing fine wire-like spindles and twists measuring ⅛" (3 mm) in diameter and under.

WORKPIECE. A prepared length of material, set up for turning, that is being worked on up to completion.

A FINAL THOUGHT

Throughout my years in the Police Force it was my natural nosy instinct and a love for the craft that drew me into many a wood shop on and off my beats. I always wondered what gave the majority of woodturners in particular, that air of resigned contentment they seemed to have when working on a lathe or otherwise.

The answer is simple, they are satisfied in what they do. From the simple process of spinning a piece of wood they can produce something that may be admired by others. They love digging around in heaps of timber in all sorts of weather looking for a find, rooting around looking for tools. With a piece of wood on the lathe and the shavings flying a woodturner is in his or her element. I sometimes think they are in another world.

I can say that as this is the way I feel about woodturning. I can also add another feeling, that of excitement, when I produce a piece of spiral work which I like and know will be appreciated by others.

To date I have produced numerous pieces of work to include a twist of some description and seldom repeat the same design. Each new piece gives me a great deal of pleasure and feeling of achievement and I am sure that I share this feeling with the many other turners and carvers who produce this attractive feature throughout the country. Whether a twist is produced by a machine or by hand makes little difference, spiral work, it seems to me, is a much neglected area in woodworking, evidenced by its absence in modern furniture or other fine woodwork.

With this book I hope to help bring alive the art of producing this attractive form. Hopefully it will be through hand production, in the traditional manner, in workshops, garages and sheds throughout the country, that the twist will become a major feature in turning.

There is one thing of which I am certain, any competent woodworker can produce a twist in a relatively short time. When one produces their first twist by hand, they will never forget it. It is an area where woodturners can enhance their work and where the boundaries of design are limitless.

'Turn' the lathes back a little and ' let's Twist again'.

James 'Stuart' Mortimer

ACKNOWLEDGEMENTS

I would like to thank my son Andrew for all the line drawings and illustrations in this book, and for all the time and effort selflessly given. To Jim Gilbert, a fellow Aberdonian and woodturner, for the photographic work and the renditions on the accordion. To Neil Hewitt, a friend and neighbour, who read the manuscript. To Tony Bonner, a pal from way back, who has given me help countless times, particularly when I lost the book somewhere in the computer. Thanks are also due to John Lenihan, a friend and fellow turner for a quick course on modern technology and a splendid back-up service. To Allan Beecham, who needs no introduction to woodturners, for checking and confirming the terminology in the Glossary. And, for getting me started, my thanks to my Father-in-law, Eric Harvey, for my first lathe, a lot of shavings have gone under the Bridges since then. And, not least, to Linda — my right arm.